# The University in the Global Age

**Universities into the 21st Century**

*Series Editors: Noel Entwistle and Roger King*

Research-Enhanced Teaching: Bringing Research and Teaching Together
  *Angela Brew*
Research-Based University Teaching   *Noel Entwistle*
The University in the Global Age   *Roger King et al.*

*Further titles are in preparation*

# The University in the Global Age

Roger King

with contributions from Svava Bjarnason,
Kenneth Edwards, Michael Gibbons
and Yoni Ryan

palgrave
macmillan

First published 2004 by
PALGRAVE MACMILLAN
Houndmills, Basingstoke, Hampshire RG21 6XS and
175 Fifth Avenue, New York, N. Y. 10010
Companies and representatives throughout the world

PALGRAVE MACMILLAN is the global academic imprint of the Palgrave Macmillan division of St. Martin's Press, LLC and of Palgrave Macmillan Ltd. Macmillan® is a registered trademark in the United States, United Kingdom and other countries. Palgrave is a registered trademark in the European Union and other countries.

ISBN 1–4039–3467–3 hardback
ISBN 1–4039–1130–4 paperback

This book is printed on paper suitable for recycling and made from fully managed and sustained forest sources.

A catalogue record for this book is available from the British Library.

A catalog record for this book is available from the Library of Congress.

10   9   8   7   6   5   4   3   2   1
13  12  11  10  09  08  07  06  05  04

Printed and bound in Great Britain by
Creative Print & Design (Wales), Ebbw Vale

# Contents

# Acknowledgements

We are very grateful to Roger Brown, Michael Moran and Lawrence Stedman for comments on earlier drafts.

# Notes on the Contributors

**Svava Bjarnason** is Head of Policy and Research at the Association of Commonwealth Universities (ACU) based in London. In this capacity she is also the Director of the joint ACU/Universities UK initiative, the Observatory on Borderless Higher Education, which is an international strategic information service. Currently she is working on a project that examines the engagement of universities with their wider societies, taking a number of countries as case studies. Prior to joining the ACU, she was an independent research consultant in UK higher education, and was also a major contributor to the Universities UK Report on *The Business of Borderless Education: UK Perspectives* that was published in July 2000.

**Kenneth Edwards** was Vice Chancellor of the University of Leicester from 1987 to 1999. During that period he was also, for two years, from 1993 to 1995, Chairman of the Committee of Vice Chancellors of the UK. From 1998 to 2001 he was President of the Association of European Universities. Before the Leicester appointment he had been in Cambridge University for over 20 years, for most of the time as a Lecturer in Genetics, but from 1984 to 1987 as Secretary-General of the Faculties, the senior academic administrative post in the University. Currently he is Chairman of the Observatory of the Magna Charta Universitatum based in Bologna.

**Michael Gibbons** has been Secretary General of the Association of Commonwealth Universities since 1996. From 1992 to 1996 he was Dean of the Graduate School and Director of the Science Policy Research Unit at the University of Sussex. Prior to this he was Professor of Science and Technology Policy and Director of Research Exploitation and Development at the University of Manchester. He has authored and co-authored several books, including *The New Production of Knowledge: The Dynamics of Science and Research in Contemporary Societies*, and *The Evaluation of Research: A Synthesis of Current Practice*.

**Roger King** was until 2000 the Vice Chancellor of what is now the University of Lincoln and has served on many university-sector committees, including for the British Council. He has been a Visiting Professor at the Queensland University of Technology and the University of the Sunshine Coast in Australia. He is Visiting Fellow with the Association of Commonwealth Universities.

**Yoni Ryan** is Associate Professor and Head of the Educational Design Group at Monash University in Australia, having previously worked at Queensland University of Technology. Her education experience covers secondary school and further education as well as universities. She is the co-editor of two books on postgraduate supervision: *Quality in Postgraduate Supervision*, and *Supervising Postgraduates from Non-English Speaking Backgrounds*. She was operational manager and lead author for two Australian Federal Government projects and subsequent published Reports on *New Media and Borderless Education* (1998) and *The Business of Borderless Education* (2000). Currently she is working on a research project on the globalization of services in the vocational education and training sector.

# Series Editors' Preface

*The University in the Global Age* is one of the first books in the new series *Universities into the 21st Century* and is intended to introduce the reader to a range of issues concerning universities at the start of the new millennium, some of which will be picked up and examined in further detail by later works in the series. As such the book offers a broad comprehension of contemporary higher education systems in a world characterized increasingly by processes such as globalization and supranationality.

The series is designed to fill a niche between those series on universities and colleges that focus on the skills or techniques of teaching and learning, and those that concentrate on detailed research evidence to substantiate propositions for more effective pedagogy. It also seeks to draw out managerial and policy issues where this appears to be appropriate, and to examine higher education systems and organizations.

This series is designed to produce reasonably compact and readable books that bring together research findings, good practice and policy issues at a conceptual level. Underpinning the arguments with research-based conceptual analysis should make the books of interest to academic practitioners as well as to a wider audience interested in the social and policy sciences, and also to those readers who are simply interested in knowing more about an organization that seems to be attracting considerable government and media attention. In part this follows from the growing recognition that investment in higher education – indeed in education more generally – is the key to national comparative advantage in increasingly knowledge-based societies.

The current pressures on academic and administrative staff, and university managers, mean that only rarely can they justify the time needed to read lengthy descriptions of research and other findings, nor are the majority familiar with the research methods of the social and policy sciences. The aim, therefore, is to produce manageable and integrated books that in many parts offer valuable synthesis and oversight of often seemingly disparate issues. We intend also that the books are written in an accessible and attractive manner.

The issues in the series will cover a broad range, from the activities of teachers and students, to wider developments in policy, and at local, national and international levels. Some of the earlier books, such as *The University in the Global Age*, are deliberatively broad in focus and conceptualization, while others generally seek to examine what constitutes 'best practice' on the basis of the research evidence available.

*Edinburgh*                                                                NOEL ENTWISTLE
*Battle, East Sussex*                                                       ROGER KING
*May 2003*

# Introduction

The university as an institution attracts more public attention in many countries than it has ever done. Issues of funding, or social access, or institutional stratification and standing commonly attract newspaper headlines – at least in the broadsheets – and politicians feel constantly obliged to make parliamentary or electoral statements about these matters. To use a description from political science, university systems and their governance have a higher salience for the media and governments (and therefore for the wider public) in recent years than previously.

In part this reflects the amount of taxpayers' monies expended by governments on universities. As participation – the numbers of students entering universities – has increased worldwide since the ending of World War II, for the most part in the industrialized countries this has occurred through public sector growth (except for Japan which is predominantly a private sector system). This has usually involved growing quite small and elite systems of higher education into mass forms by expanding existing universities (apart from in the US which has had mass higher education for many decades, and characteristics of it since virtually its inception). In some cases new public institutions have been created. In Australia and the UK this latter approach consisted in the early 1990s in turning existing colleges and polytechnics into new universities. Most of the developing world has also increased higher education enrolments by growing or expanding public institutions, although in the past two decades or so there has been a rising trend towards having more private and for-profit institutions in these and other countries.

It is unlikely that demand for university education will slacken in most countries, even if private charges, which seem to be on the rise, multiply. It still provides expectations of increased social mobility, while the private rates of return for individuals for possessing a university degree still appear to be quite significant. Developing countries are likely to want to follow the example of the industrialized world by encouraging a greater proportion of their populations to have higher education, although this raises significant questions about capacity when birth rates in many of these populations continue at higher levels than are now found in much of the West. In all countries the movement to lifelong and continuing occupational training and education will only serve to increase the need for greater university capacity. An indication of how much and in what forms some of this increased requirement will be met from private and from for-profit institutions, rather than from publicly funded conventional universities and colleges, is outlined by Svava Bjarnason in Chapter 7.

Although even the traditional universities have taken on some of the characteristics of more commercial bodies, for example by expanding entrepreneurial activities, seeking more diversified funding streams, and enrolling more full-cost and 'top-up' tuition fee-paying students, public funding is still the primary source of financing for most. The amount of government funding has risen to comprise a significant component of national budgets and inevitably this attracts democratic and other forms of scrutiny and accountability. The level of funding per student may be dropping, and in some countries more strikingly than in others, but overall expenditures have generally increased. When governments seek to replace or boost declining unit funding with private contributions from students and/or parents, usually involving the students at least taking out loans and incurring sizeable debts that require subsequent repayment, then such actions also excite media and public attention, including controversy and protest.

However, increased amounts of public funding is not the only reason why universities appear more interesting to the wider population than ever. We live in an age of increasing global competitiveness for nation states, particularly over the means for securing economic development and prosperity, and universities are seen as key elements and facilitators of our now predominantly knowledge-based societies. That is, rather than investment in physical or financial capital providing the best means for economic pay-off, investment in people – in enhancing their knowledge, ideas, and abilities to use signs and symbols – is regarded as increasingly more efficacious. That means that people need to be more skilled, and that businesses have to be more innovative, to meet the increased competitive challenges of the global economy. Universities are viewed as key agents in aiding these processes, through their teaching of future (and, increasingly, current) employees, and by the research that they undertake, which is turning more to that which is applied and in the service of corporate innovation and competitiveness.

Not everyone would accept these purposes for higher education, not least many working within it. Harnessing universities to the objectives of national comparative economic advantage would appear to some to be too utilitarian a purpose and ignoring wider social, individual and democratic well-being (which are perceived as 'public goods' that justify governmental rather than private funding). It is arguable too whether the widespread policy belief in many governments, that applied research is more productive economically than basic, curiosity, or fundamental research, is always correct, particularly if the 'seed corn' on which applied research is often dependent is too ruthlessly undernourished. Others, too, such as Alison Wolf (2002), have argued that there is no substantiated causal link between investment in universities and economic development. Some, such as Barnett (2000) and Delanty (2001), see distinct prospects for universities, rather than as agents of economic development, to be sites of open and dialogistic communication on behalf of society as a whole, including on a global scale, to help further the processes of national and international democratic institutions and governance. The universalism of knowledge in these views inevitably chafes at the restrictions and requirements of place and national governance, and the university appears in consequence to be more in tune with globalization and its opportunities, than with the national limitations of territorial leaders.

Apart from the public focus on universities that stems from increased governmental funding, and from the view that universities contribute vitally to comparative national economic advantage in the highly competitive global economy, there is a third factor at work. Increasingly we note, in many different types of society, reluctance by citizens, consumers, the media and democratic politicians, to accept at face value the actions and autonomy of, what are perceived to be, secretive professional associations. In a range of occupations, where associations representing independent professionals, such as solicitors, health doctors, or financiers, have long enjoyed an effective licence from government to regulate their own affairs, there have been introduced more legally binding, transparent and accountable forms of regulation, often with direct lines to parliaments and governments. Scandal and popular fears of heightened risk from science and mushrooming organizational complexity have helped to fuel calls for more open and public accountability of such groups than ever before. And while universities may have escaped the headline traumas of, for example, healthcare breakdowns, they have not escaped all the calls for greater scrutiny and rule-bound accountability. The growth of the regulatory state increasingly impacts upon higher education, not least in areas such as quality assurance, wider social participation, and finance, and can lead to some of the greatest resentments from those individuals and their organizations that are being regulated.

Universities, however, do not always lose out to the regulatory tendencies of governments. They are as adept as any in invoking state powers when it comes to protecting their own positions. For example, conventional universities have been able to insist that new private or corporate (and also public) entrants to the higher education sector conform to traditional models, particularly for quality assurance and for scholarship, and that governments reflect these as conditions in their accreditation and regulatory frameworks. This is not to suggest that such actions are solely self-interested, as reasonable doubts exist about such matters when new providers are characterized by narrow spreads of provision, low cost, little or no research, and 'moonlighting' staff. But it does indicate that public universities can often benefit from the regulatory state, even if this may hinder the introduction of innovative types of provision.

Universities themselves, however, are taking on some of the characteristics of private sector, for-profit bodies, not least in their management forms. In many countries, especially such as the UK and the US and other liberal market societies, universities are corporate bodies. These higher education organizations are no longer simply agglomerations of individual academics, or even disciplines, but are treated as having unitary identities and therefore collective responsibilities. And as modern organizations are managed, then so are universities, even if they remain more loosely integrated, restless, unionized, and critical bodies than those found in other parts of the private sector. Many academic staff cannot be sure whether they believe that corporate management is functionally irrelevant to universities, or whether they simply wish to have leaders that are reasonably competent managerially and which allow them to research or teach without being disturbed too much.

These and other dilemmas we explore in some detail in the following chapters. Although there are several contributors all the chapters have been written in the context of frequent meetings of the writers and around common themes. They do not simply consist of a set of essays but aim at a more coherent if not entirely seamless approach to key issues. These include the tension between the state and universities, not only over funding and social 'engineering' objectives, but also between the national concerns of governments, and the international and increasingly global interests of a number of major universities. There seems to be a heightened tussle in several countries these days between the idea of a nation state increasingly seeking to direct the university to accomplish national goals, and the notion of universities as corporate, transnational organizations, pursuing their own private and corporate interests.

Nor is it clear that nation-state policies for universities in the face of global challenges will be similar. Although the evidence is modest to date, countries have different state traditions – they have not all been converted to the liberal model – and their responses to globalization, and to how they perceive state–university relations, will not all be the same. And yet often their policies do appear to converge, and we are unclear why this is. Is it because of the operation of 'epistemic communities' of likeminded policymakers and advisers, in bodies such as the Organisation for Economic Co-operation and Development (OECD), which influences virtually all its member governments? Or are the challenges facing countries so clear that the prescriptions available to governments inevitably are quite limited, especially as nation states have lost much of their sovereignty, not only to the multinational corporations in the economic realm, but also to the rise of multinational – global and regional – layers of governance in the political realm?

The objective is to provide a book on the contemporary university that analyses these matters and that is accessible to those directly involved, as student, teacher, researcher, policy analyst, or government minister or official, or to those that may be simply interested in the modern university. It is not intended solely for the specialist – that would keep the academic 'secret garden' veiled in the mystification that has prevailed for far too long – but for a much wider audience in many countries. To do this successfully requires that the book is also comparative and up-to-date. We have not focused, therefore, only on one hemisphere or a limited range of countries, but we have tried to be wide-ranging and internationalist. And, of course, we examine such supranational phenomena as the corporate and 'for-profit' private university – one of the agents that are helping to form the so-called borderless world of higher education – and assess the role of communication and information technologies in these developments. We seek to take account also of the increasing role of higher education as a tradable service, and the implications of it falling within the competences of bodies such as the World Trade Organization (WTO), and particularly its moves toward the greater liberalization globally of such provision (through the General Agreement on Trade in Services, or the GATS).

Understanding these and other issues confronting the contemporary university requires a sense of history and knowledge of the reasons underlying its origins and subsequent development. In Chapter 1 we point out that, often contrary to popular conceptions and the hold of images of ivy-covered towers, green lawns and enclosed courtyards, most universities in the industrialized world are not medieval creations but were formed in the second half of the nineteenth, and in the twentieth, centuries. Their histories are entwined with those of nation-building leaders and the industrialization, militarization and democratization of the major powers. These processes have not followed identical trajectories in every country and therefore the historical development of university systems has also varied. Continental Europe, the US, and the UK, for example, display different characteristics, not least in their attitudes to the idea of the university as a public service or as a private enterprise, and these differences also feature in the variable nature of their state–university relationships. Attitudes to the importance of research and its relationship with teaching have also varied significantly in these countries.

A more explicit comparison between the university in continental Europe and in the US is provided by Kenneth Edwards in Chapter 2. One clear difference emerges in the relative lack of national or federal governmental direction or involvement in the affairs of universities in the US, in comparison with continental Europe, and where local state pride, funding and involvement have been among factors that have produced a mass but diversified system, with significant public and private university sectors, and where social access and world-class research can both be found. The Continental system is more state-bound, although, as Edwards points out, it is more heterogeneous than is often appreciated, but increasingly it exhibits a closer realignment with the US and the UK in its attraction to market forces. Interestingly, the US federal constitutional design is of increasing attraction to those in Europe who have federal ambitions to create a significant 'European space' for higher education, and who see in the US a successful reconciliation of governmental levels and functions. The Declaration of Bologna in 1999 by a number of European governments seeks to provide greater compatibility for European higher education systems, including length of courses, accreditation and quality assurance arrangements, and credit transfer mechanisms. Yet it is doubtful that strong federalism is ever likely to be welcomed by many national governments or universities, the latter already harassed enough by increasing bureaucratic intervention at national levels without wishing to have additional supranational layers with which to contend.

A major challenge for both universities and nation states is provided by globalization. In Chapter 3 we seek to establish what the processes of globalization actually are, and how they differ from internationalism. Universities have long been international bodies – universalism, after all, has characterized the nature of knowledge and its validity for centuries – but it is not clear that they are, as yet, global organizations as found, for example, in the business finance sector. The changing nature of knowledge production through networks spanning wide territories has provided the university, through the research function, with its most global characteristics. Teaching and learning, however, despite the growth of globe-circling communication and information technologies that have spurred the development of the borderless world of electronic delivery, is more territorially bound, although this is changing. Yet we are uncertain how to operationalize globalization and to describe how we would know – against which indicators – whether university systems are becoming more globalized or not, and the chapter seeks to address this issue. Nor are we clear of the impact of globalization on national policy makers, and the chapter calls for more work in this area.

In Chapter 4 we examine one of the most distinguishing characteristics of a number of polities in recent years, namely the rise of what is known as 'the regulatory state', and its impact on higher education. Regulatory agencies for the purposes of supervising and coordinating a range of stakeholder interests in particular sectors have been more common in the US than other countries. Yet the decline of public ownership of key sectors of the economy in the UK and elsewhere has helped to promote the notion of state regulation through functioning and allegedly independent agencies in the services of consumers in countries outside the US as well. The growth of democratic accountability, popular suspicion of professional self-regulation, and the rise of a scandal hungry mass media have been among other critical factors behind this development. However, little is known about the processes of regulation, and of de- and re-regulation, and the various and sometimes conflicting principles upon which such frameworks are based. The chapter consequently looks at a number of these principles as found in the business world, including those that are apparent in forms of global business regulation, and examines their likelihood and appropriateness for higher education. The approach and possible consequences of such frameworks in fields such as intellectual property and global tradable higher education services are also analysed.

Inevitably the theme of globalization and its consequences for university systems runs through a number of the chapters. Michael Gibbons, in Chapter 5, takes the notion of globalization as a process of competition that may arise from any quarter or country for businesses and that stimulates innovation as a response, but which in turn further animates global competitiveness. Universities are becoming key actors in enabling governments and companies to innovate through their increased involvement with an array of other bodies in networks of research activity and in their increasing turn to applied and commercially competitive forms of research. In these mode 2 forms (which are distinguished from mode 1 or basic or conventional research), knowledge is conceived and made applicable instantaneously as part of problem-solving. In this sense knowledge has become more widely or socially distributed, and, at the same time, it needs also to be socially as well as scientifically robust or justified. This raises important questions for universities in defining their specific role in these new types of research collaboration, and Gibbons argues that it is important that universities hold on to a purpose that is more socially aware, 'public good' oriented, and less profit-driven than is possible for commercial enterprises.

Globalization also figures increasingly in discussions over the benefits or otherwise of greater institutional differentiation in university systems, which are matters taken up in Chapter 6. The recent White Paper in England (DES: *The Future of Higher Education*), and Commonwealth Government consultation documents in Australia (DEST: *Higher Education at the Crossroads*), both argue for institutional diversity as part of a process for creating world-class universities. The US is often looked to as providing a successful model of institutional diversity, in which many different types of university meet the many and multifarious requirements of a fast-moving and dynamic society.

Yet such notions often run counter to the pressures of the market, and the stratification of hierarchical prestige, that are now ingrained in university systems. They also tend to run counter to the policies of governments themselves, despite the diversity rhetoric they espouse. The theory of competitive realism is advanced as a form of parsimonious explanation for the desire of the weaker and less prestigious universities to emulate market leaders. This 'power gap' between institutions in a self-reproducing or 'managed market' is a critical impediment at institutional level for state-sponsored efforts to seek greater university differentiation. The policy key may be to focus less on creating what may become ossified or static stratification systems of universities through misplaced emphasis on institutional diversity, and to encourage innovation and dynamic competition, particularly in teaching and learning. This may better resolve the problems of mass higher education in a manner that eventually may lead to greater rewards and prestige for those universities predominantly engaged in the teaching and learning function. Eventually such an approach may also give so-called 'league tables' of university prestige rather less predictable outcomes than currently.

In Chapter 7 Svava Bjarnason examines the notion of borderless higher education and, particularly, the recent growth in new providers of higher education. Often these are unabashedly 'for-profit' private bodies, utilizing the corporate form and the latest communication and information technologies, and increasingly seeking wider global reach. In some cases, however, they are corporate universities – often re-branded and expanded human resources departments of major corporations – although consortia of traditional universities are beginning to feature as they explore the best means for extending their own commercial and international activities. An important issue is whether these new providers, who are often welcomed by national governments, not least in parts of the developing world, as they help increase higher education capacity without calling heavily on the public purse, offer a major challenge to the traditional university. The picture that emerges is one of both competition and collaboration, and Bjarnason explores likely future scenarios, not least in the context of the GATS, that are characterized by the extent to which these two principles predominate.

Yoni Ryan, in the concluding chapter, looks at changes more generally to the teaching and learning function in the global age. She offers a more micro-analysis of the impact of globalization on universities than found in the other chapters, and examines closely the pedagogic implications of its processes. Increased international student mobility, alongside the mass characteristics and large student populations of many contemporary universities, are changing the assumptions, approaches and definitions of the academic role in quite dramatic ways. The consequences of the new information and communication technologies for learning practices are also explored, and Ryan suggests that their application are not simply hindered by protectionist and reactionary academic attitudes, but that positive implementation is more widespread than conventional surveys indicate and that new technologies are often embraced within what are quite limiting institutional and other structures.

In conclusion, however, all the authors are agreed that the university in the global age is one of the most important and fascinating of institutions, but that many of the changes that are occurring in higher education systems virtually everywhere require more extensive research and more sophisticated policy analysis than is available currently. We hope that this book may help to sustain such an argument.

ROGER KING

# List of Abbreviations

| | |
|---|---|
| **AVCC** | Australian Vice Chancellors Committee |
| **BBC** | British Broadcasting Authority |
| **CHEA** | Council for Higher Education Accreditation (US) |
| **CNAA** | Council for National Academic Awards (UK) |
| **COL** | Commonwealth of Learning |
| **CPD** | Continuing Professional Development |
| **CRE** | Association of European Universities |
| **CVCP** | Committee of Vice Chancellors and Principles (UK), now Universities UK (see below) |
| **DETYA** | Department of Education, Training and Youth Affairs (of the Commonwealth government of Australia) |
| **EC** | European Commission |
| **ECTS** | European Credit Transfer Scheme |
| **ERASMUS** | A student mobility programme of the European Union |
| **ERASMUS WORLDWIDE** | As for above except for non-European international student mobility |
| **EU** | European Union |
| **GATE** | Global Alliance for Transnational Education |
| **GATS** | The General Agreement on Trade in Services (part of the World Trade Organization's processes for liberalizing world trade) |
| **GATT** | General Agreement on Tariffs and Trade |
| **HEFCE** | Higher Education Funding Council for England |
| **HGMP** | Human Genome Mapping Project |
| **ICTs** | Information and Communication Technologies |
| **IDP Australia** | The International Development Programme (of the Australian Vice Chancellors Committee) |
| **IMF** | International Monetary Fund |
| **IMS** | Instructional Management System |
| **INQAAHE** | International Network for Quality Assurance Agencies in Higher Education |

| | |
|---|---|
| **LEONARDO** | European Union student mobility scheme |
| **LMS** | Learning Management System |
| **MBA** | Masters of Business Administration |
| **MFN** | Most Favoured Nation |
| **MIT** | Massachusetts Institute of Technology |
| **NGO** | Non-Governmental Organization |
| **NT** | National Treatment |
| **NYSE** | New York Stock Exchange |
| **OECD** | Organisation for Economic Co-operation and Development |
| **PSHE** | Public Sector Higher Education (UK) |
| **QAA** | Quality Assurance Agency (UK) |
| **QUADS** | US, EU, Canada and Japan |
| **R and D** | Research and Development |
| **RMIT** | Royal Melbourne Institute of Technology |
| **SOCRATES** | European Union student mobility scheme |
| **TNU** | TransNational University |
| **TRIPS** | Agreement on Trade Related Aspects of Intellectual Property Rights |
| **UGC** | University Grants Committee (in the UK, but now replaced by Funding Councils) |
| **UNESCO** | United Nations Educational, Scientific, and Cultural Organization |
| **WIPO** | World Intellectual Property Organization |
| **WTO** | World Trade Organization |

# 1 The Contemporary University

*Roger King*

## ▶ Introduction

There is a longstanding story, often regaled by vice chancellors in trying to explain to lay audiences the essence and background of the modern university, that points out that of the 80 or so institutions that have survived from medieval to contemporary times, over 60 are universities. Other remaining bodies include the Catholic Church and the British monarchy. The lessons drawn from this homily vary, usually depending on the attitude of the particular vice chancellor, the type of university that she or he leads, and possibly the composition of the audience. For some, the moral of the tale is that universities are adaptable, resilient and, in some ancient cases, have an authority that pre-dates and is superior to that possessed by the government of the day. Others more wryly conclude that it is harder to supersede antiquity than anyone might imagine, and that to drag universities into the modern world is going to take an effort of Herculean proportions.

Yet the story is misleading. Most universities are not medieval creations but were established in the late nineteenth and twentieth centuries. Their histories reflect the concerns of industrialization, nation-state formation and democratization, and, more recently, postmodernist critiques of authoritative claims to knowledge, and also the issues surrounding globalization. Certainly the origins of the word 'university' can be traced back to the European fifteenth century, when it referred to a range of corporate entities, including the guilds. Universities such as that at Bologna go back to at least the eleventh century. The early ecclesiastical and medieval origins of ancient universities, such as those at Oxford and Cambridge, still can be found in some of the pageants and practices today, including the persisting influence if no longer outright dominion of the fellows and the colleges, and their antipathy to the executive assumptions of vice chancellors and chaired professors as found elsewhere.

But the university usually is seen best as the fairly recent creation of modernity, and particularly as one of the instruments for the consolidation of territorial nation states. And because the origins of democracy and the nation state have varied by country, then so have the historical trajectories of university systems, even if today they increasingly confront a similar set of dilemmas. Continental Europe, the United Kingdom, and the United States – to take some important but not exhaustive examples – exhibit different characteristics in their higher education systems and culture, not least in their attitudes to the idea of the university as a public service or a private enterprise, going back many years, which markedly colour views of the appropriate relationships of universities to their central states.

A key issue for the chapters in this book is whether the decline in sovereignty and influence of the territorial state, and the growth of international and supranational jurisdictions, alongside the increased globalization of the world economy, also heralds, if not the end of the university, then its profound transformation. If nation states lose their ability to influence directly, and predominantly fund, universities operating as increasingly independent commercial entities on a worldwide scale, in pursuit of what they see as their own corporate advantage, then how are universities to be 'steered' in the interests of the country? Or is it possible, as we have seen in the business world, for governments to regard national advantage as accruing more from the successful economic activities of 'their' independent transnational universities than from the exercise by these institutions of public authority in the service of broader social objectives?

These matters are particularly germane as the proportion of public or governmental funding in the overall budgets of many universities in places such as the UK or Australia, where traditionally it has been quite high, continues to drop. In comparison to that derived from commercial and other sources, not least from private fee-paying international students, it is now generally below 50 per cent in both countries. Moreover, some of the traditional preserves and authority of the university are also being challenged. The notion that the university is the essential and unique depository of unique knowledge, which is produced by strong scientific and intellectual communities, and adherence to appropriate and well-attested (and well-policed) methodologies, alongside the personal and social disinterestedness of practitioners, is being undermined by postmodernist critiques of universal knowledge propositions and their counter-claims of the essential contingency and social constructivism of what passes as objective and scientifically generated truth. Moreover, as Michael Gibbons argues in Chapter 5, science increasingly has to be socially relevant as well as objective for its contemporary acceptability, while the growth of globally distributed knowledge production and its application is occurring on a greater level outside the university.

To understand better these trends it is necessary to examine the histories of university systems and to understand why they originated in the first place. It is doubtful that one could find any country these days, at least of moderate size and above, that does not have some universities and which does not regard them as significant in national development. But why should this be? What functions do universities perform, and what has been the nature of their relationships with emergent nation states that has allowed them to attain the significance and status that are still afforded to them today? And is this likely to continue?

## ▶ The origins of the modern university

The early beginnings of what we might recognize as the contemporary university are located in a handful of European countries. The European growth of the universities, and systematic scholarly activity generally, from around the twelfth century, leading to the later explosion in scientific thought in the sixteenth century, occurred in the absence of the later idea that the university engaged only in free intellectual investigation. This is not surprising given the ecclesiastical and particularly monastic origins of the early colleges, and the emphasis on the transmission of unchanging and revealed truth. It was also long regarded as commonplace before modernity that the university should undertake other and wider social purposes, too, than simply intellectual activity. In continental Europe, including Scandinavia, quite early on the position was established that the state legitimately could turn to the universities and require that they supply the necessary educated personnel for the growing needs of government rule, particularly those trained in administrative and other forms of law (Torstendahl, 1993).

In the seventeenth and eighteenth centuries it was still the case that academic and other innovators were as likely to be found outside the university as within it. The different 'disciplines' had yet to form themselves into exclusive 'life-worlds' and members of universities did not seek to separate themselves in their workaday endeavours from other educated people. Moreover, the self-educated amateur moved freely and participated fully within the scholarly and scientific work of the various European countries. The hurdles of formal credentials and paper qualifications for entry into the realms of academe had yet to appear, and nor had fully emerged the full-blown legal–rational or bureaucratic forms of state and other organizations which Weber (1968) was to describe as confronting and overcoming 'dilletantism' or amateurishness because of its superior effectiveness and efficiency.

During this time, however, nation states became clearer about the type of specialized skills that they required to operate their growing administrations and their extending forms of social intervention. There developed quite a close relationship between rulers and universities and a shared view that universities had practical import in educating public officials. In some cases states were active in establishing additional, often regional, universities to provide the theoretical understanding necessary for increasingly sophisticated statecraft. Following a university education state rulers felt that subsequent practical application could be developed on the job – 'in-house' to use modern parlance – or in non-university, dedicated and specialist institutions. Consequently broad subject range and an emphasis on theory (albeit capable of relevancy) were characteristics already beginning to distinguish universities from other forms of more specialist education and training provider.

With the rise of the German research universities in the nineteenth century was added the significant function of knowledge creation to that of teaching and the supply of educated personnel. This was a model – in which the university undertook both teaching and research – that had a wide international impact by the turn of the twentieth century, not least in the fast-expanding system of the US. However, while for many on the Continent the implication was that teaching and research were quite different, including in importance, and could function quite separately, for others, especially in the UK, the slower development of the research function was much more closely aligned to the prospect of invigorating and keeping updated the transmission of knowledge to students, than the creation of new knowledge for its own sake and with its own rationale. The two functions of teaching and research instead were regarded as synergistically related.

With the growth of scientific reasoning, and the self-organization of disciplinary and other intellectual communities to formulate and legislate on accepted methodologies and procedures, came the claim that institutional autonomy and academic freedom were necessary conditions for further scientific, and therefore military and industrial, advance. It was an assertion that national governments, increasingly caught up in the pressures of international rivalry and seeking improvements in warfare, found hard to resist. There developed a tacit if not formal agreement that universities were to have relatively privileged forms of corporate autonomy, provided that they delivered the goods with educated and trained personnel and forms of applicable new knowledge that contributed to the economic and military success of the nation. The extent of this autonomy varied by country, with it being quite marked in the UK, whereas on the Continent the stronger 'public service' notions associated with the universities saw staff, for example, as employees of the state. Yet, in most places, critiques by academics and students of existing political and social arrangements could be tolerated by rulers provided that they were not too revolutionary. And as long as universities were not entirely self-supporting and relied on public expenditure, as was generally the case, although again the levels varied in different countries, any such radical tendencies could generally be regarded by the state as manageable.

Of course, institutional autonomy and academic freedom are not necessarily the same. We shall see that in the last decade or so of the twentieth
century, reforms of university systems in many countries strengthened the
corporate independence of the university but increased the variety of managerial and other external controls over the working practices of academics.
Irrespective of whether systems centralized (with stronger forms of state
accountability and evaluation, to overcome the local powers of the professors, disciplines and fellows), or decentralized (with functions and responsibilities devolved from government to stimulate institutional competition),
executive teams became ever more authoritative.

In the middle of the twentieth century, the view of the necessary freedom
of science found its most explicit theorization in the work of Popper (1945),
who linked its necessary conditions to the notion of political liberty and
democracy prevailing more generally in society – in comparison with, say,
the totalitarian dogmatism of the Soviet Union. Intellectual freedom, in his
view, could hardly operate in a self-enclosed vacuum, marked out in its own
territory or enclave within a wider societal and political repression. The
nature and structure of scientific knowledge – which is refutable, provisional,
revisable and uncertain – is connected in its anti-doctrinal character to the
'open society' of liberal democracy.

Nonetheless, conservatism and dogmatism have also been found within
as well as outside the university. For this reason, in nineteenth-century
Prussia (later Germany) academics became civil servants and part of the state
payroll, with the purpose of making them relatively free from the patronage
and hierarchies of the professors. It was a move that reflected the benign
Continental view of the state as a neutral and socially benevolent instrument,
in comparison with the greater suspicion of it to be found in the more
market-dominated US, but also, to a lesser extent, in the UK. In the latter,
until relatively recent decades, a more personal and informal set of relations
– more clubbable – characterized the elite conversations of university leaders
and members of other state institutions, rather than either formal antipathy
or dependence. This reflected the dominant governing ideology, in the age
of the still small state, of self-regulation and autonomy for the professions
and key parts of business, in part as a form of a rather fearful oligarchic
defence against the prospect of popular democracy, and which utilized the
cultural norms and subtle social controls of the Victorian ideal of the well-
behaved 'gentleman' (Moran, 2003).

In a number of key developing university systems – Continental Europe,
the US and the UK – universities were increasingly seen in the nineteenth
and into the first years of the twentieth centuries as helping the establishment of elite cohesiveness and a wider sense of national (although still
predominantly exclusive) culture as part of territorial consolidation. They

promoted the spread of literacy and other skills recognized as essential for security and prosperity in the competing economies and state systems of the world. The result was that universities came to enjoy high status. They were seen as educating the social and intellectual cream of the nation. Although they enjoyed no monopoly in providing for all the new skills required for expanding industrial societies – professional education in growing competencies such as engineering and accountancy, for example, generally started outside the universities in specialized institutes and schools – it was a feature of the social aspirations of new professional occupations that their education and training should be undertaken within the universities. It was a sign of having arrived.

As with other organizations, universities generated 'collective personalities' and became more than simply an accumulation of their individual members, such as professors and fellows. In the UK and the US, universities were clearly corporate employers of labour. Scientists and other theorists, in their roles as teachers especially, had to reconcile their loyalties and commitments to their employer and institution, however tenuous, with a wider, increasingly transnational disciplinary identity. The universalizing tendencies of scientific and rational thought have ever since constantly chafed at the boundary limitations of employing organizations and nations.

However, it is not possible to discern one 'essential' relationship between universities and the state, based for example on autonomy and self-jurisdiction and justified as necessary conditions for scientific progress, for these relationships have varied between countries and over time. In the Continental system we find the greatest commitment to the notion of the university providing a public service, necessitating extensive state funding and with academics employed as civil servants, while in the US the market and the local state have predominated. In the UK we find rather a form of halfway house, with a strong tradition of private status and intimate relations with national elites being overtaken after World War II by extensive central governmental funding and with state intervention accompanied increasingly by forms of 'market-like' and consumer-oriented practices. It will be useful to consider these three types in further historical detail.

## ▶ The Continental model

What we recognize as the modern university, with both teaching and research as the primary functions, began to become established during the nineteenth century throughout continental Europe (Wittrock, 1993). Its most notable characteristic, particularly in what emerged as the new consolidated nation state of Germany in 1870, was the view that knowledge production through research and discovery was an essential function of the university, not simply the transmission of existing knowledge through teaching to upcoming generations. The churchly origins of earlier universities had been characterized more by the function of revelation (of ancient texts and verities) than by novel or propositional assertions, based on critical investigation, which were challengeable and changeable. The subsequent advance of Enlightenment thinking, however, and the application of rationalist methods reinforced the notion of the university as the locus of science broadly conceived.

The development of basic and curiosity-driven research in universities was the logical next step in the development of rationalist ideas and functions. The Continental, particularly Germanic view, increasingly regarded research as the essential activity of the university and these notions particularly influenced scholars from the US. Veblen (1962), for example, writing in the early years of the twentieth century, felt that teaching undergraduate students was a pale and insipid undertaking in comparison with the excitement and societal value of path-breaking research. The Continental tradition, too, has been much more relaxed about the claimed necessary relationship between research and teaching, and has not recoiled from the prospect that they could be undertaken within different institutions. The UK belief in the essential synergy of teaching and research, as almost uniquely found within the university, was much less prevalent across the English Channel. In Continental eyes, research could quite easily, and without loss, be undertaken by specialist research institutes in the service of the knowledge requirements of the fast-expanding nation state.

Somewhat contrastingly, for a long while in the UK the role of research became associated with the view that research mattered because it refreshed teaching, rather than being justified as an important activity in its own right. Stimulating and up-to-date teaching benefited from being closely and institutionally located with innovative and creative research. Teaching was the primary university function – for the training of elites and the transmission of their culture – while research was potentially distracting, rather industrial, and potentially subversive of established customs and canons. After all, as Newman (1996) once famously observed in the Victorian age, why else should universities have any students at all if their sole function was simply to undertake research.

In France, an important variant of the Continental model was to locate the formation and education of top leaders outside the university. The *grandes écoles* were special bodies established in the nineteenth century for the development of technical and high-level administrative training. This followed from the urgent need in post-Revolutionary France in the first decades of that century to establish a credible and efficient system of national, central administration. Key education and training for the administrative and scientific elite, as well as lying outside the universities, also in this way were to be prised out of the hands of the churches and secularized in new modern organizations.

Nonetheless, national ruling requirements for a better-educated governmental and economic leadership were regarded as less compelling and rather lowly purposes for university endeavours in some of the early 'ideas' of the university, found particularly in Prussia and in the work of influential theorists of the university, such as Humboldt, Kant and Hegel (later also Weber), and which lay behind the development of the renowned University of Berlin in the first part of the nineteenth century. German idealist philosophy eschewed 'narrow' and infertile technical vocationalism in favour of a more humanistic, rounded approach to university education, which recognized the power of the link between teaching and research. The development of the critical power of reasoning and the general powers of the mind were seen as much more important for robust intellectual and civilized advance than an obsession with skills and discrete specialization. It was an idealist conception of unified knowledge and cultural cohesiveness that increasingly chimed with a sense of nationhood in the new Germany in the latter decades of the nineteenth century.

Yet, somewhat paradoxically, German universities became characterized by virtually the opposing set of characteristics to that of humanistic idealism. They became instead renowned throughout the world, and particularly in the US, for their scientific and disciplinary specialization, emphasis on research, and focus on graduate education rather than on undergraduate teaching. As in other parts of continental Europe, the development of the research-orientated university was contiguous with the establishment of the nation state and increasingly its need for national identity and new forms of applied knowledge. Throughout the twentieth century, especially after the two World Wars, science was seen as the source of wealth, power and expansion.

Although the research-driven and disciplinary specialist university is apparently the antithesis of humanistic idealism, it is arguable that the earlier claims for academic freedom of the German idealists such as Humboldt and Kant helped to generate the institutional space and freedom for the protection and advancement of increasingly departmentalized science, even if idealism, as a cognitive structure and theory of knowledge, proved much less influential. It provided a sound organizational justification for scientific freedom and as such helped stimulate the rise of the modern university. As Wittrock (1993) has noted, the impact of German idealism was not the preservation of a particular conception of appropriate scientific endeavour but the creation of autonomous institutional contexts that aided the emergence of the knowledge-producing university. For many, the ultimate rationale for the university can be traced back still to the Germanic idealists, in that in comparison with other forms of education provision, it remains the place for free and untrammelled critical discourse.

## ► The market model

It is commonplace to remark that the US is a liberal, market society with a distrust of, and indeed with a weak, central government. This can be seen in its system of higher education that, from the first, diverged from both its English foundations and also from many aspects of the Continental model (despite the later influence of the German research universities). Initially, as Keohane (2000) has observed, the institutions of higher learning established in the early seventeenth century by emigrants from Britain were similar to those with which they had been familiar back home. As with national state formation elsewhere, the colonies were also in need of educated and trained personnel to service the needs of the colonial administration. The first colleges, such as Harvard, and William and Mary, that were granted degree-awarding powers, had the residential and architectural settings of Oxford and Cambridge. The earliest curricula focused on a liberal undergraduate education, supported critically by libraries in an age and location when other sources of information were not easily available.

This colonial heritage had at least two significant consequences. Each colony and (subsequently) local state had an authority and pride in its own colleges that persisted and militated against any sense of strong federal intervention. And, second, any notion of a single national university never really took off. Rather, the approach, as in society generally, was pluralistic and committed to the institutional diversity appropriate to a fast-changing, immigrant-based society, with its multifarious needs. Different communities were felt to have different requirements that could only be catered for by various types of institution. But higher education was regarded as a democratic and economic necessity, whatever its form.

Within these institutions, given their virginal beginnings, it was hardly surprising that constitutional models derived from elsewhere, involving either the authority of the chaired professoriate (Continental), or the democracy of the fellows (Oxford and Cambridge), would attract initial consideration. However, the lack of a built-up academic eminence ruled out these designs, and paved the way for a novel approach based on strong presidential authority supported by trustees and boards with considerable local and external representation. In time this model was underlined in the twentieth century by the magnetism that private business executive and leadership styles exercised over the universities, reinforced by the reliance of universities on corporate endowments and student fees and the close links engendered with corporations as a result. Unlike much of continental Europe, for example, presidents and faculty were members of an autonomous 'state-free' profession, rather than public employees, and this may have contributed to the enterprise and innovation that came to characterize the US 'multiversity' and its many links and functions with a wide range of social interests. This included an early embrace of subjects and studies that were new and had a distinct practical bent, such as engineering and food production, and that helped to emphasize that universities had a wider sense of obligation to the whole society than simply to itself or to intellectual enquiry alone.

After World War II, the GI Bill, which assisted many war veterans to go to college, helped to modify popular perceptions of who should attend universities and at what age. As in other countries, the need for educated personnel and continuous scientific discovery and application brought federal government intervention in the form of aid for poor students and sponsorship of research and development, often for military purposes, as the Cold War intensified in the 1960s. But, instructively, when it came to undergraduate teaching and learning, the intervention was on the demand side through financial support for students rather than on direct supply-side subventions to institutions, and reinforced the student-as-consumer- approach of the American way in higher education.

The growth of federal funding, however, eventually may have helped to constrain levels of institutional diversity in the US and stimulated convergence between the public and private university sectors. Today private institutions depend more than they have before on public money, while public institutions are encouraged to expand the range of their charitable and entrepreneurial activities in order to supplement their incomes. Nonetheless, despite the strong tradition of wide social access, recognizable 'brand' institutions, such as Harvard and Yale, have worldwide renown. The top universities continue to find ways to socialize as well as to educate students in the intimate ways that conduce confidence and good character – those dispositions appropriate for elite and 'get-up-and-go' leadership positions.

From the outset the American system of higher education has been characterized by its orientation to many kinds of markets, and the requirement for institutions, if they were to survive, to respond adequately to those markets. Unlike the UK and continental Europe there was no central state largesse to fall back on, or a tradition of an Established Church that wished to maintain its higher education influence (and protect its sources of clergy supply) through donations to universities. Free, if a little insecure in some cases, might be an accurate description of most universities and colleges. But responding to the market, with its growing appetite for higher education, not least among upwardly aspirant immigrants who often possessed only sketchy educational preparation for university entrance, meant that the notion that all degrees were of a comparable standard – the claim strongly adhered to in the UK, for example – could never be realistically entertained. The maintenance of a common and high standard, in the absence of a public funding 'safety net', of the kind purported for UK universities, would have meant that many colleges and universities would have 'priced' themselves out of the market. Institutional survival dictated diversity, not commonality, in standards. Lower fees and lower standards were a market option that was justified by increased access and volume, and which enabled some institutions to find their own particular niche and to be financially viable.

One reason, therefore, why institutional diversity, as characterized by both varying standards, curricula and wide social and geographical access, is to be found in the US is located in the institutional requirement to stay in business in a market environment where funding generally has been provided by the direct 'out-of-pocket' consumer, rather than by the proxy third-party arrangements of the state ('simulated market'). Yet it is a diversity created as much by need as by desire. The poorer institutions would dearly like the prestige and market power of the high status universities – and with a fairy godparent handing out large amounts of finance, they would surely emulate the market leaders, whatever their mission – while the well-off always feel the competition from their near or foreign rivals to want to attract more status and funds. The elite behave consequently as though they too were poverty-stricken.

Martin Trow (1979) makes the interesting point that the US had a system of mass higher education over a century ago, well before it had the numbers that today are used to define whether a higher education system is mass or not. That is, it was institutionally open and diverse, welcoming to a variety of aspirants, and without the need to maintain a common 'gold standard' of degrees in sustaining a select or elite cohesiveness. Skill rather than culture was the driver. Student number growth has consequently not presented the problem of systemic switch or transition found in those systems such as the UK or Australia where elite purposes have had to be grafted on alongside greater numerical massification. In the US the basic structure for mass higher education was designed into the initial architecture of the system.

Moreover, the competitive market in the US has been repeatedly strengthened in the absence of a central government able or willing to regulate the colleges and universities. For the most part, the states rather than the federal government have taken powers over higher education, and decisions and resources have generally been pushed close to the consumer and those institutions most responsive to the consumer. It is only in recent years in the UK that the introduction of tuition fees for full-time domestic students and the abolition of maintenance grants have produced more 'customer-like' behaviour along the lines of the US, but central governmental funding remains, despite its recent attenuation, for most institutions a major source of income. In the US, public funds to support teaching are mostly funnelled to universities and colleges through their respective state governments rather than directly from the federal government, and there is little evidence of the strong central management of higher education policy by the state that is found in both the UK and the rest of Europe.

One aspect of the competitive search for students in the US (and increasingly in UK) is that that they come to be regarded as having 'chosen' to attend the university of their choice. Consequently universities come to feel some sense of ownership of their students, less perhaps these days in any patronizing way, but rather as a private or commercial company might feel in seeking to consolidate and build upon customer and brand loyalty. For the most part, in contrast, the Continental practice has been to view student attendance at university as almost a public welfare entitlement. Elsewhere, such as Australia, where user pays has also introduced more consumer-like characteristics, there is a practice for students to attend universities in their local state, which has constrained geographical mobility by students and hampered competitive efforts by universities to attract the best undergraduate students from a wider national pool. Continental universities also have tended to find students allocated to them, often in large numbers, and they have been largely disinterested (until recent public expenditure and other reforms) in how long it took for undergraduates to achieve a degree.

US universities and colleges have a long tradition of autonomy and independence. They appear to value their local roots and identity. In contrast, the behaviour of new provincial institutions in the UK, from the creation of the 'civic universities' in cities such as Manchester, Leeds and Nottingham at the turn of the twentieth century, through the university designation of the Colleges of Advanced Technology in the 1960s, and then of the polytechnics in the 1990s, has been for institutions to seek national and central governmental refuge from the perceived insecurities, pettiness and parochialism of their local origins. The lure of the bright academic lights of Oxford and Cambridge, of national and international prestige, of being at the top tables (in London), and of guaranteed central funding, have combined to prove an irresistible siren to most institutional leaders. Support from the centre, including government funding and regulation, for these largely provincially established universities has been viewed by vice chancellors as an act of liberation not of oppression, at least at points of transition. The result has been much greater and long-standing homogeneity in the UK than in the US of what a 'proper' university looks like.

## ▶ Managed markets and central regulation: the UK

A feature of the university system in the UK has been the reputational dominance of Oxford and Cambridge, who for long have contributed a major share of personnel for elite positions and, more recently, regularly have topped various 'league tables' of university performance. As we noted above, for most of the twentieth century, regional and other universities have sought to orient themselves, and aspire, to the academic distinction and style of Oxbridge. The latter has exercised a gravitational pull that has helped to drag the 'civics' away from local concerns to becoming part of a national system with common entry standards and a common salary scale. One outcome has been that the power of the professors has been less marked than found in Continental Europe. Corporate bodies of dons – the 'fellows' – have comprised the democratic governance of the colleges that make up the Oxbridge system. It is only very recently that the Oxbridge Universities have sought more executive authority along the lines found now in other universities in the UK and the US.

Formally, a national system in the UK was initiated with the establishment of the University Grants Committee (UGC) in 1919, a body that formulated a common public expenditure requirement to its sponsoring department – the Treasury – and allocated the subsequent block grant. Yet before then, the universities were subject to various interventions from central government, including over the granting of charters and the instigation of reviews into the purposes and administration of Oxford and Cambridge in the 1860s and 1870s, and also into the consequences of the reform of civil service examinations. These were actions in the second half of the nineteenth century that helped to emphasize that university development in the UK was beginning to be part of a clear national framework with central controls. Nonetheless, the predominant model at the turn of the twentieth century was that of state-backed professional autonomy and self-regulation, rather than public accountability or policy interventionism, in which gentlemanly and informal ideals of elite behaviour were seen as the most effective means for guaranteeing appropriate institutional governance in the national interest. The age was one still of oligarchy rather than popular democracy and this was reflected in government–university relationships.

The development of a national university system in the UK, and the changes to institutional governance and aims, was quite complex (Wittrock, 1993). As in the rest of Europe, the modern university took shape during the second half of the nineteenth century and at the turn of the twentieth. It was comprised of three particular, and interrelated, processes. Initially, around the 1850s, the notion of the importance of a liberal education that was relatively uncontaminated by the limiting perspectives of utility and vocationalism, was forcefully articulated by writers such as Newman and Mill. Rather like the German philosophical idealists, they argued that character development through close and intimate teaching and contact with 'gentlemen' was the prime purpose of the university. This had a particular resonance, as not only were the British Isles in need of continuing and enlightened governance, but the increased requirement to provide administrative rule to the growing dependencies of colonies and other parts of the expanding British Empire underlined the necessity for a growing cadre of well-educated – that is, well-formed – public servants.

The university teachers in the colleges of Oxford and Cambridge generated residential communities, characterized by what these days we might call their 'totality', on a 24-hour basis. This form of mannered but intimate living helped shape students in a more complete fashion than had been achieved before, either by the universities, or by the Church, and probably more so than by the family home. The outcome was a cohesive ruling class with a homogeneous culture, relatively protected from the vicissitudes that prevailed upon more ordinary folk, and sustained by clubbable and intimate forms of social interaction.

A second characteristic of university development that occurred in the second half of the nineteenth century in Britain, even in Oxford and Cambridge, was the rise of education for the growing professional occupations. It involved a deeper embrace of the needs of science, and gradually of research, and saw the construction of new schools for medicine and engineering. In a physical sense, the university campus became more recognizably modern, with buildings for lecture halls, laboratories and museums. The result was not the suppression of the collegiate system but the development of a more complex mosaic, with different types of educational practice and governance emerging but operating, cheek by jowl, in a relatively complementary way.

The third feature refers to what we have described above as the emergence of the 'civic universities' in the major towns and cities of Britain. These were new institutions that were formed at the turn of the twentieth century by local dignitaries who saw in a university for their area a source of pride, economic development and rising status. (These feelings are still around today, of course, as university developments in places such as Lincoln, Cornwall and the Highlands of Scotland testify.) It is often claimed that the rise of these civics helped to develop a more professional and even vocational curriculum in the universities. The closeness to provincial trade and local economic roots seemed to imply an alternative, perhaps more American, sense of what a university was meant to do, and which appeared to differ from the traditional Oxford and Cambridge model.

Yet it is easy to exaggerate these new influences. In a centralized, status-conscious system, such as that of the UK universities, there are major constraints on university leaders of all kinds to conform to the practices of the market leaders. The measure of success is achieving excellence in standards, recruits and, increasingly, research. Moreover, as we have seen in the later parts of the twentieth century, that is what the student/parent/employer apparently wants. They wish to be associated with the 'best' universities possible. And the 'best' university is a powerful, traditional, and green-lawned concept in the mind, whatever the everyday reality, which may be more urban and shabby.

The new provincial universities were no real exception to these influences. Their development underlines the proposition that, while institutional diversity was a characteristic of the historic development of the university system in the US, the situation in the UK has been much more one of institutional convergence, despite the rhetoric of many politicians and others who talk the diversity talk pretty well, but whose policies and actions appear to reflect quite the opposite. In any case, the description 'civic university' perhaps exaggerates the dependency of these institutions on local sources. It was not easy for them to attract local funding and members of local governments were by no means united in a view that a near-at-hand university was an undisguised blessing, a perspective reinforced by the often down-at-heel nature of the some of the accommodation that the new institutions were provided with in their early days.

In any case, all UK universities have had to take on board broad national, and not just local, needs, particularly to supply professional training and to undertake scientific research. The success of the German research universities and the enthusiastic adoption of more populous versions of the model in the US meant that internationally reputable universities in the UK – and those that aimed to be – could simply not ignore such developments. Disciplines and departments were the organizational reflection of these changes, resulting in universities beginning to include a mix of approaches, ranging from the generally liberal to the strictly scientific and applied.

World War I, and especially World War II, indicated the importance of science for military and economic progress and success. They also highlighted both the demand for higher education after the end of hostilities, and the need for states everywhere to encourage the output of more educated and trained personnel for global economic competitiveness. But in the UK the expansion of the system was a slow-burn affair. Although the influential Robbins Report (1963) advocated incremental student number growth it seemed to be within the need to not alter fundamentally the nature of how this was supplied from traditional university models and structures. However, the growth of an alternative form of higher education in the polytechnics and colleges in the 1960s and 1970s that was 'owned' and developed by the state – public sector higher education (PSHE) – and its accompanying 'binary line' (to distinguish it from the existing universities), stimulated considerable student expansion. It also generated arguments as to whether more efficient, user-friendly, teaching-orientated, vocational, locally responsive, multi- attendance mode and socially accessible forms of university education, as found in the polytechnics, were possible on a wider basis, including in the universities.

The designation of the polytechnics as universities and the formulation of 'mass' student growth targets in the 1990s have confirmed the increased salience and cost of higher education for governments, and the acceptance of the belief that 'human capital' investment was the most economically effective form of investment (in comparison with that in physical or tangible capital) in increasingly knowledge-based, postindustrial societies. But with expansion in the UK (and elsewhere), and the increase in the public funding of universities, has come regulation and a form of consumerism that has sought to make the universities more accountable in public terms than ever before.

## ▶ The accountable university: the UK experience

In the UK overall, the so-called Age Participation Rate (APR), which is the recruitment rate to universities from each cohort of school leavers, remained for a long time at around 15 per cent until 1985, before rising to reach 31 per cent in 1992. (In Scotland and Northern Ireland, however, the rate rose to over 40 per cent, with that in England correspondingly lower). Kogan and Hanney (2000) point out, however, that if mature students are included, the level of growth was even higher. The proportion of entrants over 21 years had grown from around 15 per cent to nearly 30 per cent between 1986 and 1995 (see also Robertson and Hillman, 1997, tables 1.3 and 1.9). The Dearing Report (1997) into higher education also reveals that expenditure on higher education increased by around 45 per cent in real terms between 1976 and 1996–7, but fell by about 40 per cent for each student over the same period.

Although the Robbins Report in 1963 reflected an increasing consensus in the post-World War II years that higher education was an important economic resource, it took some time before the nature of that education and its direct relevancy for the economy was challenged. Employers particularly complained about the 'anti-enterprise' and non-vocational character of the typical university curriculum, and the apparently greater interest of academics in basic and curiosity research than in that of greater applicability to industrial and commercial innovation. Consequently, governments of all persuasions began to take a greater interest in higher education in the 1970s and the possibility of steering it in directions that had the potential for greater economic pay-off.

At the same time there was an increasing belief that greater efficiency as well as effectiveness was possible from the university sector. Part of the problem was that there existed few levers available to governments both to test these notions and then to make policy interventions that worked. The secret academic garden, and the apparent control of institutions by staff rather than by managers, was seen as part of a general problem in public organizations that required more market-based forms of management. Moreover, the unwillingness of the electorate to pay high direct taxes, the end of the long boom 30 years in world economies by the mid-1970s, and yet the need for higher education expansion, meant that governments were always going to seek both greater cost efficiency from the universities and other public institutions, as well as exploring ways in which more private money, including student tuition fees, could be introduced. Greater accountability to the government on behalf of students, taxpayers and other users of university services was inevitable in the political climate of the 1980s and 1990s when there was a turn away generally from reliance on professional self-regulation and culture, to more transparent and numerical forms of public evaluation and democratic accountability.

Consequently, the introduction of a body of higher education law during these years helped reduce the formal autonomy of the universities (although, arguably, it increased the freedoms of the new universities, the ex-polytechnics). Statutory provisions created a prescriptive instrument for higher education funding, gave greater means of direction and influence to ministers, and provided for the formal assessment of the quality of the university output. A consequence was the view that funding, particularly for research, should aim both to reward and to promote excellence (rather than relevance, which was primarily assigned to the teaching function). The introduction of what turned out to be regular Research Assessment Exercises was a means of coping with the increased funding needs of 'big science' through selectivity in research allocations based on track records, but with a methodology that applied to all subjects.

Kogan and Hanney (2000) suggest that universities have shared a special place in the governance of British public institutions that is confined to a few institutions, including, for example, the British Broadcasting Corporation (BBC) and national museums. They are mostly charter institutions with an (almost) independent status, but fall under public policies that constitute the basis for their funding. As such they differ from those public bodies that have a virtual direct line of command from a government department – such as found with the armed forces, the inland revenue and social security – and also from more intermediary arrangements, such as those provided for the local authorities, which are bodies intended to follow national policies but while also taking account of their local electorates, and also utilizing the specialist and professional expertise found within their administrations. The proposition advanced by Kogan and Hanney is that this relatively privileged position for universities has been hacked away at and that it remains under further threat. The longstanding discretions allowed to universities and their academics have been increasingly whittled away by new accountability procedures (not least for assessing quality), although it has not entirely disappeared. Rather, an at times uneasy collaboration and cooperation between academe and officialdom, the latter in the form of institutional and governmental leaders, prevails. Institutional and professional freedoms are still felt to be necessary for the successful operation of core university functions, particularly in the laboratory and in the classroom, although it has become subject to both greater external evaluation, and to changes in learning and teaching methods, which now tend to focus on team efforts and student choice (as found, for example, in modularization).

These relationships are often described by reference to the 'triangle' of forces between professional–collegial, governmental–managerial, and the market (Becher and Kogan, 1992; Clark, 1983). In the UK, there seems to have been a movement of power from the base of the institution – the working academic – to much higher up: to institutional leaders, the market, and national authorities. The result has been a range of allegations that the essential collegiality of university decision-making (necessary for creativity, disinterestedness and so on) has been forfeited. In its place now stands executive control along the lines found in corporate commercial organizations.

Yet it is not clear that a pure form of collegiality, with a minimal level of organization to control entry and standards and to allocate tasks and funds, while avoiding control over working practices, has ever really existed. Conditions for the receipt of public funding, and the need to ensure that university clients, particularly students and employers, are not short-changed have always ensured some level of top-down constraint, even if it was exercised in ways that worked with the collegial grain.

Moreover, the status of universities and the use of the 'university' title has long been a prerogative of the centre. A Royal Charter granted by the Privy Council on the advice of government ministers, or statutory legislation in Parliament, have been the instruments by which government has maintained part of its protectorate. However, relationships between universities and the state have become increasingly formalized. Although it could be argued reasonably that the closeness of the universities and government was even more pronounced in the 1930s than it is today, then it was based on cosiness, mutual elite respect, and intimacy. Now it is characterized by greater wariness, formality and transparency.

As Kogan and Hanney (2000) have acknowledged, there is a conundrum for the state in determining appropriate levels of both institutional autonomy and political constraint for universities. The importance of the universities to the economy leads to a stronger governmental curiosity in it, while the argument that knowledge creation is best served by academic freedom works in the other direction. For the most part, despite the sometimes onerous impositions of the Quality Assurance Agency (QAA), arguments in favour of intellectual and scientific independence have generally carried the day. Unlike many parts of the Continent, academics are not civil servants or direct state employees, with all the constraints which (formally at least) that entails. Comparatively in the world, UK universities still enjoy high levels of market and professional deregulation, although quality regulation has increased. The notion of the university, not as a part of the state bureaucracy, but as an independent corporation and community of scholars, still prevails.

Although it is often remarked that universities became part of the general reforms of the public sector instigated by the Thatcher administrations of the 1980s, including market deregulation and devolution, it has to be remembered, as we noted above, that the existing universities started from a position of strong autonomy. They were always much more likely to be subject to the other side of the Thatcher reforms, namely stronger regulation of product and other outputs as a means of protecting the general public from pure market freedoms. It was the polytechnics, through the granting to them of incorporation, the abolition of the restriction on the use of the university title, and the abolition of the Council for National Academic Awards (CNAA) – a body that regulated the standing of polytechnic degrees, although with increasing liberality – who gained most from the economic deregulatory aspects of the new public management. External quality regulation, also, was not new to institutions that previously had come under the auspices of HM Inspectorate for Education (even if they had not liked it much).

The traditional universities, therefore, have experienced greater changes (and shocks) from the introduction of a stricter external evaluative framework that effects both funding (particularly for research) and reputation (including from teaching quality grades and their publication in newspaper 'league tables'). A difficulty with a stronger regulatory position towards the universities that the new approaches reflects, derives from the historic special position of the universities in their relationship to the state. In part, governmental models of standards and protections generally are aimed at external constituencies, such as consumers, and the belief that greater quality assessment would lead from, and contribute to, better and more information being available in the public domain.

'Naming and shaming', 'league tables' and the like are processes designed to reinforce the notion of the student as a consumer, who is able, through improved choice, to exert greater competitive pressures on the higher education system. There is much less reliance in contemporary governmental measures on the professional commitment of either the institution collectively or the individual academic. Yet, as Williams (1999) has noted, the critical information feedback loops of efficient markets are absent in higher education. The repeat customer is missing and students of school-leaving age often have difficulty in assessing both their needs and the claims of competing universities.

The consequences clearly are intended to be punitive where that is deemed to be appropriate by the market. Yet quality methodologies also have been introduced (by both the QAA recently and by its predecessor body, the Higher Education Quality Council) with a different approach in mind. These are aimed at auditing (not assessing by grading) institutions own processes, and where the purpose is the production of information for the institution (rather than for the consumer directly) to use. In comparison with other methodologies, the purpose is to work with the grain of institutional autonomy and self-regulatory and professional practice. Governments seem unable to make up their minds as to how far universities can be trusted and left to their own processes, and the result is oscillation in state–university arrangements, particularly on quality arrangements that show little sign of stabilizing.

Moreover, the strong executive authority possessed by governing parties in the Westminster parliamentary system, unlike federal or consociational regimes, grants considerable and relatively unrestrained freedom for governments to experiment with policies. In the UK this has contributed more widely to hyper-policy and institutional innovation by the state, particularly as part of efforts to halt economic decline in the past three decades or more, in which the introduction of ill-informed policy reform results in negative or perverse feedbacks and unintended consequences. This, in turn, leads to even more unstable and increasingly formalized regulation, without an adequate level of support from those being regulated, and lacking enhanced effectiveness (Moran, 2003). Higher education is a notable exemplar of such processes.

In part, this oscillation stems from the need for a constant balance to be struck between the 'invisible colleges of academics', to use the telling description from Kogan and Hanney, and the formal governance of universities, including external governmental constraints. It is academics that still confer substantial legitimacy and prestige on the system, and who are incorporated into the formal peer reviews of colleagues and their work that are required by government policies, and which have major funding consequences. Although governments and funding bodies establish the policies and frameworks for evaluation and funding, the substantive judgements and allocations are made – and effectively legitimized – by academics. Curriculum and research objectives still remain largely the prerogative of the practitioner.

The greater formality and transparency of government evaluation of universities have extended market-like behaviour in institutions and reinforced competition for public and other resources. This has also allowed institutional leaders to find a basis for their own internal resource allocations – potentially more formal and externally validated than the outcomes of internal 'turf wars'. Departments, too, are allocated resources against measurable outputs, such as publications, external commercial income, or student numbers, and may have to purchase services within an internal market from other departments of the university.

There is little doubt that these changes have reinforced the role and power of institutional managers, particularly at the top. The developments have generated data useful for internal planning and control, as well as for meeting external reporting obligations. Vice chancellors and their teams are acutely aware of the competitive environment in which they operate and have to be very conscious of the quality of service provided from their organization, especially in the form of client satisfaction. They cannot simply leave these matters to chance, for institutional funding and their own executive and fiduciary responsibilities would be placed at risk. But the need to produce more – graduates, publications, commercial projects – with fewer resources has probably been at least an equal source of the greater executive responsibility and authority to be found in universities these days than simply competition itself. It is arguable, too, that the rise of managerialism is also the rise of rational and more objective ways of running large organizations. It is not simply a power play to impose order on recalcitrant academics. The sheer size and expansion of the higher education system has produced changes that may have reduced the mystique and special status of the university academic. The remorseless decline in their salaries would seem to suggest that this has occurred, at least in part as a consequence of increased supply.

## ▶ Non-western countries

A number of developments that we have described as part of the UK experience can be detected in other countries. There are patterns and convergences to state–university relationships that suggest that governments are facing similar problems and, because they move in similar policymaking and epistemic communities, that they come up with similar responses. More particularly, developing countries also seem to be adopting measures that are similar to those found in the West, such as greater corporate autonomy for their higher education institutions as a means of encouraging motivation and innovation for greater commercialization and private income generation, and the introduction of shared costs between governments and students and other users of university programmes. Although the outcome of national liberation movements generally resulted in state monopolies of tertiary education – and which have lasted over 30 years and more – the World Bank (2002) has noted a marked growth in the number of private universities and colleges, in response especially to population growth and rising demand for higher education which is outpacing the funding capacities of national governments.

These developments are stronger in the non-western world than in the relatively prosperous countries of, say, Europe and the US, and are leading to quite radical changes to the historic pattern of predominantly state financing and provision. For example, between 1990 and 1999 in Sub-Saharan Africa, the number of private sector institutions grew from an estimated 30 to more than 85. In other African countries with a strong commitment to economic liberalism generally, such as Kenya, Tanzania, Ghana and Uganda, there has been a similarly large expansion in private institutions, although the trend is less marked in the French-speaking nations. In Africa generally, however, real public expenditure on education dropped 25.8 per cent between 1995 and the end of 2000 (Maxwell *et al.*, 2000).

Elsewhere the growth of private universities has been more recent and sometimes unexpected. The Islamic Republic of Iran, where private provision commenced in 1983, has over 30 per cent of the total student population in such institutions, while Jordan, without a private tertiary sector as late as 1991, in 1999 had over 35 per cent of student enrolments in the private sector. In post-Communist east Europe and central Asia, without private tertiary colleges in 1990, there are over 350 such bodies today teaching a quarter of a million students. In south and east Asia many countries are following the Japanese path and private universities are mopping up a large part of increased demand for higher education. According to the World Bank, in the Philippines and South Korea the private sector represents around 80 per cent of total enrolments, while India and Indonesia, with tiny private sectors only a few years ago, now have around 50 per cent in private institutions. In South America, enrolments in private colleges now exceed 40 per cent of the whole student community, which is second only to east Asia. Even among nations in which the state provides and funds the majority of tertiary education, such as Egypt, Morocco, Tunisia and Yemen, governments are slowly setting up regulatory frameworks that allow for the expansion of private provision.

In part this caution in this latter category stems from the entrenched opposition in many countries to such developments, not least in the public universities, not simply on the grounds of vested interests but often because of well-founded concerns about quality control and the fears of too strong a foreign influence if the private sector is permitted to grow without adequate standards. In South Africa, a tight regulatory regime operates for the registration of private and foreign providers, reflecting suspicion about the commercial motives of such bodies and the dangers that they pose for the building up of a national tertiary capacity that would act as a key lever of economic development and national and cultural cohesiveness.

Yet the expansion of private provision is likely to continue to grow. Governments generally lack the fiscal resources to respond to rising domestic demand for a university education with more state supply, and largely they feel that global contacts, innovation, and the building up of international research networks are likely to flow more easily in a sector characterized by competition between the two sectors. Moreover, in a world of increasing global human resource mobility, the fear of 'brain drains' to the more powerful West, and especially the US without the flexibility and rewards offered by private provision and competition, looms large in higher education policymaking. A critical issue for the developing world especially, however, is to construct regulatory regimes towards universities that encourage private expansion but which insist on financial and quality safeguards in the interests of their citizens. In Nigeria, where the higher education sector was freed to the private sector in 1979 without regulation, 26 low quality 'universities' opened within six months and the policy had to be revoked. Undoubtedly, in both the West and the developing world, a shift is occurring away from the notion of higher education as a publicly funded social good to one that sees it more as a private investment in a better career and life generally, which reinforces the view that users should pay a substantial part for such opportunities. With constrained funding, public universities struggle to meet rising demand for higher education, and private institutions often appear to be the remedy.

Moreover, the increasing convergence in national tertiary policymaking in both the developed and developing world, which reflects in part at least the growing integration of worldwide economies, polities and cultures to be found in globalization, is likely to be furthered by current rounds of the World Trade Organization (WTO) liberalization of services processes. This suggests that such convergences may continue, irrespective of continuing differences and traditions of state–society relationships found in different countries.

## ▶ Conclusion

It is a moot point whether an increase in the amount and the quality of information on university competency made available to prospective students and other purchasers of university services will actually improve institutional performance. The choice by prospective students of undergraduate courses appears dependent on a range of factors, notably location and the potential for a reasonable nightlife, rather than solely on the courses that a university offers. Student satisfaction with programmes and staff appears to be consistently high, at least as derived from regular surveys. However, universities undoubtedly, as a result, have to be much more careful about the public claims that they make.

The growth of the external evaluation of university quality and standards, including the greater provision of information to third parties, marks a decline in governmental – and possibly wider – trust in the claims of professions to guarantee competency and customer protection. The emphasis instead is on publicly available data and transparency, rather than on intimate or 'inside' knowledge, in an age where complexity, size and distance make it difficult for purchasers of services and goods of all types to be confident that they have sufficient information on which to base their decisions. Public institutions of every variety are subject to these processes. The high profile incidents of medical failings by some consultants and doctors in recent years have contributed more generally to wider public demands for greater controls over standards and reductions in risk. Although the choice of a university may not fall into the life and death category of many medical purchases, it is generally a once-and-for-all decision of fairly momentous importance.

Four models of medical care have been outlined (see Harrison *et al.*, 2002, for example) that can also be utilized to cast light on changes in governmental attitudes to universities. The first model may be called reflective practice and is based on the idea that an individual professional should be constantly examining his or her practice in an open and critical manner. It includes the notion that this process can be aided by frequent audit of particular practices for patient outcomes, and that both audit and the corrections based on it are best supported by an open and peer-confident collegiate approach involving other professionals as equals. A second but related model, is based on the formulation of 'good practice' guidelines by professional communities, generated at meetings and conferences with the aim of achieving professional consensus, but largely lacking in systematic scientific underpinnings.

The third model has been styled as critical appraisal as it generally involves interrogation of published research findings. It differs from the above approaches in being more suspicious of personal experience – even if critically appraised – and aims at enabling practitioners to attain the skills to find, interpret and apply research outcomes. The purpose is to use research findings to produce evidence-based policy change. The fourth model is sometimes referred to as scientific-bureaucratic, as, like the third model, it is based on the view that valid and reliable knowledge is primarily drawn from an accumulation of well-evidenced research undertaken by experts, in clinical trials for example. However, it differs in that the result tends to be manifested in government-approved and official clinical protocols that are conveyed to practitioners with the expectation that they be followed. Both these latter two models operate on the assumption that good practice cannot be judged simply on the basis of consumer demand. However, the movement from the first through to the fourth models can be described as a move away from trusting the practice and experience of the professional to a greater reliance on external guidelines and protocols that are generated through scientific research and promulgated with the use of state authority.

One of the reasons why the scientific-bureaucratic approach has found favour recently is that it has been viewed as both generating greater consumer confidence that professional practice is being updated and is consistent in its good standards, and as enabling costs (especially the purchase of drugs) to be kept under some form of control that would be difficult if they were simply practitioner-led. As the government is the main 'consumer' and purchaser of medical services on behalf of the general public (as it still tends to be in higher education, too) it has a strong interest in the use of apparently objective and aggregate data on good practice and performance through a framework of external evaluation.

As in healthcare, university practices are generally not driven by individual consumers, as payments are made by third parties (predominantly the state) rather than directly by out-of-pocket or individual expenditures. (To use an expression, the consumption and purchase is 'collective'). Naturally those that pay the bills also to want to exercise the main influence, not least on costs. This results in the imposition of external constraints on professionals by governments not able to rely on the incentives and sanctions of an individually driven consumer market, but having to use proxy market indicators of performance (audit, aggregate data analysis and target compliance), which are much more intrusive, instead.

It is an interesting point whether a movement towards more direct out-of-pocket individual purchasing of higher education would lead to less formal and intrusive controls over institutions and academics than is the case with the current third-party payment arrangements through the state. One way of exploring this issue further would be to examine public policy processes in a number of different sectors. Is there evidence that state payments on behalf of the consumer lead to the gradual imposition of stronger forms of external and state-imposed governance on institutions and practitioners, and a distrust of the professional, and does the obverse also apply, namely that direct user-pays processes enable a greater consumer or market constraint on professionals but less governmental impositions of often very irksome and excessively formal external frameworks? And, if there was such evidence, which form of constraint would institutions and their academics prefer?

These and other issues that have been raised in this chapter will now be explored further in the chapters that follow. They are intended to try and comprehend the nature of the modern university in a realistically holistic manner and therefore to be valuable to both policymakers and practitioners who sometimes feel that they lack an overall perspective for sorting out the wood from the trees. The approach will be historical, contemporary, comparative and global. It will also, where that is appropriate, seek to challenge some of the everyday assumptions about university systems found in political rhetoric.

# 2 The University in Europe and the US

*Kenneth Edwards*

## ► Introduction: the development of the idea of the university in Europe and the US

In the opening chapter Roger King describes the development of the university from the medieval period to the present day, and points to the important influence of the nation state, particularly in modern times. Nation states have long regarded their universities as resources of great significance in implementing national economic and social policies. As we shall see, this continuing importance, and the pressures that it produces, presents universities with one of their major dilemmas. They rely on the state for much of their funding, and are subject to an increasing range of social and political objectives, and yet they are becoming both more internationalized and corporate in their activities. It is not yet clear how these tensions will be resolved, or in which direction.

This is not to suggest that university–state relationships are broadly the same in all countries, as has been noted in Chapter 1. The political aims of individual nation states differ, and consequently university systems have become heterogeneous, not only in the legal and regulatory frameworks operating in various countries, but also in many aspects of their structures and cultures. It is not that difficult to identify the specific national characteristics of individual higher education systems.

Nonetheless, as was also illustrated in Chapter 1, there are many features that are common across the university systems of continental Europe, but are not found in the US. Moreover, the universities in the UK (as with many aspects of UK life) are in some ways intermediate between both. Having described in the previous chapter the historical and cultural factors that have been responsible for these transatlantic differences, we now attempt to examine them further in the context of responses by institutions and governments to increasingly sharp global challenges.

Universities across the world face similar problems, most of which combine both pressures and opportunities. It will be useful to highlight three of the most important. First, reductions in public funding are common in many countries, at least in terms of the funding provided on a per student basis, even if the absolute sums may have risen in partial response to expansions in the overall size of the higher education system. Perhaps para-doxically, and undoubtedly to the fury of some universities, the increase in total government expenditure, if not in unit terms, as countries move towards systems of mass higher education, generates enhanced govern-mental expectations and demands of university performance, despite the fact that government is funding a lower proportion of the total cost. These assumptions lead to increasing state controls over universities, including measures aimed at making more transparent their accountability for the use of public funds.

Second, challenges for higher education arise from the rapid development of communication and information technologies, which create what is usually referred to as the knowledge society. These impact directly on pedagogy and raise issues as to how best they are applied in teaching for generating the best learning experiences for students, and for equipping them with skills for the 'wired-up' global world. This includes the ability to keep on learning for a lifetime in order to acquire new skills as old ones become obsolescent at an ever faster rate. In return universities are required to develop programmes appropriate for the needs of adults at all ages.

Third, globalization, and particularly the growth of transnational higher education, poses major tests for universities. As will be detailed further in later chapters, expanding university provision across national boundaries arises in part from the increased potential created by technological change for institutions to undertake this activity, and in part because there is rising worldwide demand for highly educated people generally, and for the employ-ment skills that are necessary for competitive organizations and nations. Transnational higher education is a Janus-faced spectre, for it is seen as a threat by some universities but as an opportunity by others.

There are differences in the nature of the responses to these challenges, both philosophically and practically, by universities in Europe and the US. In Europe they are coloured both by the effects of history and culture, and by the unique influence of the European Union (EU). The Union, and the programmes of its executive arm, the European Commission, provide a powerful stimulus to rethink the idea of a European university and, more importantly, to consider the opportunity for universities to increase the level of their cooperation and to create a more coherent higher education system across Europe. A discussion of these European developments will constitute a major part of this chapter. But since any changes in universities are always conditioned by history, we need to examine their distinctive backgrounds in Europe and the US to understand better the contemporary variations in their 'idea' of the university.

## ► Continental Europe, Bologna and the modern university

In September 1988 the University of Bologna celebrated 900 years since its foundation with a series of events around a meeting of the Association of European Universities (CRE). The value of the conference was enhanced by the party atmosphere and wonderful Italian hospitality, in the light of which it seemed churlish to even raise the question of what actually happened in 1088 to create a 'university', a retrospective concept which clearly has evolved over time. When asked how he could be sure that the date of birth was 1088, a senior member of the university remarked that they had good evidence to indicate that in 1888 the University had celebrated the 800 years anniversary!

The moral of the story is the strong sense of continuity that is felt within the University of Bologna, and which is also found in other European universities, that have their origins in the medieval period, such as Paris and Oxford. But, like the great medieval cathedrals, while we are impressed that they have lasted so long, we are aware only of those that have survived. And many have not lasted. Let us look at a few examples.

In the thirteenth century a university was set up in the English town of Northampton by a group of scholars who had migrated from Oxford to escape from battles with the civic authorities. In 1261 Henry III formally approved the title of university, but the town, and with it the university, was unfortunate enough to back Simon de Montfort (the Earl of Leicester) in his dispute with the King. When Henry won the Battle of Northampton in 1264 he ordered the dissolution of the 'heretical university of Northampton'. Nearly three-quarters of a millennium later the town and the current University College are still seeking full university status!

Other universities have had phases when they have been closed for periods by war, by Imperial decree, or by order of political or religious authority. For some this involved temporary sojourns elsewhere. The now Palacky University in Olomouc, in the Czech Republic, began life in 1573 as a Jesuit college and became a State University two hundred years later. It suffered a temporary removal to Brno for 2 years before returning to Olomouc, but with the reduced status of Lyceum. In 1827 it became the Emperor Franz University, but was closed by Imperial Decree in 1860 for a year. It re-opened as a Theological Faculty with the power to award degrees, until, in 1946, it was established by law as the present university.

Although the longevity of the ancient universities is impressive, it should be remembered that they have undergone considerable structural and functional changes over their lifetimes. The University of Bologna at its creation was a Law School, while Paris at first had only Faculties of Law, Medicine and Divinity. These early universities provided trained lawyers, doctors and priests, only later increasing the range of subjects taught. Furthermore, as pointed out in Chapter 1, the majority of universities now in existence are of relatively modern origin; indeed most were founded in the twentieth century. Universities, even within Europe, have very different histories and remain at the present day very diverse in their traditions and in their ambitions. The question of the formal definition of a university is constantly debated, usually inconclusively. Individual states produce pragmatic definitions for purposes of accreditation and funding, but these differ between countries. From time to time there is a major attempt to identify the essence of a university, if not to produce a formal definition. Two such contributions made in the nineteenth century have had great influence on thinking about the essential elements of a university, and indeed continue to do so, especially, but not only, in Europe.

In the early 1800s, the Prussian diplomat and philologist, Wilhelm von Humboldt, was a leading light in setting up the University of Berlin (which since World War II has carried his name). Founded in 1807, the University was dedicated to the scientific approach to knowledge, to the importance of combining research and teaching, and to encouraging a proliferation of academic pursuits. This school of thought developed the conviction that investigation and research were the main functions and responsibilities of institutions of higher education. Two important concepts arising from these ideas were *lernfreiheit*, the freedom of students to choose their own programmes, and *lehrfreiheit*, the freedom of professors to develop subjects and to engage in research. The view that research is an essential element of any university, and that research and teaching are inextricably linked and synergistic, has persisted to the modern day, particularly in continental European universities.

The second major contribution came from John Henry Newman in 1852 (1996) in his discourses on the 'idea of a university'. He believed that the main function of a university was to educate students into a coherent body of knowledge, in which religion was an essential part. Knowledge was important for its own sake, and the well-educated student produced by this learning would be a civilized citizen. This notion of a university was one that provided a liberal education; it had no place for vocational training or, indeed, for research. Newman had to leave Oxford when he became a Roman Catholic in 1845 and he was subsequently invited by the Archbishop of Armagh to establish a Catholic University of Ireland in Dublin, at which he attempted to give form to his 'idea'.

Newman's views have had a persistent impact on thinking about the fundamentals of what a university should be in Britain, and also in Commonwealth countries, and have had a considerable influence on the development of universities in the US. But over time the ideas associated with Humboldt and Newman, although placing contrasting emphases on the basic purpose of a university, have become incorporated in the widespread (and dominant) view that universities must be involved in research *and* in the provision of liberal education over a wide range of subjects. This rather loosely defined idea underlies the criteria used by the Association of European Universities in considering membership applications from institutions, namely that they must cover a reasonably wide subject range, have good academic resources (particularly in the library), and have accreditation to award PhD degrees, along with a good track record of successful doctorate awards.

## Universities in turmoil

The varied histories of universities, and the differences in assumptions about fundamental roles, mean that any pragmatic attempt to define a university must hide important differences in approaches to their relationships to society, and in the way that they are likely to respond to new challenges. During periods of relative stability, it may be acceptable to talk about the 'university' as if this represented an institution with many common features that could easily be recognized both from within and without. But in periods of rapid change, underlying differences become more apparent as individual institutions reflect their specific traditions and cultures in reacting to changing environments. This seems to be happening at the turn into the twenty-first century.

It is perhaps arguable whether universities have ever gone through a period of such rapid change as is occurring now. To those actively involved these historical questions may be becoming less relevant, for the current forces of change are both large and diverse. For many years a traditional university had two main functions: first, to educate young people – usually a small elite proportion of the immediately postsecondary age group – in liberal arts and sciences; and, second, to pursue research on topics chosen by the academics themselves. Of course there were exceptions to these generalizations, with technical universities concentrating on vocational education (although still principally for young people) and carrying out applied research, but the traditional view was widely regarded as representing the activities of an 'ideal' university. Providing a liberal education for the young, and undertaking 'curiosity-driven' research, were regarded as important public goods that justified the structural and financial support provided by the government in what was an implicit contract between the state and universities.

During recent decades, however, there has been a sea change in the expectations that states have of the contributions by universities to the public good. The new expectations include universities:

- widening access, so that higher education is available to a much larger proportion of young people from a broader social base;
- providing lifelong learning to all postsecondary age groups, especially through continuing professional development;
- emphasizing applied research, both technological and social, in areas regarded as important to national economic success and social cohesion;
- acting as a substantial economic agent in a variety of ways, such as creating spinoff companies or providing specific training to local companies; and
- reducing social exclusion in the community by widening access and providing specialized training programmes for the unemployed and unskilled.

While these increased expectations from government may be found around the world, their articulation in Europe is generally through the nation state, or a sub-component thereof. National governments regard their universities as very important resources and spend considerable amounts of tax revenue on them (although not nearly as much as the universities would like). In many cases governments have recognized that effective university performance, in the service of the comparative advantage of nations, requires that institutions possess a high degree of independence and considerable scope for autonomous decision-making. However, reductions in central forms of microplanning have usually been followed by increased levels of regulation and accountability, undertaken often by state-backed independent agencies. The upshot of these changes is that, while the relationships between national governments and universities have altered, differences between national systems remain considerable. And, in turn, this creates difficulties for international cooperation.

**Internationalism**
Universities have a long-held and fundamental belief that they are essentially international institutions, notwithstanding that most are creations of individual nation states and that all are regulated to some extent by national governments. They believe that the truths that they seek about the natural world, about human societies, and about human nature itself, are universal. They are also committed to methods of investigation and learning that are believed to be universally valid, such as intellectual rigour, disinterested analysis, and freedom of communication. Thus universities have always sought to operate internationally, whether through research collaboration or by teaching international students. The European universities of the medieval and Renaissance periods experienced considerable student mobility, facilitated by the use of Latin as the language of higher education. Subsequent political and linguistic barriers, erected by territorial rulers and states, have

fragmented a wider European system to a large extent, but international cooperation between universities remains a fundamental ambition.

Academic scholarship is essentially competitive and individual academics strive for excellence as recognized by their peers. International recognition particularly is prized – the pinnacle is a Nobel Prize or an international medal. The important implication is that academics regard what they do as universal. The methods of study appropriate for a particular discipline apply wherever the investigation occurs. Conclusions likewise are regarded as widely applicable, and there is a general understanding that the processes of observation and evidence-gathering will scrupulously follow accepted conventions, that the analysis will be rigorous, the debate honest, and that communication will be open. These beliefs in universality apply across all disciplines, even those where the objects of study are local, or are mostly culturally or historically dependent. Furthermore, because academics see themselves and their subjects as members of a worldwide community, so universities inevitably operate on an international scale. Thus internationalism is an aim of universities because that is what is necessary to be true to the fundamental values of scholarship.

However, a new, and not always welcome, force has now entered the university environment in the form of economic globalization. In one important sense, if internationalization is traditionally what universities seek to do by voluntary collaboration, globalization can be regarded as a form of internationalism that is much more involuntary and increasingly compelling. The pressures of globalization arise indirectly from the impacts of information and communication technologies on business and commerce, and also more directly through the potential for electronically assisted learning.

The rise of the knowledge economy, and perhaps also its wider perception, are helping to create a greatly increased demand for higher education worldwide. In many countries growing applications exceed the capacities of domestic universities, and the gap tends to be filled by foreign providers. These may be overseas extensions of established universities from other countries, perhaps operating through local institutions, or they may be commercial organizations, many with overseas links forged through financial investment and making use of the material or personnel of foreign institutions. This development of essentially commercially driven international activity has a very different character from traditional international cooperation, and is seen as threatening by many in universities, although some see it as an opportunity for collaboration and resources gathering.

### European universities and the Bologna Declaration
In Europe the challenges of educational globalization have given additional stimulus to moves to make the national systems in Europe more harmo-

nious. European Commission schemes to encourage and support mobility between nations have operated for more than a decade and have had considerable success. The aims of these mobility programmes are to provide linguistic and cultural experiences for students as well as more comparative academic knowledge. However, the volume has been disappointing and the proportion of eligible students involved has fallen well short of the 10 per cent target. There are several reasons for the relatively low take-up, including the limited funds available and, in the case of UK students, a low level of linguistic achievement.

One of the major reasons is the diversity of systems determining accreditation and quality assurance. Negotiations to establish credit recognition for studies undertaken abroad have been lengthy and often inconclusive, and the outcomes have confined student movements to universities that have made bilateral agreements, particularly on credit equivalences, without which students cannot be confident that they will not be academically disadvantaged by a period of study in another country.

It was against this successful but limited background that the ministers responsible for higher education in France, Germany, Italy and the UK met in Paris in 1998 and signed what became known as the Sorbonne Declaration (which was the precursor to the 1999 Bologna Declaration), committing their nations to take steps to improve the level of harmonization between their national systems, especially towards greater portability of degrees. In particular they recommended that the lengths of study for levels of degree awards should become similar, based on a 3 + 2 + 3 system. Thus, a first degree would normally last for 3 years; the next degree would normally take a further 2 years; finally, 3 more years would be required for a doctorate. This proposal generated a great deal of interest, and also controversy, especially among those European countries which had not been included (most of them!), and within the European Commission (EC), which had been marginalized.

As a consequence of intensive discussions involving many countries and the EC, a larger follow-up meeting took place in Bologna in 1999, at which 29 countries signed the Bologna Declaration. This proposed a broad range of developments to create a *European Higher Education Area* to cover the whole of Europe, including those outside the European Union. This 'Bologna Process' has three major aims: first, to improve the compatibility of higher education qualifications across Europe; second, to stimulate the idea of European citizenship among the young; and third, to increase the worldwide competitive strength of European higher education. This third aim overtly acknowledges the forces of globalization in higher education, while the first and second can also be regarded as significant in potentially enhancing the social cohesiveness and economic strength of Europe.

The Bologna Declaration states the aims of the process: but what mechanisms are suggested to achieve these ambitions? The first is implementation of a 'two-cycle' structure based on modification of a proposal in Paris a year earlier. Since the rules about periods of study are in many countries determined by law, government action often is required to make changes. This can make progress patchy, as it is subject to wider political currents within states, which sometimes can slow it down. Despite this potential inertia, in Italy the necessary legislation has been introduced to enforce the change and the two-cycle system is being introduced. In Germany permissive legislation allows universities to introduce a new shorter first degree, and such programmes are being introduced alongside existing courses. Active debate is occurring in other countries where a much longer period than three years to the standard first degree is also the norm, but the proposal is generating much opposition, particularly within academia.

The second mechanism is to encourage a greater take-up of the European Credit Transfer Scheme (ECTS) that has existed for some time and has been widely accepted in principle, but not greatly used in practice, as a tool for encouraging multinational mutual recognition. The third mechanism is to develop the extensive use of the 'Diploma Supplement', which is an attempt to produce a standard format for describing course content and student achievement to enable them to be recognized internationally. Finally, the fourth mechanism is to try to produce some harmonization of the diverse quality assurance schemes found within the various European countries.

The high ambition of creating a European higher education area, within which there would be general mutual recognition of university qualifications, is to allow the free movement of students both during their courses and also on completion, either to further study or into employment. How likely is it that these ideals can be achieved? Progress is spasmodic and uneven. There continues to be strong criticism of the two-cycle proposals in many countries, and there is also a reluctance to make use of ECTS or of the Diploma Supplement. Meanwhile, national quality assurance systems continue to evolve so that differences, if anything, are becoming greater. Some of this reluctance is due to innate academic conservatism, but there are also fundamental objections to the idea that a 'one-size-fits-all' scheme can ever be appropriate to universities that are becoming ever more diverse as they adapt differentially to new challenges and opportunities.

The concept of a market is one that is not readily acceptable to many academics because it implies a commercial view of higher education. Yet the current characteristics of university systems in Europe, as indeed in the rest of the world, are at least quasi-market in that competition is forcing universities to think hard about strengths and weaknesses, and about how best they could specialize to match their strengths to new opportunities. Thus universities, despite the homogeneous tendencies of stratification and prestige hierarchies, are likely to become more heterogeneous, and government policies are likely to seek to reinforce this direction. For example, some will aim for (or seek to maintain) a world reputation in fundamental research, while others will concentrate more on teaching. Some institutions will be primarily campus- or residentially based, while others will focus more on the development of distance education programmes to all age groups. Institutions are also likely to vary more in their local or international outlooks and student bodies. This diversity exists *within* countries, but when the structural and cultural differences *between* nations are added as another dimension, the difficulties of creating a comprehensive Higher Education Area across Europe are immense.

So, is the effort to do so worthwhile? The answer is yes – but with an important proviso. The systems created by governments, whether through the EC itself or by agreement of national governments, will need to recognize the existence, and indeed the desirability, of the heterogeneity that currently exists, and the need for the innovative formation of partnerships and alliances between universities across national boundaries. Associations of institutions to share teaching programmes or to create new joint programmes are good examples, and follow when universities recognize that they have much in common and will gain mutual benefit from working together. In other words, the development of a 'common area' must be driven by the spontaneous activity of universities, with government actions designed to generate frameworks that will encourage and facilitate experiments that help to identify experience which has been successful and the conditions in which is has flourished, and that assist in the dissemination of good practice.

**University diversity in Europe**
Discussion of the Bologna process often appears to pay little regard to the considerable differences that exist both between nations and between universities within countries. National systems differ within Europe on several dimensions that are important in determining the potential for harmonization. First, there is great variation between countries in the formal and legal relationships between universities and the state. This may involve direct ownership of universities by the state, as happens in many continental European countries, or the universities may be legally independent institutions, as in the UK (although the government exercises considerable regulatory control, through the laws affecting universities and the conditions that attach to public and other funding).

Where universities are formally state institutions, academic staff may be governmental employees or have employment contracts with the university.

In the former case the nature of the contract may be more or less detailed (for example, in the level of specification of teaching activities). There is also variation in both the proportion of university income that is provided by the state and the level of autonomy granted to the university in decisions about spending that income. For example, in Greece, state funding is by far the most important source of income and the individual university budget is a result of microlevel negotiation between the institution and the government. In the UK, by contrast, state funding provides a much lower proportion of total income and is provided as a lump sum with the university having considerable freedom as to how the money is allocated.

The internal governance structures of universities also vary between European countries in important ways that influence their ability to respond to new challenges. In some countries each university will have a governing board, with some members who are not employees of the institution, while in others the most direct line of authority will be to the minister of education. This variation is reflected within procedural differences for appointing rectors or presidents. Where a governing board exists it is likely to have an important voice in these appointments, whereas those universities without such a board usually appoint academic heads through a wide election process, with the outcome possibly requiring confirmation by the minister. Significantly there are also important differences in systems of accreditation and quality assurance, which are formidable obstacles to moves for greater European harmonization. Variation in accreditation systems, along with other factors, allows scope in some countries for considerable increases in the number of private universities. The continued salience of these differences is recognized by the recommendation in the Bologna Declaration that the harmonization of quality assurance and accreditation systems is crucial to the overall objective of creating a common European higher education 'area'.

Differences between countries are therefore considerable and represent major hurdles to the prospect for a European higher education area. However, this is only part of the story, for there are, in addition, also major differences between institutions within countries. One of the most obvious structural variations is the existence in some countries of a formal binary system, with one set of institutions at university level providing teaching over a wide subject range and also undertaking research, and another distinct group offering mainly technical education and carrying out applied research. An example of such a system is that in Germany, with universities on the one hand, and the *fachhochschulen*, or 'universities of applied science', on the other. These 'sectors' have different, politically determined expectations, and they operate in distinct legal frameworks and with separate funding streams. Stratification and specialization among different institutional tiers exist in other countries in Europe, but it is generally informal and, at least on paper, a unitary system operates, with all higher education institutions treated in terms of national policy and legal status in the same way. In the UK, for example, there was a move in 1992 from a binary system (of universities and polytechnics) to a unitary one. But even here there are institutions (university colleges) that do not have full university status, being restricted by law from, for example, awarding doctorates, but which yet provide university equivalent programmes. These colleges have been regarded as potential universities that are not yet ready for full university status, rather than institutions with distinct functions. However, recent UK governmental proposals indicate that such institutions may find it easier in future to adopt the university title on the basis of being distinct 'teaching institutions' with little or no research, in a move that clearly breaks the hallowed nexus between teaching and research that has been long-regarded as essential for university designation (DES, 2003).

The existence of a 'standard' form of higher education gives a false impression of uniformity, not least in former binary and now unitary systems, for there are major differences between institutions that have the title university. The legacy of past activities and traditions persists between the old universities (those in existence prior to 1992) and the 'new' universities (the former polytechnics). There is a much greater volume of research, particularly basic research, in the former, while the latter have many more vocational subjects in their teaching programmes. Given the increased level of competition within the system, for funding and for students, informal associations of distinct types of universities have been created, with 18 of the most research-intensive 'old' (that is, those that were universities before the ending of the binary divide) universities forming the so-called 'Russell Group' (named after the London hotel where they meet), while the former polytechnics have created the 'Coalition of Modern Universities'. Thus, even in a country that has a unitary system, deep divisions recur, which makes cooperation in teaching programmes more difficult.

It is too early to say whether the Bologna Declaration process will be successful. Indeed there is as yet no agreement on the criteria and associated metrics to allow a judgement of 'success' to be made. What level of harmonization would be regarded as a satisfactory achievement? What volume of student mobility would be satisfactory? Yet there is already considerable interest in the rest of the world in the European attempt to produce a greater degree of harmony between the different national HE systems within a particular geographical region. There is no doubt that progress has been achieved; the stimulation provided by the EC-sponsored student mobility schemes has been marked, although not to the extent that was initially expected. But are the developments in Europe repeatable elsewhere

where there is no equivalent of the European Commission as a form of regional government? Would universities in other world regions ever wish to have a similar supranational entity with an equivalent influence on higher education? A comparison with the US may help to provide some of the answers.

## ▶ Comparisons between Europe and the US

Comparisons are often drawn between the higher education systems of continental Europe and the US on the supposition that they represent the two axes of a state-led/market-led continuum. However, the US federal constitutional design is also of interest to some in Europe who have ambitions to create a Continental federal structure (the term 'United States of Europe' is occasionally used). But the more important reasons for making a comparison are that American higher education is regarded as being very successful, and that it is politically controlled largely at a state rather that at a national level. It is extremely diverse and yet it appears to operate in a harmonious way. So, important questions include whether there are lessons to be derived from the American experience that would be helpful to European leaders, and whether, conversely, recent developments in Europe have any relevance to US higher education?

To European eyes the diversity within US higher education seems huge. There are, for example, many private universities which together account for 20 per cent of all student enrolments. These include some of the most prestigious universities in the world, such as Harvard, Yale, Princeton and Stanford. Recently more private universities have been created, but these are 'for-profit' institutions, such as the University of Phoenix. In the mainstream, higher education institutions are differentiated into those that deliver two-year programmes and those that teach four-year courses leading to bachelor degrees. There is enormous diversity also in the volume of research undertaken by different institutions, ranging from the highly research-intensive universities, such as Harvard, Stanford and the University of California at Berkeley, with research budgets running into many hundreds of millions of dollars, to the many state universities and private liberal arts colleges that undertake little research (although the maintenance of 'scholarship' is a high priority for the latter).

As always this diversity reflects the historical development of US universities, beginning in colonial days, but mainly occurring after the country's independence. The oldest university is Harvard, which was founded in 1636 by the Board of the Colony of Massachusetts. It was named after its first benefactor, John Harvard, who died in 1638, and who left his books and half his estate to the institution. The tradition of large private benefactions to universities, which subsequently has grown in the United States, has enabled institutions such as Harvard, to become successful private universities with large endowments. There are no parallels in Europe, for even Oxford and Cambridge in the UK have, by comparison with Harvard and the other 'Ivy League' private universities, only small benefactions.

The formation of state universities followed later, particularly during the nation-state building era of the first part of the nineteenth century. The University of Virginia, for example, opened in 1826, and the many more state universities that followed in subsequent decades reflected the importance attached to universities by state politicians and other leaders in helping the economic, social and democratic development both of local regions and communities, as well as of the nation more broadly.

These developments were further stimulated by a federal government that, from the middle of the nineteenth century, granted federal land to individual states for the creation of higher education institutions that would concentrate on agriculture and the mechanical arts. These 'land grant colleges', as they were known, have generally evolved today into state universities, or significant parts of state universities. Individual states have developed often quite distinctive systems of higher education, usually incorporating several types of institution into an integrated overall scheme.

California, for example, follows a higher education 'master plan', which constitutes and plans for three levels of institution. At one level, community colleges provide two-year courses, many of which are clearly vocational and which equip graduates for specific types of employment. The state universities (originally known as state colleges) comprise a second level and offer four-year programmes leading to bachelor degrees. They also provide programmes for master's degrees, but do not award doctorates. The third level is essentially the University of California. This has nine campuses, awards PhDs, and operates very large research programmes. The system overall is integrated in considerable part by a well-established credit system, which allows considerable mobility between levels, particularly for students completing a two-year course and who wish to transfer to the final two years of a four-year programme at institutions on the next step up.

Individual states determine the policy frameworks within which the American public higher education system operates and they provide considerable funding. The federal government only has limited direct impact on the development of teaching, but it has great indirect influence through the provision of federal student aid. For research, by contrast, the federal government, through its funding agencies, such as the National Science Foundation and the National Institutes of Health, has a very powerful direct influence on the research programmes of all universities. The overall effect, therefore, is that higher education policy in the US is a composite reflection of state and federal powers and interests.

The governance of American universities involves a Board with a substantial external membership. The Board of a state university will usually be appointed by the state Governor. Private universities have Boards of trustees appointed in a variety of ways: Harvard University, for example, has a 30-member Board of Overseers elected by the alumni of the university. These governing boards are responsible for the appointment of the university president and for major institutional policy decisions.

Although state governments and legislatures control the financial and policy decisions of the public universities, formal accreditation of all universities differs fundamentally from that in Europe in that it is essentially self-accreditation. Formal recognition of a university as a university, and of its degrees, is exercised by peer review, that is, by fellow academics and representatives of other institutions passing judgement on each other. In the US there are more than 3000 general, or 'comprehensive', universities and colleges, each providing a range of courses. They are divided into eight regional groups, for each of which there is an Accreditation Board elected by the institutions in that group. A Regional Accreditation Board carries out regular reviews of each institution in its group by creating panels of academics and others.

In addition to these Accreditation Boards for comprehensive universities and colleges, 98 per cent of which are 'non-profit' and with many being state institutions, there are *national* Accreditation Boards for the approximately 3000 institutions that teach within a single field, such as business studies, and of which about 80 per cent are 'for-profit'. These subject-specific Boards operate in much the same way as the Regional Boards and in all there are 59 boards, and together they form an umbrella organization, the Council for Higher Education Accreditation (CHEA). CHEA provides services, including information, and examples of good practice, to its members, and also has an important advocacy role with governments, employers and other external stakeholders in making the case that self-accreditation is the most effective form of regulatory system. The federal government, however, also has a stake in institutional accreditation in that it has a mechanism for the recognition of individual accreditation boards for the purposes of determining eligibility of institutions for student aid grants.

As we pointed out earlier, there is a well-established credit transfer system in the US that allows students to transfer between universities to complete degree programmes. This is effective and widely used within individual states, particularly for transfer between levels of structured or multilevel systems, such as that in California. However, there is relatively little interstate transfer. An important element in inhibiting movement of students between states is the existence of higher fees in many state universities for out-of-state students. An interesting comparison with Europe arises from the requirements of European treaty law that students from another EU country must not be discriminated against by being charged differential fees, although other elements of student support remain nation-specific.

The diversity within the US seems bewildering to the European observer, but it is worth pointing out that there is also considerable national variation within Europe, with which the Bologna Declaration process is trying to cope. (Whether diversity is likely to increase or reduce in both regions is a question that is taken up in detail in Chapter 6.) The range of opportunities open to universities is now so large that it would seem very probable, and indeed desirable, that universities should focus on their strengths and for the overall system to become more diverse. On the other hand, national governments seek increasingly to direct their universities to satisfy national objectives, such as wider access or stronger links with industry, by a series of incentives. And because, whether through a sense of fairness or for bureaucratic convenience, these incentives are usually offered to the entire system, there is a pressure towards uniformity, although governments will usually pay lip service to diversity as a desirable objective. Despite the homogenizing tendency of many government policies, governments will continue to place inexorable pressure for universities to become more diverse. It is not clear, however, whether the US (already considerably diversified) and Europe (more homogeneous) will, in time, develop university systems which have much more in common than the differences that characterize them today.

### ▶ Conclusion

Universities throughout the world are attempting to meet the challenges of globalization. They are doing this in many different ways and in a more competitive climate. Many realize too that any one university is only a small player in a big market, and so are forming associations to work together. In a few cases mergers are being discussed. These usually involve neighbouring institutions, while looser-coupled alliances are more likely to be nationally based. The national, rather than a wider regional or global focus, is not surprising given the pressures on higher education institutions from national governments to satisfy national aspirations. It is much easier to work with a partner operating within the same framework of government policy, funding arrangements and quality assurance systems, than when these differ markedly.

Nevertheless, the number of international alliances of universities is growing. A current example is *Universitas 21*, an association of 17 universities from 10 countries (and which is examined in greater detail in Chapter 7 by Svava Bjarnason). All are research active universities and believe that collectively they can be more successful – as individual institutions – than if they were all to act alone. Initial plans are to produce joint courses at Masters level in subjects for which there is a large worldwide demand from students willing to pay fees, for example, in business studies and information science. The joint organization (*Universitas 21*) will seek accreditation to be the international degree-awarding body for these joint programmes. The alliance is also setting up a commercial organization with a publishing company to market the existing courses of its members.

*Universitas 21* and other similar international associations are usually worldwide in their membership rather than regional. What are the prospects for regional associations of universities developing? Will the implementation of the principles of the Bologna Declaration create conditions conducive to the creation of such bodies? We have described the considerable mix of institutions within Europe, both between nations and within. Comparison with US higher education, however, shows that the heterogeneity between institutions there is even greater than in Europe. Yet the system as a whole seems to be more coherent.

There are two major factors at work. The first is that the system in the US has evolved in a collective way in that each state, while seeking to create a higher education provision which would best serve the interests of that state, has been prepared to accept the basic structure of teaching programmes (two-year community colleges and four-year universities) and a nationally accepted system of credits. Second, nation-wide influences are quite strong, despite the predominantly state-based structure. Accreditation, although operated by a considerable number of separate agencies, some of the most prestigious of which are regional, is effectively a national system. Furthermore, the federal government exercises great influence through its funding of both teaching, albeit indirectly though payments on the demand side to the student, and of research. If this analysis is correct, what, if any, lessons can be derived for Europe as it attempts to make its higher education 'space' more coherent?

One conclusion, at first sight, could be to suggest that what is needed in Europe is strong federal action at the European level to create a framework of funding and quality control. But that would be mistaken and impracticable: it is most unlikely that national governments would allow the EU to acquire funding and other controls over university systems in Europe, at least in the foreseeable future. Universities are regarded by all states as vital contributors to their economic and social development. Such a proposal would also be strongly opposed by the universities themselves, on the grounds that national governmental bureaucracies are already too intrusive and remote, and an even further removed supranational administration would be much worse. The American experience leads to the conclusion that plurality of funding, while producing problems in managing overall institutional budgets, gives greater decisional autonomy for universities in determining policy and strategy. Attempts to impose a European top-down accreditation and quality assurance system would be even more strongly resisted.

Does this mean that little can be done and that the Bologna Declaration process is bound to lead to disappointment? Not necessarily. There is a great deal of innovation taking place within European universities as they adapt to the many changes occurring in their environments, and much of this involves acting on the realization that cooperation between institutions is an important part of competing successfully in a more competitive world. International collaboration particularly is of considerable and growing importance. The significance of the Bologna process is that it gives recognition to this development and provides a further stimulus to it on a European scale.

It would be especially helpful if the European activities of national governments, whether through the European Commission or through joint action by national education ministries, included a more regular and structured involvement from the universities and their national and regional associations, particularly to identify and to help establish potentially innovative collaborative activities, to recognize successful experience, and to create frameworks for its wider dissemination. This will require modest financial support to encourage experiments and to transpose the results of good practice. But, more importantly, it will require working with universities to frame quality assurance arrangements that work with the grain of successful university collaboration and practices, and which take account of the changing modalities and delivery systems in our more global and technological age.

Ultimately, quality assurance procedures will only work towards encouraging greater cooperation between universities if the academic staff members who have to operate them have confidence and trust that they are appropriate. Governments, whether national or at European level, will need to encourage, facilitate and support innovative forms of university cooperation, but should not attempt to determine it. This is the overriding lesson from the United States in seeking to produce a more effective collaborative European higher education system.

# 3 Globalization and the University

*Roger King*

## ▶ Introduction

Among the first questions about globalization that need to be answered is 'how is it to be defined?' and 'how does it differ from internationalism?' The term 'globalization' appears everywhere. There hardly passes a day without some reference to globalization in the newspapers and it appears everywhere in academic journals and books, too. Yet it is invoked to describe a myriad of phenomena, some with only very loose connections to each other. Clearly the term 'globalization' refers to a process – to a journey or direction – although some see it as a description of an end state. The destination presumably is some form of 'global society' or 'global age', but there is considerable controversy as to whether this outcome is inevitable or similar for all locations and spheres of life, or as to its key features and its causes.

A further problem is that globalization is seen by some as a form of explanation for a wide array of circumstances, while for others it is a process that itself requires explanation (by, say, theories of capitalism, or the constant creation of new forms of technology). It is increasingly clear, however, that the processes of globalization do not provide standard or similar outcomes across the world, but are shaped and adapted by a variety of local cultures and structures. In Chapter 5, for example, Michael Gibbons argues that globalization enhances the competition and differences between indigenous capitalisms and cultures (it does not simply produce western 'sameness' or homogeneity in economies, polities and culture, as is sometimes claimed), and spurs on the diffusion of innovation and its worldwide adaptations, which, in turn, further reinforces the processes of globalization.

Before considering these matters in further detail it is worth recalling that universities have long been considered international bodies. As far back as the eleventh century, universities that generated a particular reputation would attract scholars from far and wide. The University of Bologna, for example, became known at that time for its discovery and re-interpretation of Roman private law. Such was the increasing importance of this rich conceptual storehouse and systematic codification of legal principles for trade and governance, that Bologna's expertise made it a magnet for students throughout Europe and wider. Moreover, the 'reception' of Roman law throughout the burgeoning territorial states of medieval Europe was carried via scholastic channels and through the mobility of its practitioners. At this period, universities were primarily concerned with passing on accepted knowledge to others, rather than being engaged with its creation, which has since become a vital part of its modern function. Theology not science was king and it was the task of the scholar to receive and understand accepted wisdom. In the absence of the printing press and the means for objectifying and thereby widely disseminating this knowledge away from immediate 'presence', the location of physical collections of manuscripts and other learned artefacts, and their keepers and interpreters, had a particular attraction. They drew people to them, rather than their knowledge being conveyed to the learners, as is often the case today. By itself this was a powerful source of the international travels and wanderings of the medieval scholar. So, too, of course, were the standard use of Latin as the language of instruction and what we might describe as a common, theological-based curriculum between universities.

With modernity came the notion of knowledge as rational and secular, as having the basis to be tested and built upon. The template of truth was forged in this world rather than the next, and, as such, scientific and humanistic progress involved demonstrating universalism. Knowledge came to be viewed as international in its essence and as not contained by the sentiments and territorial constraints of nationalism. This posed a potential problem for the increasingly powerful rulers of the developing national states of the eighteenth and nineteenth centuries. Rational knowledge and the means for its pursuit were essential for both devising and utilizing more effective means of military warfare in an age of territorial aggrandizement, and for formulating more efficient instruments for national administration (as recognized spectacularly by nineteenth-century Bonapartist France). Yet there is a disregard for national and territorial ambitions in the very idea of rational and universalistic modernity that always carries potentially ominous implications for those in authority.

This dilemma was managed in the exchange by which universities were granted a critical licence and autonomy by the state not extended to most other institutions, in return for which they developed in a relatively compliant manner the scientific advances necessary for economic and military competitiveness. Additionally, they provided the teaching of succeeding generations in apparently open and meritocratic ways that legitimated the allocations of individuals to the increasing specializations of the occupational order. But it was a deal that protected the view of the university as a universalistic and international force – because that was the nature of knowledge – even though it also provided essential service to territorial and national rulers. At some point it was perhaps inevitable that the corrosive impact of universalism, especially when mixed with the social and political demands of a more democratic and often revolutionary age, would lead to greater tension in these relationships. If anything, internationalism and, more recently, globalism, seem to sit easier with the universal scientism of the academy than the territorial limitations of the nation state. They also seem more compatible with the increasing sense of the university as the site of democratic and global contestability.

Internationalism, of course, means just that. It is an exchange between nations or, more accurately, between nation states. As such it is predicated on the existence of territoriality and the benefits of cross-border exchange, in both commerce and ideas. Linked to the notion of internationalism, especially in trade, is that of liberalization and the removal of barriers to increased cross-border movement. Internationalism and liberalization are generally regarded in both commerce and higher education as conferring greater value than nationalism or protectionism. Both wealth and knowledge are seen to benefit.

With the notion of the university as an innovator, a researcher, and a developer of new ideas, rather than just the transmission belt of that already known and accepted, the international exchange of people – staff and students – has been regarded as essential to the development of truth, or the unfolding of the essential universalism of knowledge. Additionally, international educational mobility has been seen more contemporarily as vital for the process of modelling – the transposition of good and, if possible, world-class, practice – and for the generation of national economic competitiveness and advantage. For some, such as the European Union, it has become a means, although somewhat haphazardly, for developing a sense of European community and citizenship. Staff and student mobility, as facilitated by programmes such as ERASMUS, SOCRATES and LEONARDO, have been viewed as critical instruments for developing wider senses of both regionalism and its global integration.

Such internationalism, however, has stressed the academic value or 'not-for-profit' character of the cross-border exchanges of people and knowledge. More recently, the notion of transborder or borderless education has been used to describe the growth of internationalism as a commercial enterprise. As the university becomes more privatized, and its services regarded as tradable and a source of income to replace declining public funds, internationalism is seen more in terms of overseas markets. 'Exports' in the form of international fee-paying student recruitment, or in local commercial partnerships abroad, help to give the notion of higher education internationalism an added entrepreneurial twist.

Yet university systems, irredeemably internationalist in orientation, may be one of the least globalized sectors. In comparison with, say, financial services, or the pharmaceutical industries, universities appear rooted in the nation state. As organizations they lack the reach and coordination of worldwide operations found in the activities of multinational corporations in some other sectors. Their markets may be more globally distributed than before, although not by much, but institutions and the regulations that govern them, are not globalized. Why is this? To begin to answer this question we need to look more closely at what we mean by globalization.

## ▶ What is globalization?

For many globalization is primarily an economic phenomenon – it refers to the increasing worldwide integration of economies over recent decades and is associated with the triumph of liberal capitalism as the dominant economic mode. Territory means less than it did. These days, for example, the financial markets operate on a 24-hours a day basis. When an investment order is phoned, say, from Germany to bankers in New York, the transaction occurs straight away, irrespective of the location of offices and the vast distance between them. Moreover, an investment decision in, say, Washington, could have potential reverberations in Wollongong. In this sense, globalization is different to internationalization. Internationalization refers to exchanges between nation states – across borders – and has occurred over the centuries. It is not new. Globalization, however, refers to exchanges that transcend borders and which occur instantaneously and electronically, and is new.

In some approaches there is a common focus on globalization as 'flows' – of capital (financial and physical), people, information, culture and so on (Hay and Marsh, 2000). These objects move along various global forms of 'highway' and terrain, or 'scapes' (Appadurai, 1990), which create new patterns of inequality of access between people and their locations. These flows have been made possible by technological change, especially the growth of electronic forms of communication, as well as by the development of worldwide economic integration and its encouragement in recent decades by neo-liberal economic policies in many states. The development of rockets and satellites, when combined with the telephone and the computer, has generated reliable global communications, liberated from essentially local coverage.

We can usefully characterize the impact of globalization processes at three levels: economic, political and cultural. Economically, globalization refers to more than trade liberalization, but to the development of a world market, powered by global corporations, in which local economic and political actors are increasingly losing influence, and where these worldwide companies are characterized by globally coordinated business strategies (production, distribution and retailing) and accelerated flows of commodities. Strong adherents of the globalization thesis hold the view that globalization is historically unprecedented, recasting world stratification, global governance, and the nation state in quite novel ways. The nation state loses a substantial amount of its sovereignty in these views, no longer being able to modulate exchange and interest rates, while the mobility and worldwide location options for the multinational corporations restricts governments' abilities to raise taxes, increase social expenditure, and generally manage their economic and social policies as they would wish. The primary role of the state becomes that of accommodating the structure of the domestic economy to the imperatives of international competitiveness.

There is evidence that the case for economic globalization, and particularly its impacts, is often overblown. Nation states remain powerful actors, both in terms of their domestic economies, and in relation to international economic agreements and schemes of governance (Hirst and Thompson, 1996). Through elections, too, they remain the critical agencies of popular representation. Nor is there empirical substantiation indicating that nation states are inhibited overmuch by globalization processes in their public expenditure policies, as there is no clear correlation between a country's openness to foreign direct investment and social spending. Indeed multinational companies often welcome high public investment in education and training, for example, particularly if they are part of the high technology or knowledge-based industries (Hall and Soskice, 2001).

There would appear to be a number of policy options for countries wishing to compete effectively in the global economy, including social democratic corporatism based on agreements with trade unions, in which wage restraint is exchanged for labour-friendly welfare measures, and spending on externalities or infrastructure, which are seen as benefiting the economy or allowing change to occur without too much protest and with adequate compensation for the displaced (Garrett, 1998). In some northern and central European countries the systems of social protection created throughout most of the last century have not been dismantled. Social corporatism, inclusive electoral arrangements producing coalition governments, and federalism are among the factors that give those opposed to global neoliberalism the opportunities to exercise vetoes and other brakes or leverage points on globalization policies, in comparison with polities in the US or the UK, for example, where fewer such opportunities occur (Swank, 2002). More generally, nation states seek to secure economic growth within their territories through comparative advantage for the capitals operating within these territories, whether these are domestically owned or not, by encouraging innovation, competitiveness, and the research conditions for knowledge-based commercialization.

At the political level, nonetheless, globalization generally refers to the decline in the sovereignty and importance of the nation state, to increased interstate collaboration, and to the decline of socialism and the worldwide acceptance of liberal democracy. Undoubtedly states are required more than they have ever been to cooperate internationally, not only to find effective and acceptable ways of regulating economic globalization, but also to cope with worldwide issues such as the environment, illegal immigrants, crime and human rights. Moreover, these connections between governments are increasingly dense and occur, not only at all levels of government, but in a wide range of regional and international meetings, where representatives of non-governmental international organizations, including from global social movements based on, for example, ecology or gender, are also to be found in plentiful supply (O'Brien *et al.*, 2000). More complex global concentrations of state power now exist, with previously autonomous nation states becoming incorporated into 'blocs' for military, collective security, and other purposes, together with the presence of more sophisticated and specialized global institutions for regulating the world economy, and for promulgating international personhood norms and rights.

Culturally, globalization is often invoked to describe the increasingly pervasive influence of western consumption culture, diffused through new entertainment media, such as television, pop music, cinema and tourism, and the multinational corporations powering such media, so that people everywhere start to exhibit similar styles and tastes, and also convergent attitudes with the growth of universalistic concepts of the self and personal identity. People, in this view, are simply more aware, of themselves as citizens of the world, and of alternatives to the status quo and to conventional forms of authority and morality. They are more questioning.

Yet, while some would see such developments as liberating, others regard them as destroying local culture and its vitality. The globalization of culture not only extends western consumption culture, as found in Hollywood-produced films and fast food outlets, but also generates adverse reactions to it, as, say, with some forms of Islamic protest against globalization and Americanization. Although there is a sense of the globe as a primary identifying referent for increasing numbers of people, considerable variations in interpretations and responses are as likely to result in a more differentiated and loose-fit world as a more homogeneous one.

Globalization is best regarded as a spatial concept, in which time and space have become compressed (Harvey, 1989; Scholte, 2000). Instantaneous communication across the world levels out differences in location and territoriality, and is a historical process that stretches connections and networks across the globe. It leads to the growth of global organizations, both for economic and governance purposes, and these help to generate transworld rules, norms and regulation, such as in the field of standards or human rights.

Rationalist knowledge – the ways of explaining and interpreting the world – particularly sustains globalization by focusing on the planet as a single place, as the space of *homo sapiens*, rather than on gods or other transcendental entities, and by encouraging the view that knowledge is more widely gained by seeing the world as a whole.

The scientism and instrumentalism of rationalism facilitate globalization because both are intrinsically non-territorial and purport to produce objective truth that is universally valid. The methods of reason are open to all people and know no boundaries (Albrow, 1996). The historic coupling of nation and state expresses the historically contingent matching of the irrational with the rational (with the state, in Weber's classical view, reflecting the ultimate application of the process of rationalization, and to be contrasted with the sentiments of nationalism). It is a coupling reflected in the 'agreement' between national rulers and the universal knowledge-seeking universities; and it is inherently unstable. Rationalist, utilitarian and instrumental epistemology increasingly frustrates the territorial geography and hindrances of national borders, and eventually sustains the processes of globalization and supranationality. These issues are also central to any consideration of the university in the context of globalization.

Regulation is perhaps the key to the development of supraterritoriality in its more institutionalized forms. Legal and rule-like arrangements are necessary to regulate, standardize, 'make fair', and to promulgate the processes of globalization, and these procedures are increasingly developed through regional and transworld institutions created by states. Although many of these suprastate bodies have acquired a degree of autonomy from national governments, national states continue to have considerable and decisive inputs. Forms of transnational private sector governance through associative and voluntary self-regulation have often been supported by states, too. State policies have in many instances encouraged supraterritorial developments – not least in support of business's desire for 'fair' regulation and standardization in support of open markets, and in the recognition that rule compliance is sometimes best secured over all nation states by some form of supraterritorial decision and monitoring. In the case of universities, it is an open question whether forms of global or supraterritorial regulation (over quality assurance, for example) of the kind found in the wider business sector will develop. The increasingly tradable aspect of university services, as likely to be covered by the General Agreement on Trade in Services (GATS) as part of the WTO negotiations, suggests that elements of such frameworks are likely to emerge.

## ▶ **The university and globalization**

A number of sources have welcomed the processes of globalization as conferring considerable benefit upon universities, and would prefer, if anything, that globalization picked up the gallop in higher education. The *West Review of Australian Higher Education* in the mid-1990s, for example, welcomed the rise of the university as a provider of tradable services and as a key player in the development of free trade in education worldwide (see Marginson and Considine, 2000).

Not everyone accepts these views. Bill Readings, for example, in *The University in Ruins* (1996), argues that the publicly funded university is changing forever under the constraints of globalization. For him the function of the modern university has been that of constituting national culture and producing good citizens. But now the university is losing its social and public purpose and is becoming like any other corporation, serving its own private interests. Students are consumers rather than citizens in the making. And the nation state, debilitated by globalization, and adopting user-pays funding approaches, has no effective means of exerting wider social functions onto the university.

Yet, as we noted above, globalization does not lead to the demise of the nation state and Readings surely exaggerates the loss of its influence. National governments still exert considerable regulatory authority over university systems, including over the fees that can be charged to full-time undergraduate students, and through funding and other policies the state can seek, for example, wider social access and the promotion of particular areas of research. Moreover, nation states remain anxious to use their deep financial pockets and other levers to keep universities in harness, especially their scientific research, to help secure best comparative economic advantage.

In some developing countries, too, states are anxious that they retain the ability to use universities as key instruments to build up national capacities. In South Africa, where national reconstruction following the ending of the apartheid regime is critical to its long-term future, there is suspicion that the increased globalization and commercialization of university activities as found in the more developed world will, if allowed free rein in the developing world, result in a denuded or undernourished university sector in such countries. Partnerships by local institutions with foreign universities are regarded in many cases as simply 'marriages of convenience', enabling the external partner to enter the local market with little or no contribution to the development of the teaching and research capacity of the local partner.

Consequently these foreign universities are regarded as providing little support for South Africa's national development agenda and the nurturing of its domestic knowledge production; rather, the emphasis seems to be on securing profitable outlets by targeting white students, thus impeding de-racialization policies, and focusing on a narrow range of subjects, such as business and information technology, where capital investment can be low (Asmal, 2002). On the other hand, however, if globalization is construed as the diffusion of innovation (see Gibbons, Chapter 5, this volume), then too strong a national policy of protectionism and regulation may lead to a fortress approach that may hinder the pedagogic and other major changes that may also be essential for the successful development of an efficient and high value domestic university system.

Certainly the academic value of internationalism, and the cross-border exchange of students and staff, jostles more palpably with internationalism as a commercial operation in universities than before. As an example of what Marginson and Considine (2000) call 'the enterprise university', as the university becomes more privatized, with its services regarded as a source of income to replace declining public funds, internationalism is seen more in terms of overseas markets. 'Exports' in the form of international fee-paying students, or in local commercial partnerships abroad, help to give the notion of higher education internationalism an added entrepreneurial twist. But, as we have noted, internationalization is not the same as globalization, and university systems may be one of the least globalized, at least to date, even if this is changing.

## ▶ Research and knowledge production

It is in the area of knowledge production – of research – where globalization currently most affects higher education. Global flows of information and data seem to be an inherent feature of the emerging knowledge economy, and knowledge travels even more effortlessly than money. Globalization is absorbing universities into a distributed knowledge production system, involving universities in many more alliances and partnerships as they seek to acquire specialized and up-to-date knowledge, including from an increasing range of non-university research and development companies, and where basic and applied research are increasingly converged (Gibbons *et al.*, 1994).

Distributed knowledge production is therefore creating a world of collaborative arrangements. It is the need to possess specialized knowledge of all kinds that lies behind the current growth of networks and the proliferation of research and development partnerships and alliances. These new forms of organization are ostensibly about sharing risks and costs, but they are also about getting access to research being carried out by others. If universities intend to operate at the leading edge of research, they need to ensure that their academics are able to participate in the appropriate contexts. But these are so diverse and volatile that no university can afford to keep 'in-house' all the human resources that are needed to guarantee a presence everywhere. To maintain a position at the leading edge of research, universities have to learn how to exploit all the advantages to be had from sharing their intellectual resources.

Globalization also appears to be fundamentally 'marketizing' key parts of university research, changing the relationship between universities and the outside world, and making their boundaries more porous. The most dramatic examples of what Slaughter and Leslie (1997) call 'academic capitalism' (although it is debatable whether the description is accurate, as the notion of capitalism refers to some form of socioeconomic relations of exploitation, and Slaughter and Leslie are concerned mainly with examining the increase in market relations in the production and distribution of academic knowledge), are to be found in the public research universities, and especially in the areas of the new 'technosciences'. The biological sciences provide the best examples of the growing convergence of science and technology in the market place. Globalization has its impact through the enhanced competitiveness laid on large corporations to find and exploit new products in the increasingly knowledge-based societies that characterize a steadily integrating world economy. As companies become more aggressive they invest in areas such as molecular biology, and this has the consequence of turning a basic science into a more entrepreneurial form.

This is illustrated especially by the growth, in countries such as the US, the UK, Australia and Canada since the 1980s, of many types of interdisciplinary centres and departments, such as materials science, optical science and cognitive science, which are characterized by their commercial activities. They reflect an emerging exchange between the corporation – endlessly seeking innovations that can quickly be turned into successful commodities – and the need for universities to compensate for the declining unit of public funding by seeking more market opportunities. As national economies become increasingly subject to the processes of globalization, governments become subject to increased pressure from industry and commerce to provide incentives for universities to generate more market receptive innovations. Grants for university–industry collaboration also become more plentiful as governments look for companies to be better equipped to compete more successfully in world markets. Within public research universities, less funding is allocated to teaching, while increases are regularly made to applied research and similar activities that aid a university's potential to earn more external income.

The linking of postsecondary education to business innovation as a means of enhancing national competitiveness seems to be an increasingly striking feature of the growing global economy and is being reflected in national higher education policies. The aim is to create national wealth by developing global market shares through the discovery of new products and processes in order to expand the number of higher technology jobs that are better paid and further up the value chain of worldwide production. Higher education ministers everywhere appear to be ensuring that public funds that may be available for discretionary or marginal activities are being directed to research that is either focused directly on product innovation or on research that complements the areas of innovation in the large global corporations, such as high technology manufacturing. As a consequence, funds for teaching and for 'softer' social science or humanities research have tended to decline. The internal impact of globalization on universities is therefore quite variable.

Curiosity-driven or basic and more individualistic forms of research seem to be a particular casualty of the drive to harness university research to wider strategic national goals and to integrate it into broader plans for economic development. It is a moot point for some whether a diminution of basic research produces more non-benefits for companies than the advantages that are gained from applied investigations. The outcome might be a loss of the essential intellectual and divergent energy needed to produce forms of thought and creative property that underpin more market-based applications. That is, it is an approach that might be considered to be overly short-term and, effectively, shortsighted. In the UK, a recent report for the Engineering and Physical Sciences Research Council suggests that too close a collaboration with business and industry may be constraining the creativity of UK chemists. There is a shift away from innovation and discovery to more cautious incremental research that may reflect too strong a focus on product-related work (*The Times Higher Educational Supplement*, 13 January 2003).

Slaughter and Leslie suggest that the rise of academic capitalism is best explained by what they describe as resource dependence theory. In a parsimonious form, this argues that organizations that are deprived of critical revenues, such as declining public funds, will seek new resources. They suggest that research finances are a key resource for universities, not only because most research money is raised competitively, but also because universities generally seek constantly to maximize their prestige and overall standing. And research is the key to the status differences between universities.

Faculty turn to commercial forms of research and closer ties with industry and commerce in order to maintain levels of research funding but also because such activity appears to be increasingly encouraged and smiled upon by public and other bodies. It is a university strategy, therefore, for enhancing prestige, particularly if the company that is being allied with is a large national or global player with major standing in its own right. Indeed it is possible that over time universities may become further differentiated by the 'blue chip' ranking or otherwise of their industrial or commercial collaborators. It would appear that, while basic research is still regarded by academics as the core of science, applied commercial or entrepreneurial research is steadily seen also an important dimension of general research merit. Products as well as publications count. This is particularly the case with those academics closest to the high technology end of the market. Such staff value knowledge as much for its commercial payoff and its ability to generate added funds as for its contribution to science's worldwide intellectual heritage and explanatory significance.

A problem with analyses of contemporary 'academic capitalism' or the 'entrepreneurial university', particularly in a comparative and global context, is that the evidence that is adduced is often quite limited. Slaughter and Leslie do not provide a detailed and rigorous investigation into changing academic or staff values, using variables such as gender and subject, for example, compared to their notion of institutional resource dependency. Also, there is little account taken of specific local factors, or the differential impacts of globalization on local arrangements (Deem, 2001).

A recent comparative investigation of universities in five European countries by Burton Clark (1998), however, does appear to confirm the general outcomes of the Slaughter and Leslie project, although it is somewhat more celebratory of this than the other work. Clark observes that these European universities shared five common features: a strengthened steering core (utilizing speed and flexibility); an expanded developmental periphery, with the growth of new non-departmental units such as interdisciplinary research centres; a diversified funding base; a stimulated academic heartland in which academics accept the need for transformation; and the taking on of entrepreneurial activity and an integrated entrepreneurial culture. Yet, as Deem (2001, p. 17) has noted, the methodology employed appears overdependent on interviews with managers and administrators, the very groups that might be thought to be the most welcoming of the entrepreneurial developments described by Clark and his associates.

These developments in the globalizing world of higher education are not without their risks. It is not clear that universities possess the expertise to properly and successfully exploit both their knowledge generation and their commercial alliances. There is continuing evidence that universities do not always realize the patentable value of their research and that they allow the terms of their collaboration with the industrial sector to leave them with too high a proportion of the risk and too little of the rewards. Cost–benefit analyses that examine the distribution of gains from collaboration between the university and the corporation, not least in the context of the respective levels of risk undertaken, are scarce on the ground. The legal liabilities of such alliances often seem poorly realized and inadequately monitored, while the broadly 'non-corporatist' and devolved ('collegiate') nature of university organization leaves the prospect of staff with inadequate commercial experience forming agreements that are insufficiently tested within the institution and that may carry sizeable financial exposure. As for the academic entrepreneurs themselves, they remain largely protected from market risk and the penalties of loss by their institutional employment. They are publicly funded entrepreneurs, and few appear ready to give up their secure employment and take on contractual terms of the kind that would be normal for businesspeople in the private sector.

Globalization, in the forms that we have described above, may have significant consequences for the morale and cohesiveness of the university. It may encourage fissures between entrepreneurial faculty, increasingly used to the relatively high levels of autonomy and authority that decision-making in these new contexts requires, and administrative staff used to more leisurely styles and yet also increasingly responsible for the new and transparent corporatist forms of accountability. Among academics themselves, it is not hard to imagine resentment from those subject areas that appear to have little to offer the high-tech commercial world of knowledge-based product innovation. And as for those faculty committed to undergraduate teaching, larger student numbers drawn from increasingly varied social backgrounds are likely to produce greater workloads for less reward. Given the gender imbalances between subjects and functions in universities everywhere it is not difficult to imagine that the advantages that accrue to predominantly male academics in science, engineering and technology may become even more pronounced.

## ▶ Teaching and learning

Teaching and learning, however, at least in its publicly funded form, appears to be subject to different processes than that of research. Most contemporary universities are creations of the nation state (Scott, 1998). As national governments lose functions to global and regional agencies – public and private – they tend to see higher education teaching and learning as a means of reasserting national goals. Increasingly, however, this is less the creation of a national elite culture and more the formation of human capital – a means for upskilling the workforce to enable national competitiveness in a global knowledge-based economy. As such teaching and learning policies appear to be part of national governmental strategies to manage globalization to best economic effect.

Universities still have a strong sense of place (campus, region) and university systems display marked national characteristics. For example, they operate within national rules that quite severely restrict where academics may work. As university employment became more formalized with the development of publicly funded, national systems of higher education, and particularly as the academic professions in continental Europe became part of the civil service, academic employment mobility has become more constrained. Career paths favour the nationals of the country, either formally or through more subtle means. In the absence of more internally coordinated policies, each country has developed its own procedures and processes for selection, appointment and training (*The Times Higher Education Supplement*, 1 March 2002).

Moreover, in the EU, supranational public authority for higher education has yet to emerge (as opposed to inter-governmental declarations of intent). Although the EU may be regarded as a form of 'regulatory state', in that it operates through rules and directives rather than seeking resources distribution between social groups, unlike most states, it has yet to promulgate effective regulatory frameworks for higher education. Moreover, recent efforts, following the Treaty of Bologna in 1999 (an initiative of member countries, not the EU Commission), to develop a more standardized approach to the length of the time taken for undergraduate and postgraduate degrees, and to take steps for more common credit accumulation and quality assurance processes between individual countries, have made only halting progress, as Kenneth Edwards notes in Chapter 2. In part this reflects divided approaches to globalization and to the role of the EU in facing up to the challenges of such processes. For some countries, Bologna is a means for making European universities more competitive in the face of American, Australian and Asian challenges for international fee-paying students and commercial research opportunities. For others, however, Bologna is regarded as a form of protection from globalization for public service higher education in Europe, with its domestic monopolies, government grants and public goods ethic, and commitment to social objectives such as equity, national cultures, emancipation, and access. It reminds us, that even in an age of globalization, varieties of national capitalism and their associated political economies persist. Countries with traditions of comparative institutional advantage that derive from their more managed and cooperative forms of economy and associated consensual and corporatist political and business arrangements, are more likely to resist the liberalization of their university systems than those where more market-driven processes obtain (Hall and Soskice, 2001). But in all types of society it is not uncommon to find that higher education has lower levels of private provision than in the primary or secondary schools sectors.

Meanwhile, most individual universities lack the resources or capabilities to become global commercial players. They seem increasingly aware, however, that the costs of not developing online learning – a key component of its globalized forms – may be rising. These include losing market share to foreign (particularly American) organizations, public and private, and declining intellectual capital. Yet difficulties in operating at scales to generate cost-recovery of initial heavy investment, on agreeing workloads and other issues with staff and their unions, in changing the culture to a less individualistic and more team-based pedagogical one, the lack of professional staff development, and faculty suspicions of management motives and the fear that profits rather than educational reasons may be predominating, continue to provide high obstacles to adoption and successful implementation in university systems throughout the world. The picture raises the prospect that other types of provider, able to start from scratch but with powerful resources behind them, may take increasing shares of traditional university markets (Roberts *et al.*, 2002). (See Chapters 7 and 8 by Bjarnason and Ryan respectively for a further consideration of these points.) If the quality of provision and customer service are seen to be better in the more private sectors, these are likely to be preferred particularly during periods of rising national prosperity.

Those universities that do become involved in global online learning, do so either as part of consortia, or because they have a long tradition of distance learning (such as the UK Open University). Moreover, as well as the institutional difficulties outlined above, as long as nation states continue to subsidize higher education, the commercial and global market may continue to be viewed as marginal at best.

Nonetheless, it is unlikely that the processes of globalization will leave university teaching and learning untouched. Current discussions at the WTO on the trade liberalization of professional services (the GATS) increases the prospect that national markets and funding may become more open to foreign providers, including those from the private sector. International regulatory change is likely to introduce wider globalization exposure for teaching and learning functions in universities than hitherto.

Moreover, the growth of commercial, online and 'virtual' universities will undoubtedly continue, although its pace is hard to predict. Virtual education, building on established forms of distance education, is increasingly diminishing the importance of place, and opening the door for students to take courses from institutions on different continents. The development of 'fifth-generation' online global higher education, with features such as automatic or computer-generated responses to students, is also likely to reduce the labour costs of such operations. The World Wide Web, which is able to combine other media, such as text, audio and video, and to offer global education in both synchronous and asynchronous forms, is transforming existing and longstanding forms of national and regional distance education, and making the prospects of global education much more realistic. There is an increased compression of time and space and a deterritorialization of the learning experience. Virtual education has increasingly legitimized distance education by providing a high-tech respectability. However, in worldwide terms, many parts of the globe remain without adequate access, although this is changing rapidly with the use of local 'tele-learning' centres and the adoption of mobile telephony.

A number of persuasive arguments have been advanced to support the rise of global education. These include the possibilities for a more vibrant and multiperspective student body, wider geographical and social access (including for those developing countries without an adequate domestic university capacity of their own), the ability to distribute worldclass knowledge and practitioners to a larger audience, a broader and more international curriculum, and the prospects of lower costs and raised private/consumer income through mass – and possibly more standardized – provision to enable institutions to offset falling governmental funds. Against this, detractors fear the possibilities of western cultural domination. After all, the language used is nearly always English, the pedagogy generally is anti-didactic and student-centred as found increasingly in the developed world, and the curriculum replete with western models and examples (Mason, 1998, p. 45). However, there is evidence that more global student bodies are able in their increased interaction to effectively challenge often-assumed western interpretations of the world, although cultural sensitivity in curricula, delivery and administration have some way to go in the further development of global university education.

## ▶ What might a globalized university teaching and learning look like?

Mason suggests that there is, to date, far less global education than might be imagined from much of the media and other hype. In her researches, admittedly now a few years ago, she was unable to find a single example of an institution offering global education in all of its characteristics, such as: students in more than two continents of the world able to communicate with each other and with the teacher; an express aim on the part of the teacher or institution to attract international participation; course content devised specifically for transnational participation; support structures – both institutional and technological – to tutor and administer to a global student body; and operations on a scale of more than one programme and more than one curriculum area, with more than one hundred students.

If we are going to test propositions about the globalization of higher education we need a schema that allows some form of empirical observation. For example, with teaching and learning, this might include: a) the continental or global composition of a student body for a particular programme and its ability to use the Web to communicate with each other and with teachers; b) the curriculum seeking to generate graduate global attributes; c) course content designed to encourage transnational participation; d) technological and institutional support structures to tutor and administer a global student body; and e) a range of programmes (25 per cent? 50 per cent?) in a university prospectus exhibiting the above characteristics.

Another approach might be to test for the following in national university systems: a) the extent to which higher education policies – at systemic and institutional level – are influenced by international or global epistemic communities or networks; b) the ability for students and staff to move internationally from or to a country's universities; c) the utilization of communication and information technologies to provide learning and its administration transnationally, and around the clock, irrespective of territoriality; and d) the professional development of teachers in higher education to be explicitly global in orientation.

Currently, in comparison with the training programmes of multinational corporations, there are few examples of universities developing global support structures. Global practices seem still to be largely confined to small groups of enthusiastic staff innovators dealing with relatively small groups of students. Even the Internet has yet to be adapted to manage large numbers of university students in a satisfactory manner. Yet global activities are undoubtedly increasing, despite such difficulties as universities frequently lacking the funds for adequate upfront investment, and without the ability to devise and operate the necessary staff reward and development practices, that we discussed above.

For the most part, the private and corporate globalizers represent a slimmed-down version of a traditional university. They generally undertake no research and rely often on the 'moonlighting' activities of staff from the conventional universities to teach their courses. Yet they invest significantly in the professional development of teachers and other staff, and often rely on small groups to maintain customer satisfaction, pedagogic integrity and individual and group support. Their key resource is control of increasingly sophisticated delivery platforms and managed learning environments, plus efficient administrative staff and systems.

It is difficult to envisage that global forms of technology-supported higher education will not continue to grow in importance. It appears to be in tune with broader pedagogic movements to a more skills-based and student-centred curriculum, and to be allied to postmodernist notions of knowledge and its relative de-privileging of the position of the teacher. It also seems to be calibrated with lifelong learning processes seen virtually everywhere now, with the requirement to meet the updating needs of the time-constrained and often house-bounded adult in the most convenient and effective ways possible. The spread of the Internet will facilitate such developments, although satellite and broadcast media will be used in countries (such as in Asia) where more didactic methods of instruction continue to prevail.

## ▶ Global developments

Globalization tends to increase international and supranational forms of convergence and regulation. The forces affecting higher education around the world are strikingly similar – expanding enrolments, less public funding (per student), lifetime learning, and more private investment – and constitute global phenomena. In the business sphere, transnational standardization and regulation (including quality assurance) are seen as essential for promoting globalization. The EU Treaty of Bologna (1999) may be regarded as representing the first halting steps for higher education towards such processes. It emphasizes the likely role of high quality and its assurance as a key guide for consumers in a global market, and governments, institutions and transnational bodies are evaluating the ways that they judge the quality both of online provision and foreign institutions. However, as yet, a lack of agreed standards for initiatives, such as the development of learning objects databases, restricts the abilities of institutions to collaborate in terms of sharing costs and resources. The lack of shared standards is apparent also in the areas of academic quality and credit accumulation, which restrict the portability of skills and knowledge from one institution to another.

An important question that needs to be answered is whether increases or decreases in regulation flow from the growth of globalization. Provisionally, it would appear that global competition reduces or severely modifies market regulation, but also leads to reregulation and new regulatory regimes for customer protection. In higher education particularly, can we detect stronger regulatory or deregulatory impulses that can be traced to increased worldwide connectedness, especially with the development of higher education as a tradable and commercial activity? Global trade liberalization proposals to be applied to services such as education that are part of the current negotiations being conducted through the WTO would suggest that there are powerful influences for market liberalization and deregulation. Recently it has been estimated that there are at least seven major initiatives worldwide aimed at setting up global structures to regulate transnational education or to create international quality assurance, recognition or accreditation systems. These include such familiar bodies as UNESCO, the OECD, and the

EU, as well as the European Universities Association and the International Association of University Presidents (Williams, in *The Times Higher Education Supplement*, 5 April 2002). Globalization influences can also operate on national regulatory bodies. In the UK, the Higher Education Funding Council for England (HEFCE) has helped finance an 'E-University' to assist universities compete in the international online commercial market, but subject to clear quality controls. The government-commissioned Dearing Report into Higher Education in the UK (1997) also introduced proposals for the Quality Assurance Agency (QAA), the body that regulates academic standards, to take on more powers to control overseas and other franchise arrangements and to contribute to the recognition and standing of UK awards throughout Europe and the world. In New Zealand and Australia also, quality assurance bodies for universities have been established, at least in part to protect marketability in overseas countries.

It is doubtful that a single European higher education quality assurance and accreditation body for universities will be established. Nor is it likely that a harmonized set of standards will be promulgated and applied. This is not simply because the autonomous traditions of universities make such approaches problematic, but because international and global regulatory regimes in areas other than education often rely on the principle of Mutual Recognition (MR), formulated by the European Court of Justice, rather than on harmonization, to generate processes of convergence on standards. Since the mid-1980s this has certainly been the new approach of the EU, following earlier, fruitless attempts at creating a Single Market through consensually arrived at agreements on common or harmonized standards.

If national regulatory diversity continues to prevail in global contexts for universities, it is possible that it will reinforce tendencies for the creation of the transnational university (TNU) along the lines of the transnational corporations found in the global economy. Such universities, operating to maximum benefit in outlets around the world, would take their advantages from their corporate organizational form. This would enable them to internalize the international exploitation of their assets, in the context of locational risk and opportunity, generated by differences in national forms of regulation and gaps in international regulatory coordination. Competition between national regulatory systems could ensue (despite international efforts by governments to prevent this), with transnational universities picking and choosing their preferred regulator. At that point the historic alignment between the nation state, social purposes, and the university would have given way to one based more on global frameworks and corporate or private interest.

Yet it is unlikely that nation states would be happy with such a state of affairs. Indeed many are likely to strongly resist its arrival. They see universities as key instruments in developing the scientific and other research necessary for national innovation and competitiveness in the global economy, particularly in the technologies that have high economic value. This is part of the responsibility that governments feel to create infrastructures in their own territories to make their country an attractive partner for collaboration and which requires that technological capabilities are not jeopardized by institutional failures or inadequacies (Archibugi and Iammarino, 2001). Although transnational universities originating or based in another country may bring capital investment and knowhow into overseas countries, they will be closer to their own domestic government than to the overseas administration, and nation states are aware of this potential gap in their influence. 'National champions' consequently will be regarded by governments as continuing to be necessary for economic health, while wider social and political purposes, such as widening access and the maintenance of national prestige through possession of world-renowned 'centres of excellence', are regarded by political leaders as best advanced by universities amenable to their own state influence. A tension, however, between an increasingly transnational corporate university and the public agenda of states, is likely to continue, with its resolution unclear.

Either way, patterns of global inequality in both economic wealth and university provision will persist and possibly deepen. One of the emerging characteristics of the new global order in the economic field is that globalization can leave many developing countries on the sidelines. A recent Commonwealth of Learning (COL) Report indicates how the application of digital technology in higher education reinforces this. Not only is there an increasing 'digital divide' in terms of access to communications and information technology infrastructures between the developed and developing countries, and also differential access to scientific knowledge and its exponential growth, but little seems to be happening in developing countries by way of partnerships, consortia, or public/private sector alliances. Institutions prefer to act separately rather than form collaborative alliances to help reduce costs and to enhance capability and reach. Yet:

> the costs related to establishing a virtual learning initiative are already high. The development of learning objects databases and more online services will likely drive costs even higher. As a result it is becoming more difficult for individual institutions to go it alone. In this context, partnerships and joint venturing become more attractive as a means of sharing investment costs and in-kind resources (COL, 2000, p. 146).

Additionally, as we have noted, the western capacity to develop content in the new globalized forms creates the potential for 'content imperialism' in which the developing world becomes the consumer of learning resources produced elsewhere. The COL Report also points to some constraints on commercial, borderless and virtual operations. Their increasingly 'business operation' approaches are leading to the phenomenon of 'picking the low-hanging fruit', with particular subjects (such as business and information technology studies) and pedagogies favoured to the exclusion of less profitable and more socially interactive subjects and methods. Unless these tendencies can be changed it may mean that the size and profitability of the international market for online learning and globalized higher education will be more limited and competitive than originally perceived.

## ▶ Conclusion: globalization, the university and democracy

There seems increasing recognition that globalization impacts most significantly on universities by extending the territorial and supraterritorial bases of knowledge. Both globalization and knowledge are characterized by their depersonalized and universalistic features, which tend to burst free of national constraints. Even within nations, knowledge is more publicly available than before, and is no longer confined to elites. And everyday or lay or professional knowledge is seen as not necessarily inferior to scientific accounts but as closely intertwined with them. Both forms are subject to greater critical and thoughtful engagement – to reflexivity – by individuals, which undermines traditional knowledge authorities and reinforces validity based upon application and utility. Science is seen as requiring greater social accountability, not least as the closeness of the human and natural worlds are continuously demonstrated (see Gibbons in Chapter 5).

Consequently, it is difficult to establish agreement within the academy as to what is incontestably knowledge (Delanty, 2001). But for some this state of affairs is a source of some optimism. Contestability and the free engagement of ideas – in an age when the traditional aloofness and authority of the university over society has all but gone – provide both a new 'idea of the university' and also suggest it as the site for the development of less territorial and more global forms of democracy. Using concepts derived from linguistic and critical theory, particularly the work of Habermas (1996), in these accounts the university in the global age becomes potentially the site of ideal speech communities. Interdisciplinarity, exchanges between knowledge as science and knowledge as culture, and enhanced communication within what is still a protected and privileged institution – requiring facilitation and leadership from vice chancellors and other institutional leaders, rather than top down, stultifying and uninspiring managerialism – are the optimistic means for establishing the wider communicative competences that are likely to be essential for more global forms of democratic arrangement (Barnett, 2000; Delanty, 2001; Held et al., 1999). Universities, in these views, contain more democratic possibilities as locations for public debate and interconnectivity than the weakening public realm more generally, or the notion of vanguard classes, such as the intelligentsia or the working class, as found in revolutionary socialist theory. In these ways the university finally resolves the tension between its inherent cosmopolitanism and its service to the nation in favour of the former. Globalization, cosmopolitanism, science and the cultural, therefore become aligned and reinforcing within the university as part of the reflexive, universalistic and supraterritorial logic of worldwide identity and connectedness.

Yet it is not clear that such expectations and aspirations are not fanciful. Science is not only embedded within communication, but also within specializations, and within protected and conservative paradigms, and within departments. They are characterized by tribes and territories (Becher, 1989), and these have been reinforced by competitive assessments of research and quality externally that drive funding and rankings. Academic capitalism, as one of the consequences of globalization that we discussed above, is more likely to divide and to fracture the academy than to forge new democratic and consensual debates and opportunities. And while managers and administrators in the body corporate that is now the form of the modern university may provoke, if they push too far, a collegial revolt by the academic masses, this seems unlikely. Divide and rule, rankings and competitive funding, are instruments that are likely to conduce segmentation rather than a sense of common consciousness.

There is little sign of resistance to the instrumentalizing forces of market, bureaucracy and the state that some have envisaged. The picture is more Weberian than that as the inexorable rise and development of rationality produces not only universalistic epistemology, but also the organizational (if not necessarily the national) hierarchies and boundaries that keep universalism's democratic and consensual potentialities well under control. As Delanty (2001) has noted, globalization does not necessarily run against the state – it can strengthen it in some respects and undermine it in others. The university as an organization is still largely formed in the service of the state, even if one of those central functions – the reproduction of a national culture – has succumbed to the multifaceted forces of postmodernism.

# 4 The University and the Regulatory State

*Roger King*

## ▶ Introduction

As we have seen in previous chapters universities are relatively contemporary institutions. In the UK the majority have been created in the last 40 years or so. Although it is possible to trace the existence of universities back many centuries or more, they have developed in the main as part of the consolidation of nation states. Their culture (perhaps ideology) of institutional autonomy, and academic and critical freedom, owes less to old medieval guild notions of independence from the state than to the nature of their role in the service of nation-establishing elites. Medieval associations and corporations were largely extinguished by the new state rulers, and were generally replaced by more modern forms of business organization that were constituted by trade-based legal notions of corporate unity – the 'collective personality' – than by notions of semi-autonomous fiefdoms. Universities generally have been slow to move from older notions of themselves as collections of individuals that came together periodically for self-governance, to one where the corporate organization is the legal 'face' of the university. These developments have quickened in recent years with the need for greater cost controls, financial accountability, and a recognizable management function.

Universities provided the rulers of the industrializing capitalist states of the late nineteenth and early twentieth centuries – and subsequently – with technical knowledge, and a means for the transmission of national culture and intellectual cognitive structures, that seemed appropriate for modernity and its increasing democratic temper. In exchange the academy was granted a level of autonomy that largely insulated it from wider social movements. Nonetheless, despite this institutional protectiveness, at the individual level the notion of the independent, creative intellectual, insulated from the distractions and sirens that lay outside the musty study door and in the wider society, curiously seemed appropriately aligned with the bourgeois and Victorian 'privatism' of the individualistic capitalist entrepreneur. One consequence is the persistence of 'professionalism' in academia as very much individually conceived, which has made difficult the acceptance of more collective or 'team' notions of professionalism in approaches to teaching and learning, for example.

During the course of the twentieth century we witnessed the growth of national higher education systems, fuelled by larger proportions of public funding, as part of the aim to secure wider citizenship and social welfare, and, increasingly, supporting the goal of achieving national economic competitiveness in knowledge-based, globalizing capitalism. In turn this has led to greater public and financial accountability and the dismantling of binary and similar models of formal institutional stratification. Research began to be defined in national strategic terms, while teaching more students was regarded as part of the necessary investment in human capital. But universities in the 1980s and 1990s became tied up, too, with the application of market forces and the development of the new ideas about public management. A combination of new-right ideology, and a widespread recognition of the failures of the welfare state model's emphasis on public ownership, saw this model replaced by a form of 'regulatory state'.

The welfare state was a service-delivery state, in which government assumed responsibility not only for the provision of a wide range of services but also for their production. But the opaqueness and inefficiencies of this approach have seen the rise of the institutionally distinct regulator coordinating a variety of actors – public and private – and operating at some remove from the central state. The outcome has been greater transparency and formalism in governance, and the development of systems of rules that are often precise and at variance with the former discretions and intimacies of earlier forms of state governance. The use of competitive tenders for procurement is one example of how formal regulation helps distinguish the public responsibility for provision from the more private responsibilities for operations and production. The 'contracting' or 'enabling' state, that was reinforced in the commercial sector by the disposal of the state's ownership of assets through a series of privatizations, saw the market as providing the competitive source of greater responsiveness and innovation that was also required for public bodies to become more efficient and effective. As applied to the universities, these approaches were seen as necessary to make them more reliable in their servicing of national economic and other needs.

## ► Markets and the state

In considering the relationship between the state and markets – between public authority and private interests – it is easy to neglect how each is generally dependent on the other. They are not essentially in opposing corners; markets are constituted by political and legal institutions, and by rules (such as those to do with property, or contracts) and, in times of radical change, effective functioning may require governmental action to quell social unrest. In turn governmental administration itself is frequently these days abjured to operate along more commercial and competitive lines, as found in private business organizations. Moreover, large corporations, rather than individuals, comprise most markets, and not only do they often seek state action for the protection of their privileged and sometimes monopoly market positions, they can often act as political organizations themselves, both internally and in their often close ('network') relationships with politicians.

As we shall see, market reforms generally have been accompanied by the rise of a host of regulatory agencies. In the UK particularly, but also elsewhere, the privatization of state-owned utilities, such as gas, electricity, water and telecommunications, has been seen as requiring safeguards against the potential abuse of monopoly positions. Regulatory bodies have been tasked to ensure that the consumer interest and its protection (through price-setting, for example) are promoted. Nonetheless, regulatory agencies inevitably need to tread a fine line between producers and consumers and their dispositions one way or the other may reflect changes in the overall political environment, or indeed their relative 'smartness' in both gaining the confidence of those being regulated and yet exercising their functions to protect consumers and the wider public. Levels of accountability (including directly to parliaments, for example) can also vary.

## ▶ The regulatory state

In recent years we find the growth of regulatory agencies throughout many sectors. The changes in the relationship between the state and society, and particularly between the state and the economy that we outlined above, have led steadily to the increased use of the description the 'regulatory state' (see Moran, 2002). This refers to the development and enforcement of rules, often legally codified, to order or to modify socially valued behaviour, usually through the establishment of an independent or institutionally distinct regulator as a formal instrument of government. As with traffic regulations, the overall purpose is to improve conduct rather than to sanction offences, although regulators often undertake both tasks. Regulation is a description that conjures up the picture of a mechanical act of steering, as in cybernetics, with an overall governor (the regulator) in receipt of information about the condition of the system and its relationship with the external environment.

Regulation generally seeks an ordering between competing interests, such as shareholders, employees, consumers and the wider public, which constantly evolves. This can involve the regulator having powers to license, monitor, supervise or ban. Self- or private regulation can operate whereby a collectivity, such as a professional association, is recognized by the state as having authority to regulate the behaviour of its practitioners. As Clarke (2000) has noted, regulation involves the constitution of a form of authority to achieve order in an area of life that is displaying tendencies to disorder, perversity or excess.

The growth of regulatory authority and instruments mark a key change in the perception of the role of governments towards the economy. Outside of the US, and particularly in Europe, throughout much of the twentieth century government was associated with substitution for market failure, through the means of public ownership of enterprises such as utilities, and through high taxation and public expenditure policies. However, regulation and other recent market-based reforms are associated more with the failure of government than the market, and the need for government to be concerned more with assisting markets rather than substituting for them, including through the adoption of competition and 'anti-monopoly' policies.

The reasons for the extension of government-backed and legally supported regulatory bodies are various. They are seen as more effective and efficient operators than government, and as increasing transparency, customer protection, quality control, and technical standardization. This decentralization is ideologically attractive to market-orientated politicians and also persuasive to those on the left who seek forms of 'social steering' without incurring large amounts of public expenditure. It also helps to differentiate governmental responsibility for ensuring that a service is actually provided from its actual delivery. This does not necessarily eliminate detailed ministerial intervention, especially in countries such as the UK that have a long historical tradition of strong central governmental decision-making, nor does it necessarily overcome the more informal processes of policy formation that exist within the administration of most states.

There appear to be structural factors at work encouraging more state-directed regulation than ever before, particularly as this takes the form of statutory supervision by the state or its agencies, and the increasing formal and codified requirements imposed upon a variety of business and professional bodies. Almost irrespective of country and the political colouring of governments, the challenges of competitive and increasingly global markets, the rise of democratic politics, the growing political influence of mass media, and the propensity for consumers and others to be assertive and to mobilize, are all factors helping to create forms of regulatory state, with a corresponding decline in trust afforded to professional practitioners and their associations of all kinds.

An overriding aim for regulation is to formally generate processes of accountability and transparency that produce trust. Trust in the product or service, and trust in the provider. For long, higher education and the other professions have enjoyed a form of confidence and working autonomy (monitored by professional associations) that has been based on long periods of training and the gaining of expertise, on state recognition for their control of markets (and for them keeping out the cowboys), for eschewing the principle of commercial exploitation, and from a deep-rooted conviction that the patient or the student benefited from a close, if paternalistic, relationship in which due deference was paid to professional knowledge and standing. Customer 'knowledge', and consumer wants and desires, were regarded as unreliable and probably misinformed. Professionally assessed 'client' needs were primary and should lead rather than follow public expenditure levels.

But this rather cosy state of affairs has been rudely shattered. Intellectual and social criticism of professional expertise has grown, reinforced with the publication of scandals by a mass media more intent than before in rooting out such stories (Thompson, 2001), automatic deference has declined, and the state is increasingly looked upon to ensure adequate levels and standards of provision at costs that both consumers and the public purse can afford. Professions and their associations are increasingly subject to greater intrusion into their working practices, including state-sponsored regulatory monitoring, in return for the public money that is disbursed. The state remains as a background safeguard for the public interest in this approach. It does this by insisting on greater public accountability from professional associations in ways that come close to reconstituting such organizations as officially approved governmental bodies.

As a result higher education and other professions have been positioned closer to the state and to more market-like forces. And, inevitably, this has involved the formal generation of information and other data for consumers. Transparency not intimacy has become the basis of public confidence and trust. The notion of what constitutes a service has shifted from the exercise of professional judgement to satisfying consumers. Moreover, professional autonomy, granted to ensure expert knowledge and adequate standards, has been questioned as delivering complacency, arrogance, and an unwillingness to learn continually.

In some cases, the relationships between regulators and the regulated can be close and genuinely cooperative (perhaps even leading to 'capture' of the regulator) although in others it can turn nastily adversarial. At least some minimal level of friendly engagement and understanding would appear to be necessary for 'smart' regulation – which nearly always has a component of self-regulation – to be effective (Braithwaite and Drahos, 2000). In the UK the belief obtains that general principles and methodologies lead to the best forms of regulation, although in the US by contrast there is greater commitment to more detailed and legally binding approaches.

## ▶ Global regulation

As well as the development of the regulatory state at national level, the growth of more integrated world and regional economies has seen the extension of business and other sector regulation on a global scale. Although by no means a new phenomenon, rule-based supervision of trade and standards has accelerated in recent decades. Not only do the pace and the extent of regulation internationally vary from sector to sector (probably strongest in finance), but deregulation in one aspect (market competition, for instance) is often associated with more regulation in another (such as price controls or consumer protection standards). In banking, for example, increased market deregulation in services in a number of countries has been accompanied by the tightening up and stronger supervision of capital holding and other standards. The consolidation of the European Union also indicates how fierce determination to ensure competitiveness and a level playing field as part of the aim of a single market can result in considerable deregulation in the economic sphere but enhanced regulation elsewhere on matters such as health and safety, and the environment.

In some cases international regulation may involve a harmonization of common standards between countries; in others it may involve considerable national diversity but extensive mutual recognition. Or it may be based on affording equal treatment to both domestic and foreign suppliers (the notion of 'national treatment', which, of course, can mean applying only minimal standards to both).

## ▶ Universities

In turning to universities, therefore, it would be surprising if we did not continue to find strong state or regulatory influences on them even in the most 'marketized' of times. States determine who can use the title of university, and what fees they can charge to domestic full-time students; they secure freedom of academic speech and academic tenure (and take it away), and they can insist on the necessity for universities to engage in research (and can remove that requirement); they can shift the balance of fees and grants in a system (and modify it if it leads to unintended effects, such as too powerful a growth in student recruitment); and they can insist on a range of reporting requirements. And they act, of course, often as a virtual monopsonistic buyer of universities' main services on behalf of the student, as a single or primary proxy buyer.

These powers have not prevented governments in many countries looking for more sources of intervention, not least because, when the levers marked 'universities' are pulled in central government, they appear not to be attached to anything; or, if so, there is plenty of slack in the line. Universities, quoting autonomy and the requirement for criticality in the services of the nation, can seem to go their own way. The response by governments has been to use funding and evaluation, carrot and stick, incentives and sanctions. These have helped to diminish substantive institutional autonomy even as the rhetoric of market deregulation and the status of legal procedural autonomy have expanded. For some universities and observers, unless governments fully deregulate student fees and allow greater private funds into universities, the lack of financial autonomy will continue to subject universities to government's beck and call.

In many countries over the past few years we have witnessed a decline in government confidence in university self-regulation and professional autonomy to protect the consumer, especially the student, and to guarantee academic standards. Rather there has been a widespread introduction of national systems and procedures to evaluate quality in university programmes and to find ways of improving it (Brennan, 1999). Usually this has involved the creation of a national agency to manage the assessment and academic audit processes, although these generally do retain a fair amount of academic self-regulation at the institutional self-assessment level and in the use of peers and assessors drawn from the academic community. Considerable controversy over quality regulation generally attends its introduction – over who owns it (the state or the universities), its method of operation (light audit touch or close assessment), and the intended outcomes (are the findings for the use of institutions' self-improvement policies, or to 'name and shame' and to link to funding and accreditation decisions?).

Brennan points out that the emphasis tends to reflect differences in the balance of accountability, markets and trust in the relationship between higher education, government and the rest of society. Universities seek self-evaluation for the purpose of internal improvement; governments look for more external scrutiny, and are likely to stress purposes such as wider accountability, and more institutional competitiveness.

The universities in many advanced countries in recent years have been subject to these wider societal and state pressures for greater accountability for the large amounts of public funding that they receive. Without adequate regulation, it was felt that universities would be badly led, would lack strategies, and would be controlled by their staff and their unions. The consumer/student would lose out to staff desires to focus on their research (although this has actually been encouraged by government policies), rather than on their teaching, and staff would recoil from controls over their working time and environment without stronger external intervention. Of course, 'regulation' is an ugly word. It resonates with metaphysical pathos and seems to appeal only to the flinty-eyed and the control freak. Unsurprisingly universities react to its threat with alarm and hostility. Regulation seems incompatible with the freedom, professionalism and vitality necessary for scientific advance and intellectual creativity. But regulation is unlikely to recede. The question is whether universities will become subject more to national state regulatory modalities (such as found in the case of the media, for example), or to emergent regional and global supervision and standards (as with financial institutions).

**Globally regulating tradable services**
An important question that needs to be answered is whether increases or decreases in regulation flow from the growth of globalization. In seeking to understand the relationship (and potential relationship) of universities to regulatory authorities at both the national and international level, it is useful to look at the development of global forms of trade regulation. This will be particularly relevant in the case of the operations of the World Trade Organization (WTO), as its General Agreement on Trade and Services (GATS) includes within its provisions the view of higher education (and other levels of education) as a tradable activity that falls within the scope for greater liberalization and regulation. More generally, however, the principles that have governed regulatory and deregulatory frameworks in sectors other than business may have relevance for the regulatory possibilities for higher education.

Although global regulation has expanded in recent decades it has a long history. Examples of trade and financial regulation across countries can be found in the medieval period, as merchants and their bodies and networks formulated practices and customs that enabled their markets to function and develop effectively. Legal notions of property, contract, currency and credit, for example, were essential in providing a sound and reasonably secure basis for the expansion of international trade. In Europe, these developments were considerably aided by the rediscovery and reinterpretation of Roman private law, which provided many of the foundation concepts for regulatory regimes over succeeding centuries. This had a codified and systematic jurisprudence – conceptual depth, technical detail and a capacity to solve new problems – that proved invaluable in formulating ideas and frameworks that aided the spread of international commerce, and were quickly exploited by the merchant classes.

As might be expected, the universities had a role in disseminating the reception of Roman law. The University of Bologna (again!) from the eleventh century developed expertise and reputation in the Roman schemas that drew students and scholars from many countries. Yet the formation of territorial states (when rule and law became centred on territorial possession and authority, rather than on personality) provided a major challenge to the universalism and pan-national characteristics of Roman law. The reception of Roman law into Europe travelled initially along academic routes. The numbers of universities developing the study of Roman law gradually climbed. University-trained lawyers helped in the application of Roman law to overcome localism and universities generally were central in the process of legal transmission. The outcome was not one ideal legal system but a collection of principles and rules that worked in the direction of transnational harmonization and against the centrifugal tendencies of customary and monarchical law.

The rise of centralizing rulers, however, generated national legal formations, with laws and rules applying across a territory, rather than to individuals carrying their domestic jurisdictions with them. Customary, particularly merchant, practices were taken into national legal systems and helped give them national identity, although such systems still tended to utilize Roman law concepts. Merchants looked to the state to supplement the operation of custom with legal norms. However, the persistence of the more private and transnational commercial customs of merchant traders remained one instrument for the harmonization of laws across the main European trading nations.

The mid-nineteenth century witnessed the re-emergence of cross-border regulatory and rule-based regimes as international trade began to accelerate. The movement to standardize negotiable financial instruments (securities and other bonds and shares) internationally began in the second half of the nineteenth century, as did the establishment of specialist international organizations with the purpose of creating a worldwide commercial law. Initially, legal instruments and their dissemination – such as the spread of standard contracts – were undertaken by private trade associations. Only in the twentieth century have international governmental organizations sought to standardize and regulate the variety of privately ordered contract law.

Economic recession and war tended to force back transnational trade and other liberalization approaches, in favour of nationalistic, 'beggar-thy-neighbour' and protectionist policies, until, led by the US and Britain, the post-World War II international agreements at Bretton Woods created an international monetary system administered by international organizational bodies such as the International Monetary Fund (IMF) and the World Bank.

It was part of a worldwide provision for the internal coordination and management of currencies, the supply of funds and loans to countries with economic difficulties, and making available finance for assisting with aid for developing nations. The incursion into state sovereignty was considerable, as Bretton Woods became part of a planned global regulatory system for trade and finance. It marked what Braithwaite and Drahos (2000, chapter 8) describe as a shift away from the tacit, convention-based cooperation of central bankers to a sweeping, rule-based, multilateral cooperation of states.

Although much of the Bretton Woods regime broke down in the crisis-ridden 1970s, for example in favour of floating currencies, the last two decades of the twentieth century saw the further establishment of global and national regulatory frameworks. The integration of finance and trade, and the rise of illegal trade such as money laundering, generates systemic risk and the heightened prospect of local crises becoming worldwide ones, and therefore the need for greater global regulatory supervision. The establishment in 1995 of the World Trade Organization (WTO) particularly, following the end of the Uruguay Round of the General Agreement on Tariffs and Trade (GATT), provided a strong legal and binding process for underpinning agreed moves on worldwide market and trade liberalization. Taxation, however, perhaps like education, has generally operated in national and bilateral, rather than global, regulatory systems as governments see this as consistent with retaining their fiscal sovereignty. Nonetheless, the EU has recently sought to include taxation within its 'level-market' and competition policies, not least as differences in national tax regimes can generate competitive 'play offs' by multinational corporations and also by governments, and hinder the implementation of a single market. The spectacular collapse of large companies such as Enron and the discovery of irregular 'off balance sheet' practices not picked up by auditors, has also stimulated agreement for more extensive international accounting standards.

What are the principles and other processes that have characterized global forms of business regulation, and how might they inform regulatory frameworks applying to universities? We have remarked already that higher education appears, in some respects at least, to be among the least globalized and regulated of sectors (in national and international terms). Perhaps the exception is in the research function where international networks and collaboration seem increasingly essential in generating the creativity and funds for expensive applied and commodity science. Generally, however, nation states have regarded their higher education systems as part of national strategies for responding to globalization and the competitive economic challenges that it poses. They are likely to be wary of losing too much capacity to steer such systems through the further global commercialization and independence of the universities and colleges, and as a consequence of higher education regulatory frameworks shifting too sharply towards supra-nationalism and bodies such as the EU.

## ▶ Regulatory principles and mechanisms

Braithwaite and Drahos (2000) usefully elucidate the key principles that underlie the globalization of business regulation. As they regard such principles as key to the understanding of regulatory negotiations and outcomes generally, it will be helpful to detail these. We can then consider the extent to which they may have relevance to the regulation of higher education.

### Regulation and deregulation

Often it is common to find references to regulation or deregulation in a sector as though it was entirely an either/or affair. Yet it is rare that one finds economic deregulation without some form of enhanced regulation and supervision in the form, say, of customer protection or security. In the cases of privatization, for example, the selling of state assets to the private sector (economic deregulation) was accompanied by increased regulation to protect consumers. Banking is another sector where in global terms market deregulation has been accompanied by increased supervision and regulatory requirements. In the UK the banking sector also offers an example of national self-regulation, including the use of voluntary codes of conduct and similar guidelines, which is monitored by the government. Such cases provide perhaps some of the weakest forms of regulatory regime in terms of state regulatory involvement, although of course this is not to say that they may not be highly effective from the view of the consumer.

In the case of universities, in the UK for example, the picture is more complicated. For the ex-polytechnics/new universities, following the abolition of the binary system, the position post-1992 appears to indicate considerable deregulation. Incorporation, the ability to use the university title or 'brand', and the lessening of restrictions on student recruitment, plus the introduction of tuition fees for full-time domestic and other EU students – and on a 'full-cost' or 'market-setting' basis for many others – can be regarded as a considerable form of deregulation when compared with the restrictions ('local authority maintenance') that operated before. Moreover, the financial and quality accountability processes that were also introduced were not especially more onerous than those that had prevailed previously for these institutions. For the older universities, already incorporated and autonomous through royal charters, the regulatory imposition was more marked, and the offsetting advantages in the exchange for market freedom much less apparent.

Opposition in the UK, particularly from the pre-1992 universities, explains why recently state-backed quality assurance processes (as formulated by the Quality Assurance Agency) have been modified with the aim of providing a 'lighter', more audit-based approach. In this sense, the 'empire' of the old universities has 'struck back', not least by dominating quality assessment panels on the basis of their disciplinary leadership. (Whether this constitutes a form of regulatory 'capture' is an interesting, if yet unanswered question.) Despite this 'fightback' there appeared insufficient gain for the older universities on the economic deregulatory side to justify enhanced and what was perceived to be over-intrusive regulation of quality and standards. It is possible that a heightening of state-supported external quality assurance that might match that found in some economic sectors would only be possible if at the same time there was a considerable deregulation of university price structures. The lifting of restrictions on the ability to charge 'top-up' or full market tuition fees, for example, which would benefit those universities – mainly the older ones – with strong reputation or 'brand' positions in the student market, could provide an incentive to adopt more transparent and externally intrusive quality assurance regulations and processes. The 2003 White Paper on higher education by the UK government seems to indicate some movement along these lines, with proposals for 'top-up' fees and an access regulator. But the maximum level of additional fee would still be regulated or set by government.

Regulatory regimes not only protect the consumer but are often welcomed by producers and other suppliers. The establishment of such frameworks can form part of an agreement with government – as in the banking industry – that more market freedom is available in exchange for greater formal transparency, quality assurance and customer protection. Such accords are also useful for formulating a coherent strategy from government towards a sector. A 'regulatory deal' by universities with government, involving a mix of greater price and other market freedoms in exchange for greater external quality and other scrutiny, has not happened in the UK, partly stemming from the persisting stratification and differences in the system that make it difficult for universities to agree common positions. However, such agreements can benefit both parties.

### 'Ratcheting-up' and 'races-to-the-bottom'

A feature of both national and global regulatory frameworks is the extent to which they encourage either quality enhancement ('world's best practice') or a low-cost 'race-to-the-bottom', which may threaten standards. It used to be argued, for example, that multinational corporations would seek out the lowest-cost and lowest-taxed countries for supply or production. This would enable them to compete on price and to enhance profitability. Yet there is compelling evidence (Porter, 1990) that corporate competitiveness is increased by locations where high standards operate. Top-notch standards for environmental, and health and safety, protection, and the availability of highly skilled labour as a consequence of large public investment in education and training, are more likely than poor quality price-cutting to impress consumers. Nor does there appear to be any direct relationship between taxation regimes and the influx of foreign direct investment. Moreover, in knowledge-based societies, locating operating processes in closer proximity to research and development facilities may be more important for many enterprises than scouring the world for far-flung cheap labour opportunities.

The case of the New York Stock Exchange (NYSE) is interesting here. It operates the highest standards of probity and transparency in its regulatory frameworks, and as a consequence it is very desirable to companies wishing to list. Such a listing, despite the increase in what might be regarded as onerous disclosure and other restrictions, is seen as competitively valuable. Capitalism is less intimate and clubbable than it used to be – pension fund and other investment fund managers need open and reliable information on which to base their decisions – and high standards are regarded as more reassuring that simply low transaction costs. Insider dealing has become the most heinous of corporate crimes. For those organizations that are less concerned to operate in, say, the most advanced and richest markets, such as the US, other less demanding stock exchanges with fewer costs and less transparency may suffice. These alternative stock exchanges offer a form of cheap 'niche' provision. The value of the market aimed at is clearly a major decision for companies in seeking to decide whether to go for the highest standards or the lowest costs in 'purchasing' their regulatory regime.

For universities, there is no reason why similar processes and options cannot prevail. Clearly at least minimal levels of acceptable quality and standards must apply in whatever country or market a university offers it services. But it may be that the provision of a 'world class practice', global quality assurance body, offering to ensure compliance with the very highest standards on behalf of the (worldwide) public, could be desirable to universities seeking to operate effectively on brand and reputation in the most attractive markets (*Universitas 21* may serve this purpose eventually – see Chapter 7). Despite traditions of self-governance and collegiate autonomy, many universities might consider the extra quality regulation to be an exchange worth making. For other institutions, however, less demanding assurance processes would be sufficient for their marketing strategies. Yet, although the market would be the judge, it is a better than even chance that such segmented global quality assurance provision would start a race to the top rather than a scramble to the bottom. Universities would find it hard to justify not being judged by the highest standards available to them when it comes to international trading. The issue for a university is what plays best in its market, and whether its strategies will endure.

## Harmonization and mutual recognition

The globalization of regulation involves the worldwide extension of specific configurations of regulatory norms. However, this does not mean that all countries adopt the same set of rules and that these become harmonized. Most states now have laws governing media ownership and control, but there are considerable differences in the scope and levels of such laws by country. It seems reasonable to suggest that the more that regulatory standards are the same – are harmonized – the more we can describe the framework as globalized. Nonetheless, it is possible for the organizations in a particular sector to be globalized (that is, they operate in an integrated worldwide fashion), and for their markets to be global, but for regulatory frameworks not to be. With gambling, for example, although it is regulated by virtually every country, different states regulate it in quite disparate ways, despite high rollers being drawn from around the world.

An alternative to the harmonization of regulatory norms (and the standards that measure their performance) is the principle of mutual recognition. In such examples, states agree to recognize the regulatory norms in another country as generally producing comparable outcomes to those that operate in their own. There is in some sense an underlying acceptance of equivalence or, slightly weaker, of comparability. This is a stronger idea of globalized regulation than the operation of quite disparate normative systems by states, but not as strong as harmonization. The very weakest sense (indeed, its absence) of globalized regulation would be the existence of regulation of a sector in some countries, and its complete absence in others.

In higher education, the harmonization of both regulatory regimes and standards looks some way off. Among the strongest exporters of university provision – the US, Australia, the UK, Canada and New Zealand – the development of quality assurance regimes has followed, in part at least, concern that foreign markets would have less confidence in countries that lacked such processes. The impact of globalization may be seen in the willingness by domestic quality bodies to go 'out of territory' and to assess the standards of programmes delivered overseas by their national institutions. In part such arrangements reflect the absence of international quality assurance regimes and also the lack of confidence to allow individual jurisdictions to regulate all the provision in their territory. Domestically, too, such developments indicate less trust in 'professionalism' and self-regulation as a means of providing customer protection and robustness in standards-setting and standards compliance, and more of a turn to state-supported and market processes.

Nonetheless, these countries have not all adopted the same approach. In New Zealand and Australia, for example, the process has been holistic (covering the whole of an institution, including management and governance, as well as teaching and research) and is based on an audit methodology. In the UK, the work of the Quality Assurance Agency has been more extrinsic and has included subject assessments with numerical scores and rankings. Moreover, unlike Australia and New Zealand, teaching and research assessment have comprised two separate processes. Also, while research assessment has influenced the amount of research infrastructure money from the UK Funding Councils for each university, teaching assessments have played no such direct role in the allocation of public funds.

There is evidence, however, that the UK quality assurance process is becoming similar to the audit approaches found in Australia and New Zealand. In the US, however, a considerable complexity of quality and regulatory regimes function, largely at state level. In global terms, therefore, the situation resembles more the regulation of the media – with states having regulatory norms, but with considerable differences among them. The next global stage in such circumstances would appear to lie in the area of mutual recognition based on reasonable levels of comparability and equivalence. This appears to be the situation in the EU. The Treaty of Bologna in 1999 commits individual states to pursuing the path of the mutual recognition of awards based on a similar shaping of qualifications hierarchies (utilizing outputs, and time spent by students), rather than attempting to create one common structure.

The recent convergence in approach in the quality assurance regimes of the UK, New Zealand and Australia, and the steps taken by the EU towards mutual recognition, indicate that regulatory norms are influenced increasingly by dense, international networks of 'experts' ('epistemic communities', according to Braithwaite and Drahos) and by the mechanism of modelling, by which good practice regulatory models in one or more countries become adopted by others. Not only is this regarded as more efficient than starting from scratch, but stems from the influence of bodies such as the Organization for Economic Cooperation and Development (OECD) where opinions are formed by authoritative national decision-makers as to the advantages of some approaches rather than others. The increasing role of private finance in university systems may be seen as an example of the influence of international networks on national decision-makers.

### Transparency

Braithwaite and Drahos found, from their study of 17 different sectors or domains, that transparency was the principle that has most consistently been strengthened over recent years in negotiations on regulatory regimes (while that of national sovereignty has weakened most). They trace this to the shift in contemporary capitalism from an industrial to an informational base, and from an intimate and clubbable form of capitalism to a more impersonal one based on the risk analysis of company prospects as indicated by public information that has been properly accounted. This form of capitalism is constituted by a legal commodification of knowledge. Abstract objects, such as patents, have become one of the most important forms of property, and, as with other intangibles, their ownership and impact on balance sheets require disclosure and openness by companies to attract the risk-bearing investments of fundholders.

For universities, the impact of the spread of the regulatory norm of transparency is likely to be on those activities in the academic 'secret garden' that have generally remained immune to public disclosure. The publication or availability of marks for examination performance, the methodologies used in assessing such performance, and the opinions of external examiners and others as to the comparative quality of the award and the organization and teaching underpinning it, are likely to be increasingly disclosed (perhaps after increased legal challenges) to students, employers, government and other stakeholders. And, of course, as public corporations and independent charities, the financial arrangements of universities will be subject to accounting standards and transparency requirements laid upon such bodies and companies more generally.

## ▶ Intellectual property

The concept of property (and the related notion of contract) is perhaps the primary legal foundation for capitalism. A feature of capitalism, too, has been its propensity to commodify – to turn into private property – that which previously may have been regarded as commonly owned or simply part of the world's natural heritage. Contracts, currency, credit and ownership are the legally constituted means by which property can be exploited and turned into value. As we have seen with the fall of eastern European communism and subsequent attempts to introduce capitalist forms of economy, market relations are insufficient by themselves to generate economic growth and commercial prosperity without a properly constituted and extensive legal system that guarantees property and contract. Property and contract law have been essential throughout the ages in promoting capitalist development. This is a universal – a totally globalized – phenomenon.

With the development of abstract and symbolic capitalism the notion of knowledge as property has emerged and with it the creation of legal protections in the form of patents, copyrights, and so on. The movement from industrial to knowledge-based capitalism has gone furthest in the US. The anxiety of large multinational corporations (in pharmaceuticals and computer software, for example) to protect their large Research and Development (R and D) investments in the creation of new ideas and products has been instrumental in the search for the most effective ways globally to secure innovations and inventions from piracy and generic imitation before they have been properly exploited. The idea of intellectual property tends to run counter to both the notion that knowledge belongs to the worldwide community rather than to be stored in private holdings, and to the view, particularly in poorer and developing countries, that the cheap and non-protected (generic) distribution of, say, new medicines for Aids sufferers, should take precedence as a principle over that of intellectual property rights. On the other hand, patent holders argue that without such protection (and the ability to use monopoly positions to keep prices high) the large amounts of investment needed for the R and D to maintain scientific advance would not be forthcoming.

These issues have been of increasing concern to universities. As they have become more involved in networks of research and applied collaboration with the commercial sector, not least in areas such as biomedical and technoscience, they have become subject more to commercial norms, including those on intellectual property. And as public funding for universities falls, the opportunities and incentives for income from such commercial undertakings correspondingly rise. But notions of commercial confidentiality and the legal protection of knowledge tend to cut across the desire for peer reputation and scholarly debate that comes from the early publication of ideas and results.

The key to the rapid and extensive globalization of intellectual property regulation over the last decade or more lies with it being tied to issues of trade. As we shall see later, the location of intellectual property protection within the procedures and processes of the WTO, which has juridical authority and enforcement mechanisms, has ensured a compliance that would have been much more difficult to achieve if it had not been linked to trade. It also enabled the US – as the prime information economy and main net exporter of intellectual property – to use the prospect of denial of access to its large domestic trade market to countries dependent on the US to overcome their initial objections and to secure agreement within the WTO. The use of coercion to obtain 'non-reciprocal coordination' – so that even net importers of intellectual capital such as Australia felt obliged to support the US proposals so that they would not lack US support for their own interests in agricultural trade – demonstrated the bilateral and other trade-offs – the mechanism of linkage – that pave the way for wider multilateral agreements. The use of the WTO (as opposed to the more ineffectual World Intellectual

Property Organization – the WIPO), and of its predecessor (the GATT), to make intellectual property a trade matter, also indicates the willingness and ability of strong countries such as the US, or the EU, to 'shift global forums' to where they may be best placed to obtain their preferences.

The Agreement on Trade Related Aspects of Intellectual Property Rights 1994 (TRIPS), all of which is binding on all members of the WTO, comprises a common and enhanced collection of standards that are increasingly mandatory rather than permissive, and offers less scope for countries to determine what can or cannot be a patent. But it would be a mistake to assume that the creation of a global intellectual property regime was developed under duress or through the grudging assent of many nations. Most recognize that being signed up for intellectual property protection provides a signal of confidence to investors thinking of placing funds in their country. Even China, with at best a patchy record on intellectual property protection, agreed to TRIPS as part of its recent accession to membership of the WTO because it understood the level of investor assurance that this would provide in areas of the economy that are likely to become even more important as knowledge products and processes assume greater prominence and ultimately dominance. Low-cost location is a principle that has been largely pushed aside when it comes to intellectual property. However, the key to the global intellectual property regime lies as much in compliance as in agreement. The willingness of countries such as China to ensure such compliance is a matter of continuing vigilance for the US and some other countries.

There is little doubt that TRIPS reflected the interests of major US corporations, who have a significant comparative human capital advantage in their ownership of abstract objects. They also have a clout not possessed by most, if any, universities. The resources for lobbying and for the preparation and analysis of technical and complex cases also lie outside the powers of most university collective associations, as does the ability to attract entrepreneurial corporate lawyers who sense in global regulatory regimes the opportunity to commodify (to turn into a product 'for sale') regulatory regimes themselves. Nor are university consumers – not least students who have a direct interest in having access to new forms of knowledge – likely to be influential in debates over intellectual property, as consumers have not been players in these matters.

The case of TRIPS is an example of the harmonization of standards that comprise the clearest examples of global regulation, and is the one area that directly affects many universities. It includes the WTO obligatory principle of most favoured nation (MFN) – the same trading terms apply to all countries in the WTO – and the less completely obligatory principle of national treatment (NT) – so that foreign suppliers trade on broadly the same terms as domestic suppliers in the latter's home markets. The principle of national treatment, however, does not require a country to adopt a specific set of standards. It may have few standards, but is only required to practice non-discrimination so that the paucity of standards applies equally to domestic and foreign producers. As such it is a principle that is broadly compatible with notions of national sovereignty. Prior to the WTO Agreement, it was a notion that for a century or more had proved reasonably congenial to many nation states – including the US – as it did not prescribe the standards that had to be followed.

The inclusion of the commercial and perhaps other activities of universities within the scope of the WTO through what is known as the General Agreement on Trade in Services (GATS) – in which higher education, or at least significant parts, is regarded as a tradable professional service – raises questions for universities as to the operation of such principles as MFN (mandatory), NT (negotiable), harmonization (unlikely), and mutual recognition (likely). As with intellectual property and other sectors, the positions and forcefulness of the US and (to a slightly lesser extent) the EU are likely to be critical to the final outcomes. This dominance, given the liberalization position of the US, and some US business groups, is likely to lead to a considerable easing of national restrictions on higher education tradability.

Supranational decision-making favours the more organized world actors, not local or indigenous ones. Apart from their political clout, the US and the EU possess the on-the-spot technical and skilled personnel resources that count in the concluding rounds of negotiations. It is likely, too, that trade and perhaps competition policy ministers, rather than higher education ministers, will call the final shots. Membership of the WTO obliges members to continue to seek successive rounds of liberalization. Once started, no matter how hesitantly, the search for greater liberalization is continuous. The WTO provisions also allow states to make deals across a wide range of subject matters. It is possible that a trade minister may feel that it is in his or her country's interests to trade access to the domestic higher education market, for enhanced market access in other sectors abroad that may have significantly higher (potential) value.

This may happen over the stated objections of the higher education institutions (and even against the wishes of higher education ministers), and extensive consultation with affected interests by governments generally has not been the norm. Yet it is not clear why governments should necessarily reflect the demands of a sector's producer groups. It is arguable that a country may benefit more if consumers were offered greater opportunities at more competitive costs through allowing foreign suppliers to compete more effectively in domestic markets.

Other factors that trade and other ministers, particularly from the powerful so-called 'Quads' (US, EU, Canada and Japan), who represent the main net exporters of higher education services, have to consider is the extent to which greater liberalization may harm the capacity-building propensities of the developing countries. Opening up their university sectors to strongly commercially minded university and other suppliers from abroad may confer some intellectual and consumer advantages, particularly in the short run, but may induce a dependency, including in western cultural terms, that may cut across the development strategies of the Quads countries, and world agencies such as the World Bank and the IMF.

It will be helpful if we analyse further the implications of the WTO and GATS for the global and national regulatory implications for universities, as it represents potentially one of the most important levers of change for university systems in the context of globalization.

## ▶ Universities and the GATS

All service sectors are covered by the GATS, as well as services that in many countries are traditionally in the realm of the public sector, such as education and health care. Before considering the implications of the inclusion of higher education within the scope of the GATS provisions of the WTO, it is worth trying to understand why higher education has come to be regarded as a tradable professional service. In domestic contexts, of course, the growth of largely fee-paying lifelong and adult learning has heightened awareness in institutions of new markets at a time when their own public funding relatively continues to decline. At the same time, however, new private and corporate providers have also sprung up to take advantage of these new opportunities, both to challenge the conventional universities and also to ally with them. To date, however, their subject range is limited, confined mainly to business and technology. But the conventional school-leaver undergraduates are also increasingly likely to contribute from their private sources to their education, as education is viewed more widely not only as a public good but as an investment by the individual.

Internationally, as the OECD, a group of the world's richest countries has noted, a significant trade in higher education services has already developed, which perhaps confounds popular perceptions. It is roughly estimated to have a value at around $US 30 billion in 1999, equivalent to 3 per cent of total services' trade in OECD countries (OECD, 2001). This figure is likely to represent a sizeable underestimation as it only takes into account students studying abroad. Yet cross-border e-learning, and the establishment by many universities of foreign campuses, or joint-venture or overseas franchising arrangements, for the delivery of their academic programmes, have increased rapidly in recent years. Traded educational services are already a major enterprise in some countries. In Australia, New Zealand and the US, educational services are respectively the third, the fourth and the fifth largest export service. By 2003 it is estimated that the value of e-learning provided by the corporate sector will be some $US 365 billion. In part this growth may also reflect persisting dissatisfaction by employers with the offerings of the conventional universities, especially their relevance or otherwise to the world of work.

## The GATS framework

The GATS is a multilateral, legal agreement, and set of rules, governing international trade in services. It consists of three core components: the framework of rules that lays out general obligations (such as transparency, MFN), annexes on specific sectors (such as telecommunications, financial services), and the schedules of commitments submitted by each member country, detailing the member's liberalization undertakings by sector. Given that national policy objectives often involve specific service sectors, the GATS was designed to allow countries to shape their commitments to match those objectives. WTO members are free, for example, to omit entire sectors out of their GATS commitments, or to limit market access in specific sectors. Market access and national treatment obligations apply only to the sectors in which a country chooses to make commitments.

General obligations, such as those pertaining to transparency (which simply require members to publish trade-related information and measures, set up inquiry points for other member countries, and notify the WTO of any changes in regulations applying to trade in services), apply to all services covered by the GATS, notwithstanding whether liberalization commitments have been scheduled. Through successive negotiating rounds countries choose the sectors and modes of services' trade they wish to include in their schedules, as well as the restrictions to market access and national treatment they wish to maintain.

There are four different modes of services trade according to the GATS classification. These are:

1. *Mode 1: Cross-border supply*: This corresponds to the normal form of trade in goods: only the service itself crosses the border. Cross-border supply of educational services could grow quickly in the future through the application of new communication and informational technologies for distance learning, such as the Internet, including their adoption by private and corporate universities whose activities in these fields have grown in recent years.

2. *Mode 2: Consumption abroad*: This refers to cases where a consumer of the education service moves to another country to obtain the service in

question (such as a student who travels abroad to study). These international movements of students currently constitute by some way the largest share of the global market for educational services.

3. *Mode 3: Commercial presence*: This refers to the commercial establishment of facilities abroad by education providers, such as the local branch campuses of foreign universities or their partnerships with domestic education and other institutions.

4. *Mode 4: Presence of natural persons*: This consists of a natural person, such as a teacher or researcher, travelling to another country on a temporary basis to provide an educational service.

Education remains one of the sectors covered by the GATS for which members are quite reluctant to provide liberalization commitments. Moreover, WTO members place considerably more limitations on trade in educational services in modes 3 and 4 ('commercial presence' and 'presence of natural persons') than in modes 1 and 2 ('cross-border supply' and 'consumption abroad'), although this is also the common picture for trade in other services. The main trade obstacles by countries in respect of mode 1 include those to the awarding of financial assistance for studies abroad, restricting the supply of the service only to foreign students in the country, and nationality requirements. The principal barriers in mode 2 are actions that restrict the entry and temporary stay of students, such as immigration and foreign currency controls. For mode 3, obstacles include the inability to obtain the required licences, for example to confer degrees, foreign participation limitations, economic needs tests, restrictions on the recruitment of foreign teachers, subsidies provided solely to local institutions, local partner requirements, and discriminatory tax treatment.

Barriers in respect of mode 4 tend to be covered by *horizontal commitments* that, in addition to specific commitments, are made to cover all the sectors of educational services (and include, for example, restrictions such as investment ceilings, or on assets that can be held). These are commitments that would apply across all sectors irrespective of whether members listed them in their national schedules. They effectively move negotiations away from the 'bottom up' approach of the *request–offer* process towards a top-down approach whereby all sectors are included unless specifically excluded by members.

The OECD notes that indirect barriers also operate, such as accreditation difficulties for foreign degrees when the foreign student returns home for employment. GATS article V11 provides for negotiation of agreements between members for mutual recognition. This article tries to strike a balance between encouraging members to extend recognition of education, experience obtained, licences and certifications, and avoiding discrimination between members. Either by agreement or unilaterally, members may extend this sort of recognition. However, they must allow other members the opportunity to negotiate similar agreements.

The GATS was initially agreed as a legal framework in 1995, but negotiations only began in early 2000 in accordance with the Agreement's 'built-in agenda', namely for successive rounds of negotiations, beginning not later than five years from the date of entry into force of the WTO Agreement and regularly thereafter, with a view to a achieving a progressively higher level of liberalization. With each round, members are expected to negotiate to continue the process of progressive liberalization of services' trade, by both broadening and deepening their liberalization commitments. The aim of the GATS is to increasingly liberalize policies that prevent discrimination between domestic and foreign suppliers and prohibit national measures that would limit foreign access to domestic markets. The WTO Doha meeting of November 2001 approved a new negotiation timetable with permissions to proceed to the 'request–offer' stage that began in March 2002. During this stage bilateral negotiations took place on which sectors members requested market access and on which they were offering access. The request–offers do not need to be reciprocal, so a country could request access to educational services in one country while another country may wish greater access to, for example, telecommunications services. Members were required to file final requests for opening trade in specific markets by June 2002. The final round of negotiations began in March 2003 with trade discussions aimed at reaching agreements in the identified sectors by January 2005.

Finally, there are a number of different types of submissions made in the GATS negotiations, each with a different requirement for action. For example, a proposal is tabled either bilaterally or multilaterally for other members to consider. A request is from a member to another to liberalize or open to trade (such as on visa requirements), while an offer is something a member is prepared to bind as a commitment, but this would depend on reciprocity from others. A commitment is something a member has bound, with bound meaning a commitment to liberalization that a government intends in principle to be permanent. Unbound means no commitment, although the point of progressive liberalization is to eliminate such positions.

## ► GATS implications

Education services are a politically sensitive matter, including for the post-secondary sector. Governments and universities are wary of losing their current capacities to steer and operate their higher education systems by allowing foreign, predominantly private, suppliers to flood domestic markets, relatively untrammelled, and where the diminishing traditional distance between the university and both government and the market place, a distance that originally allowed critical and moral development to be fostered, is accelerated. Concerns by government, about implications for the shape, size and direction of local university systems, are also allied with domestic university anxiety about the likely predominance of the profit motive (leading allegedly to short-termism and little if any long-term investment), and a lack of quality supervision and practices in the new providers. Universities also fear the prospect of reduced public funding for themselves as many more education organizations become entitled to state support under national treatment and MFN measures. In extreme interpretations, public funding for higher education could potentially be subject to action under the GATS as an unfair subsidy. Private operators could challenge the public funding of existing institutions by asking for public funding themselves.

The debates over the GATS tend to be divisive. Those hostile to the GATS see it as threatening the government role and the protection of the public good and quality dimensions of higher education. Those in support feel that it will help consumer choice, raise investment more generally, and diffuse innovation. University trade unions are also concerned that further commercialization will lead to staff casualization and a reduction in academic freedom and collegiate democracy with the enhanced corporatization of the academy. Nor is it clear whether the GATS covers only the commercial services of a university, or whether their publicly funded activities fall within its scope too, as most countries also have private competitors to their conventional universities already (and GATS covers educational services supplied on a commercial basis where competition is allowed). The existence of tuition fees, private contracts, donations, and endowments could potentially be viewed as evidence that public higher education is supplied commercially. It is also unclear what are the implications for online institutions under the GATS since such institutions can be accredited in one jurisdiction yet operate via the Internet in another jurisdiction.

## ▶ Negotiating positions

By March 2002, only the US, Australia and New Zealand governments had submitted proposals setting out their negotiating positions for GATS higher education. The EU was considering its position although it seemed likely to support liberalization measures, not least because of the high involvement of the powerful Competition Directorate of the EU that zealously pursues the levelling of the EU market. More generally, there are signs that competition policy considerations ('antitrust') are being increasingly linked to trade liberalization, on the grounds that reduced or abolished barriers to entry may be less than effective unless they are buttressed by legal provisions to ensure, once entry has been made, that free competition prevails. Countries tend to pursue distinctive national policy aims, even when they all broadly support trade liberalization in higher education. Australia emphasizes the prospect of greater access for students from further GATS liberalization, while New Zealand and the US welcome the opportunity for developing new knowledge and skills. All three, however, see tradable provision as supplemental or complementary to predominantly publicly funded higher education and as a way, too, for increasing export earnings. Some developing countries appear to welcome the attraction of additional investment for education into their countries, although others, such as South Africa, are much more critical and fear that international partners will 'cherry pick' the most profitable opportunities and do little to develop the capacities of domestic universities.

Certainly in Asia and other parts of the world the great demand for higher education cannot be met by domestic institutions alone. There is a desire for international awards and courses that are globally oriented, not least as business and professional careers adapt to the increasing worldwide economic integration that is characteristic of globalization. This applies particularly to international professions such as law and accountancy, whose professional bodies can exert considerable influence on university curricula, and a range of reputable business schools are increasingly engaging in international university partnerships that help to give their programmes wider global appeal.

All perspectives, however, are likely to support the need for strong regulatory frameworks for quality, accreditation, and licensing in a more liberalizing international climate. However, regulating for more diverse provision and for cross-border delivery will not be easy. A major issue is whether governments and their regulatory modalities will change, seeking even greater controls over their university systems, or whether, as we discussed in the previous chapter, in keeping with the more enabling function of the modern nation state, they will exercise a lighter or more facilitative touch in the context of global cooperation.

The position of the US (and to a slightly lesser extent, that of the EU) is likely to be a critical factor in how far the liberalization of higher education services progresses, given its influence in WTO negotiations generally. The US, as well as being one of the biggest supporters of study abroad (in and out), by some way contains the largest number of new private and corporate providers, and possesses considerable capability to use electronic technology to deliver at a distance. A market-focused Republican presidency is also likely to support the further liberalization of higher education services. The

UK, Australia, Canada and New Zealand, as large net exporters may also be inclined to support the US position. Yet, the heterogeneity of higher education systems, not least the difference of interests internally to countries between big exporting universities and those dependent almost solely on their position in the domestic market, is likely to produce cross-pressures on both governments and on domestic collective associations of universities, who may have some difficulty in articulating common positions. Moreover, as we noted previously, in final negotiating sessions, trade and other economic ministers may be prepared to concede more liberalization than their education counterparts, as part of wider trade reciprocities and adjustments.

The US appears strongly committed to the abolition of a range of barriers to trade in education services, particularly prohibitions on education services offered by foreign entities, the lack of possibilities for authorization to establish in a member's territory and to be recognized as a degree-conferring institution, and economic needs tests, and suggests that members take these into account when making market access commitments and when taking additional commitments relating to domestic regulation in the sector.

Educational trade policies can change without necessarily being regulated through an international trade regime. In the UK there is a Prime Minister's Initiative that aims at breaking down identified barriers such as those relating to student visas and employment regulations for students and academics, while the Bologna Declaration of the EU also aims to reduce barriers to educational mobility and other matters. The Declaration is a pledge by 29 countries to reform the structures of their higher education systems 'in a convergent way', although it carefully rules out a path towards the 'standardization' or 'uniformization' of European higher education. With a deadline of 2010, its specific objectives include the adoption of a common framework of readable and comparable degrees; the introduction of undergraduate and postgraduate levels in all countries, with first degrees no shorter than three years and relevant to the labour market; compatible credit systems; a European dimension in quality assurance, with comparable criteria and methods; and the elimination of remaining obstacles to the free mobility of students, teachers and researchers. An overall aim is to increase the international competitiveness of the European system of higher education. The method employed to realize these objectives is described as 'the ways of intergovernmental cooperation'.

The OECD is among bodies that have begun to explore the policy implications of further liberalization under the GATS. Among the most important is the lack of an international framework of quality assurance and accreditation in higher education. This undermines confidence by foreign students about the quality of the service that they receive. As we have noted, however, the EU has sought to instigate a regional arrangement based on mutual recognition in the Bologna Declaration of 1999. Yet underlying the very different quality assurance and accreditation systems around the world (not least their variety within the US) are diverse views on what constitutes quality and standards in increasingly differentiated systems and in the context of the rapid utilization of electronic delivery. Also, new multinational e-learning-based institutions, with no physical presence in countries where they have students, will be more difficult to regulate using current local systems of recognition and quality assurance. The harmonization of university standards as a result, even if it was deemed to be desirable, and generally it is not, seems to be a considerable distance away.

It is possible that rather than supragovernmental, transnational quality assurance regimes, we may find that university-led or independent (Non-Governmental Organization – NGO) global accreditation bodies may be the way forward. *Universitas 21* (a network of elite universities from around the world that aims to share the production and delivery of high quality programmes over distance) and the Global Alliance for Transnational Education (GATE) are two current examples. GATE is an international alliance of business, higher education and government committed to the growth of international education programmes. Its aim is to set up a worldwide system of certification of some weight and standing that would enable higher education institutions to attach comparable levels to curriculum content, curriculum quality and the level of their graduates. GATE has developed a protocol of 'Guiding Principles' to help institutions and organizations in the development and evaluation of quality education that is mobile across national boundaries.

The GATE principles have been applied indirectly through their adoption by national bodies, and also directly when requested on a voluntary basis. A key objective for GATE is to provide some form of consumer protection as students may be at increasing risk from 'fly-by-night' international operators. Providers are encouraged to seek external certification reflecting a commitment and adherence to GATE principles for standards and quality. However, its success and authority to date have proved limited.

Nonetheless a number of bodies, such as the World Bank and UNESCO, are actively seeking to overcome the lack of a proper international accreditation and qualifications framework, including seeking to define rules that balance consumer safeguards with reasonably accessible markets for new providers, and which do not impose rigid protectionist measures against potential competititors. The World Bank (2002) suggests that governments, licensing and quality assurance agencies adopt a common set of criteria to evaluate new providers on the following: a) minimum infrastructure, facilities and staffing requirements; b) appropriate, transparent and accurate information on the policies, mission statements, study programmes and feedback mechanisms of foreign providers; c) capacity-building partnerships with local and established institutions; and d) comparable academic quality and standards, including the full recognition in the home country of the degrees and qualifications delivered by foreign providers in a developing country.

Although to date there are no official international accreditation agencies, with ever growing numbers of students looking for foreign qualifications, especially in the developing world, either through distance learning or travelling abroad, the efforts to seek to provide such bodies are likely to intensify. Two current important organizations in this area, however, are the International Network for Quality Assurance Agencies in Higher Education (INQAAHE), based in the Netherlands, and the Council for Higher Education Accreditation (CHEA), based in the US. The former does not accredit but operates as an information network for accrediting bodies from around the world, while CHEA explores international quality and accreditation issues through research publications, conferences and seminars (Maxwell *et al.*, 2000).

## ► Conclusion

The application of national and international regulatory regimes for universities in all countries is likely to increase rather than to diminish. This is despite a long (and generally accepted) position that universities need to be relatively autonomous in comparison with other institutions to undertake their key functions. Criticality, openness of views and their subjection to contestability, the need for curiosity-driven experimentation, and the privacy necessary for advanced studies – these are powerful, historical forces that cause politicians and others to pause before they go too far in locating universities within accountability structures that are regarded as increasingly the norm in other sectors. Even the steady overall growth of public funding for higher education over the decades, despite its more recent diminution at the level of unit funding, has not eroded overmuch these positions. For very good reasons, academic and institutional freedom has been seen as conducing a habitat that governments and others recognize as necessary for delivering advancement nationally in cognitive skills, and a meritocratic – on the surface at least – allocation of individuals to the stratification structure of the occupational division of labour.

Yet, even these influences are starting to ebb. The rise of mass higher education – critical although it may be for the development of human capital – makes the activities of many universities not that special anymore. Other providers have entered the secret garden and made it less hallowed. And governments can no longer afford to ignore the efficiencies and accountabilities demanded in return for such large amounts of taxpayers' money. The role of national states has changed – both domestically and internationally. They are less inclined to run things than to regulate them, often through partnerships with other societal actors. The consumer looms larger and more influential in all sectors in more market-based societies. And when the consumer becomes more involved the more chance there is that older professional norms and associations, the market-restricting practices and self-regulation of the producer, will give way increasingly to state-backed and rule-based forms of regulation. The growth of the global economy and the rise of the international university in an age of supranationality is likely also to generate comparative and, in time, global regulatory arrangements that may not be that dissimilar to those found in other sectors. Yet, neither globalization nor regulation are linear or inexorable processes, and their progression in higher education is bound to be uneven and irregular.

# 5 Globalization, Innovation and Socially Robust Knowledge

*Michael Gibbons*

## ▶ Introduction

This chapter, following on from the themes explored in Chapter 3 by Roger King, explores the nature of the relationship between globalization, innovation and the universities. These different entities are related in so far as each influences the rate and direction of inventive activity or, more generally, knowledge production. What is often insufficiently grasped is that globalization, through the pressure it puts on firms to innovate, evokes new research practices that change the way that research is performed, not only in industry but in universities as well. More specifically globalization drives these changes by intensifying competition between firms. This compels them to pursue innovation through the search for knowledge solutions of various kinds.

As will be argued later in the chapter, it is dynamic competition that is opening up the innovation process to new forms of knowledge production in which academics now play a crucial role. Further, the collaboration of academics with industry, in the search for knowledge solutions, has now achieved a level sufficiently high to modify the ways in which research is carried out in universities. These new research practices, denoted as mode 2 research, are setting up tensions between this emergent form and the traditional manner in which the bulk of university research is still carried out – which we term mode 1 research. Further, this strengthening interaction between universities and industry, increasingly filtered through their mutual participation in the innovation process, raises profound questions about the university's autonomy and social accountability. The chapter argues, perhaps somewhat controversially, that it is only by fully embracing the research practices associated with mode 2 that universities will be able to preserve their role as institutions organized to protect the public good.

## ▶ The new context

Globalization is taken here to refer to the processes of imitation, adaptation and diffusion of knowledge solutions to problems of many different kinds –

whether these are new technologies, organizational forms, or modes of working – as they are taken up by one firm after another in one country after another (Gray, 1998). In this formulation, the loosening up of markets for capital and labour, and the increasing volume of information flows that is accompanying the spread of information and communications technologies, may be less directly important for companies than the probability that competitive threats can now arise, apparently without warning, from many different sources. In other words, competition and innovation are, respectively, the stimulus and the response to the pressures of globalization. Firms must innovate continuously because they fear that, if they do not, their very existence might be threatened by others that come up with a new idea, or with a set of technologies, that might render their current operations and workforces obsolete.

The intensification of competition is also linked to a perceived shift in the driving forces of innovation itself. No longer simply a matter of natural endowments or investment capital, knowledge, it is now argued, has become a, perhaps *the*, crucial driver in the innovation process. However, the importance of knowledge is not really a new idea. The Austrian economist Hayek (1978) observed many years ago, that competition always sets up a discovery process and, therefore, any intensification of competition must be reflected in a parallel expansion of experimental (or exploratory) modes of behaviour. This includes not only research and development, and the discoveries that these may bring, but also the forms of organization and modes of work that are necessary to support them.

Viewing globalization as the competitive spread of knowledge solutions through the processes of imitation and adaptation has importance for the developing world. It highlights that much innovation, and hence economic development, is dependent, less on original discoveries, and more on the timely take up, modification, and marketing of knowledge solutions that already exist but need to be adapted to local environments. Innovation therefore remains a local phenomenon and serves as a constant reminder that globalization turns on differences in the sentiments of a population, in its particular institutional structures that are designed to achieve collective purposes, and in the cultures that give meaning and value to the decisions taken. As societies differ in their various historically endowed modes and capabilities, they will imitate, adapt and diffuse knowledge solutions differently. Without these local differences sustaining territorial competition, globalization would falter. Despite greater global interconnectedness and worldwide economic integration, the extent of globalization is measured less by the progressive diffusion of a uniform set of market institutions – the homogenization thesis – than by the emergence of specific, indigenous, forms of capitalism (Whitley, 1999).

While it is now conventional to regard globlization and innovation as elements in an emerging knowledge economy, it is not yet fully understood that this process is touching the university at its heart: in the research process itself. The following thesis draws upon the work of Gibbons *et al.* (1994), in *The New Production of Knowledge*, and by Nowotny *et al.* (2001) in *Re-thinking Science*. The argument takes this work in new directions by exploring further the links between globalization and mode 2 forms of knowledge production.

## Mode 2 knowledge production

Mode 2 can be described in terms of five characteristics (Scott *et al.*, forthcoming).

First, mode 2 knowledge is generated within a *context of application*. This differs from the process by which 'pure' science, generated in theoretical/ experimental environments, is 'applied', technology is 'transferred', and knowledge is subsequently 'managed'. The context of application, in contrast, describes the total environment in which scientific problems arise, methodologies are developed, outcomes are disseminated, and uses are defined.

Second, mode 2 is *transdisciplinary*, in that a range of theoretical perspectives and practical methodologies are mobilized to solve problems. But, unlike inter- or multidisciplinarity, in deriving from pre-existing disciplines or contributing to the formation of new disciplines, the creative act lies as much in the capacity to mobilize and manage – to externally orchestrate – various perspectives and methodologies, as in the development of new theories or concepts, or in the refinement of research methods, as found conventionally in the 'internal' dynamics of scientific creativity. In other words, mode 2 knowledge production, in this transdisciplinary form, is embodied in the expertise of individual researchers and research (and project) teams as much as, or possibly more than, it is encoded in traditional research products, such as journal articles or even patents.

Third, in mode 2 there is much greater *diversity of the sites* at which knowledge is produced and, an associated phenomenon, a growing *heterogeneity* in the types of knowledge production. The first phenomenon, it can be argued, is not especially new. Research communities have always been 'virtual' communities that cross national (and cultural) boundaries. But their dynamics have been transformed. Generally interaction within these communities has been limited by both physical constraints (the requirement for geographical proximity in order to communicate) and technical (the limitations, in the Internet age, of letters and telephones). As a result of advances in information and communication technologies, interaction nowadays is relatively easy, global and instantaneous. The old orderly hierarchies, imposed by these 'old' technologies of interaction, have been eroded by a communicative free-for-all. This shift has been intensified by a second phenomenon, that research communities now have open frontiers that allow many novel types of 'knowledge organization' – such as think tanks, management consultants, activist groups – to join the research game.

Fourth, mode 2 knowledge is highly *reflexive*. The research process is no longer characterized as 'objective' investigation of the natural (or social) world, or as a cool and reductionist interrogation of arbitrarily defined 'others'. Instead it has become a dialogic process, an intense (and perhaps endless) 'conversation' between research actors and research subjects – to such an extent that the basic vocabulary of research (who, whom, what, how) is in danger of losing its significance. As a result traditional notions of accountability, as being an external review of mature research concepts and projects, have had to be radically revised. The 'applications' and effects of new knowledge are not regarded as being 'outside' the research process. Rather, problem-solving environments influence choices of issues to research, and research-designs, as well as the uses to which the research outcomes will be put.

Finally, in mode 2, *novel forms of quality control* are emerging – for a number of reasons. One, scientific 'peers' can no longer be identified reliably, as there is no longer a stable taxonomy of codified disciplines from which 'peers' can be drawn. Two, reductionist forms of quality control are not easily adapted to more broadly framed research questions; the research 'game' is being joined by more and more players – not simply a wider and more eclectic range of 'producers', but also by orchestrators, brokers, disseminators and users. Three, and most disturbingly, clear and unchallengeable criteria to determine quality may no longer be available. Instead, we must learn to live with multiple definitions of quality, which seriously complicates (even compromises) the processes of discrimination, prioritization and selectivity on which policymakers and funding agencies increasingly rely.

## Socially distributed knowledge production

The emergence of mode 2 makes knowledge production more complex than before. The key change is that it is becoming less a self-contained activity. As practiced currently, it is neither the 'science of the universities' nor the 'technology of industry'. No longer is it the preserve of a special type of institution (predominantly the university), from which knowledge is expected to spill over, or to be spun-off, to the benefit of other sectors. Knowledge production, not only in its theories and models, but also in its methods and techniques, has spread from the academy to many different types of institutions. It is in this sense that knowledge production has become a socially distributed process. The expansion of its sites forms the sources for a continual combination and recombination of knowledge resources. Metaphorically speaking, we are seeing a multiplication of the nerve endings of knowledge, and these extend far beyond the boundaries of universities and the disciplines housed in them.

As a system, socially distributed knowledge production comprises a reservoir of skills and expertise, increasingly of global proportions, that are available for utilization in a variety of problem contexts. In keeping this reservoir topped-up, the universities play an important part by providing a supply of trained researchers. Yet this is turning them into only one player among many in determining the research agenda.

This system has five principal characteristics:

1. It contains an increasing number of places where recognizably competent research is being carried out. This can be demonstrated by consulting the addresses of the authors of scientific publications, though change, here, is taking place so rapidly that the full extent of the social distribution of knowledge production is probably no longer fully captured by the printed word.

2. These sites communicate with one another and, thereby, broaden the base of effective interaction. Thus, additions to the stock of knowledge are derived from an increasing number of tributarial flows from various types of institutions that both contribute to, and draw from, it.

3. The dynamics of socially distributed knowledge production lie in the flows of knowledge and in the shifting patterns of connectivity among these flows. The connections may appear to be random but they move with the problem context, rather than according either to disciplinary structures or to the dictates of national science policy.

4. The number of interconnections is accelerating, so far apparently not channelled by existing institutional structures, perhaps because these connections are intended to be functional and to survive only as long as they are useful. The ebb and flow of connections follow the paths of problem interest, which are no longer determined by the disciplinary structure of science.

5. Knowledge production, therefore, exhibits heterogeneous, rather than homogeneous, growth. New sites of knowledge production are continually emerging that provide intellectual points of departure for further combinations or configurations of researchers. In this sense, the socially distributed knowledge production system exhibits some of the properties that are often associated with self-organizing systems in which communication density is increasing rapidly.

In summary, the distributed character of knowledge production constitutes a fundamental change, both in terms of the numbers of possible sites of expertise, and in their degree of connectivity. As will become evident, research that draws upon the resources of a socially distributed knowledge system uses different criteria for determining research excellence than those required in discipline-based peer review. To the extent that university researchers operate within the distributed knowledge system, they may import these different types of excellence into the university and hence begin to modify what it is to 'do' good science and scholarship in academic life. As described, the socially distributed knowledge production system refers simply to the multiplication of the number of sites where recognizably competent research is being carried out. Though this change within society is not necessarily a product of globalization, socially distributed knowledge is nonetheless now acquiring a global dimension.

## ▶ Globalization, innovation and competition

We have defined globalization as the imitation and adaptation of knowledge solutions, or innovations, as they are diffused from one country to another. That a particular technological innovation might undermine, or render obsolete, the basis on which a firm stands, together with the recognition that this threat might arise from an increasing number of places located anywhere in the world, has the immediate effect of increasing competitive behaviour among firms. Further, competition always launches a discovery process, and it follows that an increase in competitive behaviour will manifest itself in the intensification of the search for knowledge solutions that might underpin future technological or organizational innovations.

Of course, one well-established way of searching for knowledge solutions is for firms to engage in R and D activities. It is perhaps because R and D is widely understood to be a source of new knowledge that it is frequently argued that, in the process of innovation, knowledge has become the scarce resource. But more than scarcity is involved. Knowledge solutions by their very nature can never be completed closed, neither can they be contained, nor protected, by patents for very long. Rather, it is far more likely, given the propensity of information to diffuse, that any particular knowledge solution will be picked up and developed by others. It is because knowledge solutions are intrinsically open-ended that they can be adapted, modified and improved in different contexts by firms with a different constellation of human and financial resources. When innovation is based upon a knowledge solution, even first movers can face the prospect of an unanticipated competitive threat arising from some quarter or other. Globalization has been described in terms of the spread of knowledge solutions from one country to another. This is perhaps a non-contentious formulation, but less well understood is that knowledge solutions arise as a direct result of competition between firms.

## Static and dynamic competition

At any given time competition between firms operates simultaneously at two levels: the level of static, and the level of dynamic, competition. The presence of static competition drives a firm to search for efficiency gains by relentlessly trying to increase the efficiency with which existing resources are allocated. At this level, the discovery process often includes R and D activity, sometimes involving universities, as firms seek to improve the processes they have adopted and the performance characteristics of the products that they make currently. The result is a stream of incremental innovations that arise within the framework of a previously chosen technology set, and within what has been described as a design configuration (Utterback, 1998).

Firms are often at their most efficient when they are competing within a design configuration that a group of individual firms have agreed upon as possessing fruitful lines of development. For example, the delivery of music through laser-based technology and the medium of the CD is the currently accepted way to provide high fidelity music. Most firms in the sector have accepted this, have adopted the relevant technology, and sell products that compete with one another in terms of slightly different sets of performance characteristics within the framework of what is possible with that technology. In a regime of static competition, markets operate to choose among products produced within a design configuration, but, because firms differ in the efficiency with which they utilize their resources, there emerges in each sector a hierarchy of firms distributed around what is sometimes referred to as 'average best practice'.

Under dynamic competition, things are very different. Dynamic competition also launches a discovery process but in a different form. Dynamic competition operates at a higher level by launching searches for new design configurations – novel combinations of scientific ideas and technologies – that might provide alternate bases for the survival of the firm, should its existing technology set – its current design configuration – be undermined by innovations from one quarter or another. In other words, dynamic competition launches the sort of search behaviour that firms must undertake to guard against the possibility that, from out of the blue, a knowledge solution will arise which might render their current technological base and, more critically their work force, obsolete. To continue with the previous example, the CD has displaced the long-playing record and magnetic tape, but for how long? The CD is currently being challenged not only by new developments in older technologies – vinyl long-playing records – but also by new technologies – the recordable mini-disc, and perhaps other technologies whose development potential is now only vaguely perceived. But since firms in the music industry do not know what these knowledge solutions will be or from whence they may arise, they deal with this type of risk by participating in alliances, often collaborative research activities. To accomplish this, they join networks, enter joint ventures, and form partnerships of various kinds.

In terms of a search process, these competition-induced collaborations form complex problem-solving sites. Solutions are pursued collaboratively, involving many participants, and, maybe paradoxically, often involve competitors. Under dynamic competition, markets still operate, not to choose between products, for there are none yet, but to discriminate between research groups. Because the performance of each group depends upon its composition and the resources available to it, they differ in their creativity and in the effectiveness with which outcomes can be operationalized to good competitive effect by their respective members. It is, therefore, of the utmost importance for firms which, and how many, research collaborations they join, and how long they persist as members of a particular grouping.

Globalization stimulates innovation, not primarily through static, but through dynamic, competition. It is the intensification of dynamic competition that drives the proliferation of collaborative problem-solving sites. The evidence for this is unequivocal: the numbers of these collaborative ventures have been expanding exponentially across a large number of sectors for many years now, and they are often committed to long-term research objectives (Webster, 1998). Of course, some of the human resources for these collaborative research ventures are drawn from the employees of member firms, but use is also made of the expertise available in the increasingly global, socially distributed knowledge production system.

## ▶ Tensions generated by mode 2 research in universities

These sites of competition-induced collaborative research act as 'attractors' for the academic community, in part because they conduct research at the leading edge of disciplinary fields, but also because, for many academics, the opportunity to work in these problem-solving groups provides an important way for them to utilize and to develop their specialist skills. The principal characteristics of these groups are that research is carried out in the context of application, it is transdisciplinary, and it uses a variety of skills. Further, they utilize flat organizational structures that are generally transient and often elaborate their own forms of quality control.

The spread of globalization is accompanied by a proliferation of collaborative research arrangements, and these ventures are the sites in which new research practices are being developed. Into this process are being drawn an increasing number of members of the academic community. In fact, the numbers of academics participating in this type of industry-driven search process are already sufficiently large for the experience to feedback into, and so affect, the ways in which research is pursued in universities (Marginson and Considine, 2000). Globalization is contributing, in no small part, to setting up a tension between mode 1 and mode 2 research in many universities.

This tension manifests itself along many dimensions:

• between academics who seek peer recognition for their participation in what is clearly a different kind of research activity, and those in subjects where such opportunities are limited or even non-existent;
• between academics and the university, as the former seek a more differentiated reward structure that recognizes their contribution to different types of research, which is contrary to conventional university practices;
• between universities, in the competition over the prestige of having faculty deemed sufficiently competent to be admitted to these, often elite, forms of collaborative research; and
• between universities and industry, over the sharing of the revenues from intellectual property that are now more likely to be the outcome, not of individual genius, but of the joint production of knowledge by experts of many different kinds.

To date, the drift of academic researchers into collaborative research with industry has not been solely the outcome of governmental policy or institutional strategy, although as has been noted in earlier chapters, this type of encouragement is increasing. The decisions of academics to join these forms of collaborative research activity have been largely a matter of individual choice. It is what academics seem to want to do, and, it must be said, it is often an attractive option for the best of them.

If universities wish to adjust to these changes in research activity – and it is hard to imagine how they might resist – they will need to modify their recruitment policies, the terms and conditions of work, and reward structures. The consequence of such modifications will have profound implications for them as institutions. By becoming so deeply involved in the innovation process, universities are being drawn ineluctably closer to industry. But, in doing this, or allowing it to happen, they are also changing the basis of their relationship with the wider society. Can universities become involved more intimately in the wealth-creation process without compromising their status as independent, autonomous institutions, dedicated to producing public goods?

## ▶ Contextualization, trading zones and transaction spaces

Though competition-induced collaboration is ubiquitous in the global environment, the effective performance of collaborating teams is not an automatic process. Let us explore this further. So far we have viewed mode 2 from the side of the research process, almost as a dynamic internal to it. The same set of practices can also be viewed from the side of society, as a modification of existing (mode 1) research practices in response to a broad social imperative for research-based solutions to a range of complex problems. This adjustment (to mode 2) can be expressed as a reciprocal response by the scientific community, or more specifically, by the university-based research community, to communications generated from society. Mode 2 research is, in this sense, distinguished from mode 1 by the degree of social participation or influence in the research process. To put the matter slightly differently, mode 2 knowledge production is more contextualized, more responsive to a wider array of inputs, than mode 1. This notion of contextualization directs attention to the openness (or otherwise) of science (or its institutions) to the needs of society. To the extent that science is socially responsive, it leads to the production of a new kind of science, primarily by altering the problems that university scientists consider it worthwhile researching, how these are investigated, and who is involved.

A number of consequences follow from this shift in perspective. First, different degrees of contextualization can be distinguished: weak, middle-range and strong. Each reflects the response of the relevant research community to wider social influences. In weak contextualization, society exerts influence largely through the voices of institutions that, with the advice of experts, interpret social concerns in terms of scientific priorities and research programmes. Perhaps ironically, most government-funded research programmes can be categorized as weakly contextualized because social demand is still communicated indirectly, often through the filters of state bureaucracy and the dominant institutions of the scientific community. Contextualization in the middle-range is the home of transaction spaces, about which more later. Finally, in strong contextualization forms, communications, not only from experts but also from the wider 'lay' society, enter directly into the identification and formulation of problems and issues (Latour, 1997). Each degree of contextualization – from weak to strong –

describes a mode of knowledge production that depends, in varying degree to the others, on the functioning of transaction spaces.

Second, to understand the function of transaction spaces it can be helpful to begin from the more familiar notion of a hybrid forum. Historically, the idea of a hybrid forum referred to a socially constructed 'space' where the risks associated with certain technological developments could be debated. These were the public spaces where, for example, the safety of certain types of nuclear reactors, or, in environmental science, where the rate of global warming, generated sufficient public concern to provoke governments into establishing a forum comprising technical experts, policymakers and, in some cases, concerned citizens. The involvement of a range of participants provides the description 'hybrid' in this context. Such forums are now commonplace and most governments consider them as essential elements in involving the public in any scientific or technical issue that is contentious. But, they are largely still creations of institutions, whether international bureaucracies, governments or lobby groups.

Third, in these forums, important new knowledge is often generated. In particular, the experience of working in hybrid forums has led to the widespread recognition that interesting and challenging science can be produced outside disciplinary structures, that this can give rise to changes in university curricula and, hence, lead to the transmission of different kinds of scientific knowledge. This is well-illustrated in the rise of the environmental sciences to the status of a respectable academic subject for teaching and research. It is possible, therefore, to regard some hybrid forums as among the early manifestations of contextualization in the middle-range. Indeed, the increasing openness and permeability of society's major institutions has also allowed the emergence of a growing number of other, less formally constituted 'spaces', in which various kinds of participants, with different interests and outlooks can, and do, come together.

Fourth, while contextualization takes place, initially in transaction spaces, the process is far from automatic. Rather, the challenge is to find ways to allow experts and others, each of whom may inhabit different social worlds, to interact effectively so as to be able to transform an issue or problem into a set of common understandings upon which a coherent research programme might be based. Such transaction spaces are essential entities if cooperation is to be promoted and consensus generated, because they provide important frameworks in which still tentative, and as yet inadequately institutionalized, interactions can take place. However, within any transaction space these interactions are more than random encounters.

Genuine transaction spaces recall some of the essential features that the historian of science, Peter Galison, has described for the 'trading zones' he came across when analysing the history of nuclear physics in the twentieth century (Galison, 1997). In this work, we are made to encounter *within the disciplinary structure* of one sub-field the fascinating exchanges and intense collaborations between three sub-cultures of the nuclear physics community – theoreticians, experimentalists and engineers (who build the machines used in nuclear physics). These traditions remained intact, preserved inside scientific collaboration, while the coordination of exchange took place around the production of the two competing instrument cultures of 'image' and 'logic', which ultimately were joined. Similar kinds of exchange can take place between two competing design configurations.

Taking his lead from anthropological theories, Galison observes how the often synchronous exchanges between the various sub-cultures of physics can be compared to the incomplete and partial relations which are established when different tribes come together for trading purposes. Nothing in the notion of trade presupposes some universal notion of a neutral currency. Quite the opposite: much of the interest in the category of trade is that things can be coordinated (what goes with what, for what purposes) without reference to some external gauge. Each tribe may bring to this interaction, and take away from it, completely different objects, as well as the meanings attached to them. An object that may have a highly symbolic or even sacred value for one tribe may represent an entirely banal or utilitarian object for another. Nevertheless, interaction and trade is possible and actually takes place – to the obvious benefit of all because, if this were not so, dialogue would cease. Trading may also give rise to the emergence of contact languages, like 'pidgin', as a means of communication that inevitably is incomplete and truncated. Galison's insight was that physicists and engineers were not engaging in translating knowledge from one sub-culture to another as they pieced together their microwave circuits, nor were they producing neutral observation sentences. *They were working out a powerful, locally understood language to coordinate their actions.* Despite obvious limitations, some kind of understanding and exchange does occur in such situations.

For Galison (1997, p. 63), then, the crucial question was not how different scientific communities pass like ships in the night. It was rather:

> how, given the extraordinary diversity of participants, in physics – cryogenic engineers, radio chemists, algebraic topologists, prototype tinkerers, computer wizards, quantum field theorists – they speak to one another at all . . . [T]he picture . . . is one of different areas changing over time with complex border zones that sometimes vanish, coalesce, and even burgeon into quasi-autonomous regions in their own right.

It is possible to extend and generalize the concept of trading zone beyond interaction amongst scientific sub-cultures to wider exchanges that take place across both disciplinary and institutional boundaries, as occurs, for example, in the search for new design configurations. Here, exchanges take place in what have been denoted above as transaction spaces. As in the case of trading zones, the idea of 'transaction' implies, first, that all partners bring something that can be exchanged or negotiated and, second, that they also have the resources (scientific as well as material) to be able to take something from other participants. Of course, the meanings attributed to exchanged objects may differ greatly for different participants. But the success of these exchanges depends upon each participant bringing something that is considered valuable by someone else – whatever that value might be. Participants usually will return to their home base with their gains, thereby re-enforcing, in typical mode 2 fashion, the links and exchanges that have already occurred by sharing with others.

We have suggested that the research practices that characterize mode 2 knowledge production can be seen either from the side of research or from the side of society. The notion of transaction space makes the double aspect of this process more specific, because transaction spaces become visible as the sites where the first tenuous interactions – conversations – between society and science take place. They are spaces (both symbolically and concretely) where potential participants can decide what might be exchanged or traded, and where they also establish the lines of communication necessary to sustain discussion, to the point where constraints become visible. Of course, if the constraints are too severe the transaction space may disintegrate. But, through further interaction, ways may be found to overcome constraints and, when this happens, a more robust research activity may emerge. The growth in the numbers of transaction spaces, some of which will persist while others will be transitory and temporary, is one of the characteristics of mode 2 knowledge production.

In sum, the idea of hybrid forums, together with the notion of trading zones drawn from anthropological research, can be extended to the notion of transaction spaces. These are spaces where different types of expertise, outlooks and interests come together, and involve local exchanges of various kinds, in which may be generated a language with which to pursue a common research agenda. 'Local', in this context, is meant to imply that the area of agreement is limited and, by agreement, some issues are for the moment left untouched.

## ▶ Policy implications

There is a further insight that can be derived from Galison's work. He notes (1997, p. 63) that:

a trading zone is an intermediate domain in which procedures could be coordinated locally even where broader meanings clashed . . . The work that goes into creating, contesting, and sustaining local coordination is at the core of how local knowledge becomes widely accepted. In other words, *rather than depicting the movement across boundaries as one of transla-tion (from theory to experiment, or from military to civilian science, or from one theory to another) it may be more useful to think in terms of work* at *boundaries*, where local languages grow, and sometimes die in the inter-stices between sub-cultures (italics mine).

This shift in perspective is crucial and its importance can be illustrated by reflecting on the mechanisms that are currently in place to render more effi-cient the translation of scientific discoveries from universities to industry. Working, silo-like, within the discipline-based structures of science and scholarship, it is often presumed that the knowledge produced by universi-ties is in some way primary. For example, scientific discoveries are commonly regarded as essential ingredients for successful technological innovation and not infrequently universities have assumed that they are the prime source of many of these ideas. Accordingly, many have thought it important to move this knowledge efficiently *across* institutional boundaries.

This language is perpetuated at several levels: with respect to cognitive boundaries it is found in the translation from pure to applied science, while at institutional boundaries in the translation from universities to industry, and so forth. Given the prevalence of the idea of translating knowledge across boundaries, it is perhaps not surprising to find that many universities and government agencies have put in place administrative structures – tech-nology transfer offices, innovation incubators, science parks, and similar – to help with the translation. *By contrast, the notion of a transaction space shifts the metaphor from translation across boundaries to dialogue* at *bound-aries.* This shift underscores precisely that it is dialogue at the boundary that makes it possible to appropriate knowledge held by others. For many differ-ent expertises to be brought to bear effectively on a complex problem, the issue needs to be formulated in a common language. As Galison has argued, common languages, when and if they occur, provide the 'evidence' that some sort of common understanding has been achieved. By contrast, simply moving information 'packages' across boundaries leaves too much unsaid and, not surprisingly, it is often the case that such translations are not successful.

As an example of work across boundaries, consider the case of the mini-computer developed by the Digital Equipment Corporation (DEC) which has been described brilliantly by Kidder in *The Soul of a New Machine* (1981). Here, what we have described as a transaction space was largely internal to the Corporation but its boundary was a highly permeable one. The author describes a process of discovery that would lead eventually to a new design configuration that would underpin the manufacture of the new computer, although the path to the design configuration was still undetermined. But, initially, there was little agreement on what the configuration might be like. In the process of 'discovery' expertise of many different stripes collaborated in the search. These included engineers and computer programmers, but also logicians, mathematicians and solid state physicists as well as finance and marketing personnel. Some of the participants in this transaction space were from universities, but others from elsewhere in the socially distributed knowledge production system that has been described above. Not many stayed for the duration of the process – as the project evolved the composition of experts shifted as different problems emerged.

Finally, the 'management' of the project, was seemingly the responsibility of one individual, whose function is perhaps better described as a knowledge broker than either a manager or an entrepreneur. He facilitated the collaboration that led to the common language necessary to develop the design configuration and moved the experts in and out of the transaction space as the project evolved. Being a knowledge broker is a subtle art and it often involves telling experts that their role in the collaboration is at an end. As Kidder makes clear, the participants in the process, including university researchers, put up with what might be called 'rough' management practice. They did so because they knew that many important and intellectually challenging problems would be addressed on the way from an idea to a final design configuration and that they could not afford to be absent from the evolving 'conversation'.

This example provides an example of the strategic importance of managing complexity and uncertainty within an organization where both areas of stability and instability are necessary. Undoubtedly DEC had to develop and improve many other products simply to remain in business and to be able to fund new developments. The point is that the strategy and style of management necessary to improve a product is vastly different from those that are necessary to develop a new one, particularly where, as in this case, it is not clear just what 'shape' the new product would have. It would be interesting to discover how DEC balanced these two necessary but very different strategies within the same organization. Some organizational theorists argue that the strategies necessary to promote creativity are often barely acknowledged within organizations; not infrequently these activities have to be carried out surreptitiously. The current dominant discourse of rational planning and outcomes management, and the like, appears a well-entrenched mindset that organizations find difficult to displace. Not surprisingly, creative people always have found ways to work around such dispositions (Lacey, 1996).

In general, the idea of exchanges at boundaries within transaction spaces captures very well what is actually taking place in the many contexts of application that characterize mode 2 research and underscores the point that mode 2 is less the application of the results of mode 1 than it is the absorption of mode 1 into new frameworks of understanding around common languages that make the pursuit of complex problems – problems that lie outside the disciplinary structure – possible. Star and Greismer (1989) are surely correct when they deduce that it is not normally appreciated just how often it is the case that the objects of scientific work inhabit multiple social worlds. All science, it seems, not only the mode 2 science that is involved in the search for new design configurations, but mode 1 as well, requires intersectoral work.

## Implications for government

The strategic implications of promoting work at the boundary are profound because, to adapt to it, policymakers have to break with the dominant discourse of the field. Conventionally policy is based essentially on establishing objectives, allocating resources, and determining outcomes. For organizations that need to operate at boundaries – those that depend upon continuing creativity – strategies based upon a resource allocation model are not only inappropriate but do not work. To remain innovative most organizations have to devote at least part of their effort to promoting creativity through collaborative arrangements of various kinds. They can do this by encouraging work in transaction spaces at boundaries, whether between departments internally or between groups in different organizations. This strategy is appropriate to the more open forms of knowledge production that we have described as mode 2.

Clearly such a major shift cannot be accommodated simply by importing the language and practices of the current dominant discourse – a new language is required to 'make sense' of what is going on in the research context. We have argued that this can be done by thinking in terms of encouraging the emergence of transaction spaces that operate at the boundaries of established activities. Strategies for this purpose need to recognize that when uncertainty and complexity are endemic, as they are in research, there has to be an acceptance of a certain amount of irreducible redundancy. Moreover, criteria to assess comparative group creativity have to be developed, and, most importantly, collaborative creativity requires managing to reduce the anxiety that researchers face when operating in essentially transient frameworks.

Governments tend to be wary of supporting programmes of the kind that we have just described. They much prefer the apparently more rigorous language of objective outcomes. Nonetheless, policy makers and strategic analysts have to accept that organizations need both stability and instability, and that each has its own criteria of effectiveness. Failure to acknowledge this is likely to lock both research-based organizations and nations into forms of behaviour and practice that, in the long term, will render them vulnerable to new ideas and practices developed elsewhere. In other words, the new mindset requires the mutual shaping of science and policy.

The language of translation across institutional boundaries has been at the heart of science policy since its inception. In its original formulation, science policy was concerned with the 'criteria for scientific choice' (Weinberg, 1963). It was about the allocation of resources to research topics by scientists themselves, since it was assumed that only they knew where and how 'good science' could be produced. It was the responsibility of others to take the discoveries beyond the laboratories and see to their application. Over the last 40 years this view has gradually changed; first with the introduction of technology policies in which science was seen as just one, albeit a crucial, input, and latterly with the development of innovation policies which attempt to put science (and technology) at the service of national social and political agendas, such as promoting international economic competitiveness and improving the quality of life.

It is with the emergence of innovation policies that the language of translating scientific discoveries into technological innovation and hence economic growth finally demonstrates its limitations. As has been indicated, at the root of the need to advance international economic competitiveness (and innovation) can be found the imperative to search for new design configurations. From the analysis so far, it will be evident that the elaboration of new design configurations is the outcome of boundary work within transaction spaces. Innovation fundamentally requires finding knowledge solutions to complex problems. This entails the binding together of myriad groups of experts who, so to speak, inhabit different social worlds and this, in turn, implies that the resources to address such problems must come from a variety of sources. As a consequence, the attempt to develop innovation policies has served to open up to closer analysis the nature of complex problem-solving and to demonstrate that the role of government policy may be less as a prime funder of research, and more as a broker between individuals, and groups and institutions that have an interest in finding knowledge solutions but that nonetheless have different perspectives on what would constitute an acceptable solution (Gibbons, 2001).

Many government innovation policies are already structured in terms of drawing in resources from the different actors involved in the innovation process. For example, the UK's research programme in biological sciences is funded in part by the Department for Education and Skills, in part by Funding Council and Research Council allocations, in part by industry, and in part by a private charity (the Wellcome Trust). Similar multi-sourced approaches now predominate in many advanced countries, not because resources could not be made available to fund research from a single source, but because innovation requires solutions to complex problems that cannot be adequately addressed from within a single paradigm. A way to ensure that the solutions found will reflect a range of perspectives is to give different actors, through their funding contributions, a place in the appropriate transactions spaces. It is this approach to the pursuit of solutions to complex problems that, in part, underlies the current tendency for governments, somewhat reluctantly, to take up brokering roles.

### The human genome mapping project

A useful example of how transaction spaces operate in research is provided by Balmer in his analysis of the UK-based Human Genome Mapping Project (HGMP). The aim of the HGMP is to catalogue the entire human genetic make-up. The maps, like geographical maps, can be of varying type and resolution, from large-scale linkage maps of genes in relation to other genes based on frequency of co-inheritance, through various types of physical maps that locate 'landmarks' in the DNA, and eventually to the highest resolution, the sequence of chemical base-pairs which make up the DNA molecule. The project has not come about without controversy. Proponents of the project claimed that it would provide a valuable resource for science and medicine, while opponents have challenged its wisdom in terms of cost, strategy, ethics, and the ultimate utility of its results (Balmer, 1996).

Balmer argues that the HGMP was not the outcome of any single factor nor does it follow the model of a typical national research programme. The fact that a mapping project emerged has to be understood, not in terms of bureaucratic politics, but as the outcome of a complex process of negotiation in which a large number of interested parties were involved. No one person, group or organization was in control and dictating the pace and direction. Moreover, UK governmental policies of 'selectivity', 'concentration' and 'value for money' did not drive the project directly but provided guidelines for a coordination with the agendas of the Medical Research Council and the gene-mapping community.

The HGMP came to function as a transaction space (in Balmer's term, a boundary object) situated at the intersection of a number of organizations and interests. It constituted a social and political entity that aligned the goals and agendas of separate working groups, and which was achieved over a period as groups and their agendas were shuffled into and out of the policy arena, or marginalized. Consequently, money flowed from the state to the scientists, and gene mapping under the auspices of a concerted programme was supported. The emergence of a transaction space was crucial in the furtherance of the project. The alignment of diverse and often divergent interests was necessary for the work to get under way, but it was not a planned, but more an orchestrated, process. Rather like an orchestra, where all the players are vying to be the conductor, there was no one fully in control and everyone was ready to improvise. The boundary object – the genome mapping project – allowed some sort of melody to be heard and elicited at least a basic commitment around which many interests could converge sufficiently to allow funds to flow. The HGMP eventually ran into problems, generated in part by the emergence of other competing boundary objects operating in their own transaction spaces and which promised quicker and cheaper scientific results.

**Implications for universities**
New design configurations are perhaps the simplest example of contextualized knowledge in the middle range. The problem is that, for many, this context is still too narrow. However, as Nelson argues, it is perhaps time to acknowledge that the selection environment that determines which new products will emerge and be developed is now hedged about by increasingly articulated regulatory structures. These require firms to include in their new product developments, *ab initio*, a wider range of social and health-related concerns than is normally covered by the conventional use of the term 'market' (Nelson and Winter, 1982). It is here, at the interface between economic and social imperatives, that a new research opportunity for universities presents itself.

Given the vast range of knowledge resources that they currently possess, universities are ideally placed not to act reluctantly but to take the lead in brokering the search for complex knowledge solutions. Universities ought not to waste energy denigrating the integrity of mode 2 research practices and continually re-affirming the singular value of discipline-based research practices that are commonly associated with mode 1. Universities do not need to abandon mode 1. On the contrary, they need to embrace mode 2 more fully. In other words, they need to take their participation in collaborative research beyond the relatively narrow horizons of the business/economic context that currently predominates in the search for novel design configurations. Rather, if they embrace mode 2 forms of research, they will be in a position to insist that the 'price' of their participation in competition-induced collaborations depends upon the aim of finding solutions that are valid beyond the narrow imperatives of conventional market economics.

Further, they will be more convincing in this if they develop, in-house, the experience, knowledge and skills that will enable them to develop capabilities in facilitating the emergence of, and managing, the outcomes of the many transaction spaces that are required in mode 2 research. Taking the lead will, of course, also require the development of administrative arrangements, organizational forms, and reward structures that will attract and hold scientists. These will need to be sensitive, to the public imperative for solutions to complex social problems, to the requirement to take the search for knowledge solutions beyond a dialogue of experts (in the market), and to an approach that supports wider social participation in the research process.

## ▶ Conclusions

Stated simply, universities need to make a commitment to move from the production of merely reliable knowledge to the production of socially robust knowledge; that is, knowledge that has been tested and re-tested in a variety of contexts. This will, by their very involvement in that process, provide a basis for public trust on which continued social and financial support for universities depends. At their best, the research practices associated with mode 2 – particularly those that imply wider participation, enhanced social accountability, reflexivity, and expanded forms of quality control – could be used to establish in universities an ethos for the production of socially robust knowledge. And it is socially robust knowledge that society is increasingly demanding of all its scientific institutions.

It is by greater openness to the wider community in the development and pursuance of research agendas that universities will be able to retain their integrity and impartiality as institutions. Withdrawing into an ivory tower is no option, but by entering, more comprehensively and deliberately, into the *agora* – those myriad public transaction spaces where issues are discussed and their research implications explored – universities can move not so much into, but *beyond*, the market. Finally, it will be by embracing the production of socially robust knowledge that universities will be able to remain truly critical participants in the process of globalization. To the extent that universities fulfil this role, they will be able to put beyond doubt that they are the crucial institutions that, not only in their aspirations but also in their policies and research practices, are mobilized to serve the public good.

# 6 Differentiation and Diversity in University Systems

Roger King

▶ **Introduction**

There is little doubt that the notion of diversity in university systems is regarded as a good thing. Indeed Robert Birnbaum (1983), in writing of higher education in the US 20 years or so ago, described institutional diversity 'as one of its major ideological pillars' and as having 'a strong ethical component'. In England a regular feature of the government's annual letter of guidance to the body that funds the universities – the Higher Education Funding Council for England (HEFCE) – is the requirement that the Council seeks to find ways of enhancing institutional differences. In November 2001, for example, the Secretary of State for Education wrote to HEFCE stating that she looked to the Council to 'help support increased diversity among higher education institutions'. The government's White Paper on higher education for England (DES, 2003) argues that that it is unreasonable to expect all higher education institutions to sustain all functions at an excellent level and that individual institutions should focus on what they do best. In Australia, the recent review of higher education by the federal government (DEST, 2002) strongly emphasizes the benefits of diversity in promoting choice, flexibility and the prospects for creating 'one or two world class universities'. Indeed it is rare to find a country anywhere that does not invoke diversity as a major aspiration for its university system.

Recently HEFCE has reiterated that its key strategic objective is to devise a funding methodology that, while allowing all universities the opportunity to engage in all the 'core functions', will produce greater diversity by encouraging institutions to develop or excel in only some of these functions. Yet neither the government nor HEFCE have evidenced the claimed advantages of such a policy or clearly examined different kinds of diversity. This could be in the range of institutional types, characterized particularly by the balance of activities between teaching and research, in specialization by universities in undergraduate programmes or subject disciplines, or areas or forms of research (basic and applied). Normally in the UK and often elsewhere, the notion of diversity is not extended to questions of quality. At least a broad comparability of standards, and particularly at a minimal or threshold level, for all universities is deemed essential to justify the autonomy and monopoly of degree-awarding powers. In the US, however, variability in university standards has been much more acceptable – some might say, more realistic – than in the UK, and is regarded as helping to sustain university responsiveness to new and variegated clienteles.

Particularly ministers and officials have not addressed the problem that research-focused traditional universities will continue successfully to chase the funds that enable them to be in every game – not least because the emphasis on 'quality' used in the discrimination of funding allocations tends to favour such institutions, even when it is teaching or commercial linkages that are being encouraged. Not only do such universities need to safeguard their finances as public units of funding continue to decline, but they are also increasingly subject to exhortations and incentives from government to widen social access and to focus more on their teaching. Moreover, resource and student market pressures, and increasing criticism from government, have forced the older universities to become a little more like the newer universities and to introduce modern management and marketing methods, to actively promote more popular and vocational courses, and to develop extensive partnerships with industry. The newer universities, traditionally characterized more by their focus on teaching and learning, and the provision of opportunities to those without a family or peer background of higher education, face strong exhortations from ministers to turn away from research and to become excellent as teaching institutions, yet, as we shall see, there are powerful reasons why they are unlikely to do so. The result is increased convergence rather than diversity, perhaps closer to the middle in some respects, rather than to one end, although the pressures tend to lead to emulation of the older universities.

We need to understand how diversity is to be defined, what it is intended to achieve, and the best means for securing it. This might seem obvious but it does appear to be a remarkably elusive concept. For example, if we confine our focus to institutional types, according to what functions are universities to be differentiated? Is it by levels of teaching and research, the form of research (basic or applied), size, the social class of most of its students, or something else? Does it matter much if system diversity is achieved by every university getting larger – perhaps through mergers – and uniformly undertaking the full range of identified functions – what might be termed internal or programmatic diversity – or is institutional specialization a more preferred outcome? And what is diversity meant to accomplish, and does it matter what means are used for securing it?

Strangely, the evidence from universities in the UK – and probably elsewhere – is that they do not much care for the system to be diversified. This is despite the public pronouncements of many vice chancellors to the contrary. Universities seem remarkably similar in seeking more research funds – even the ex-polytechnics – and in being attractive to wider numbers of undergraduate students. Since the creation of the new universities in the early 1990s they have sought the research base and prestige of the older universities. This is hardly surprising perhaps, given that the higher education policies of New Labour have generally supported the research-focused and scientific-based older universities, rather than those that have lesser prestige and are predominantly concerned with student learning and the teaching function, and which attract many students from the lower social classes. Additional government funding to universities mostly has been targeted at research rather than for teaching.

The result of this (and a similar pattern can be found in other countries, such as Australia) is that public funding for teaching has been compressed. The scope for innovation in learning is thus reduced once time and money fall below certain levels. And although the increase in fee-paying students in countries such as the UK, Australia, New Zealand and Canada, has provided increased income for teaching, this tends to be confined to a limited range of subjects, such as business and information technology studies. In the UK the Labour government's obsession with 'top' or 'the best' universities, including highly public calls for the widening of access to Oxford and Cambridge, as though other universities with stronger track records in such endeavours were hardly worth getting into, is at odds with its rhetoric of more generally wishing to 'modernize' the whole of the university system and of facilitating the different strengths of universities. Both old and new have great difficulty in passing up any initiative with potential marginal increments to their income, whatever their so-called missions. Cash is hard to pass up when resources are tight, and getting tighter. The proportion of public funding top-sliced from general operating grants and earmarked for special initiatives, which must be applied for competitively, has increased, which means that universities are evermore obliged to bid in order to protect their finances, whatever their mission. Not only does this raise the transaction costs for universities in obtaining funds, but it seriously hampers government strategies for system diversity.

This is not to imply that new university leaders speak with forked tongues when they talk the diversity talk but yet seek to emulate the more prestigious and research-based universities in their actual strategies. Rather, arguments for systemic and institutional diversity are 'public good' statements that inevitably differ from the actions required in an increasingly market-based order if institutions are to survive and even prosper. This order is formed from the self-interested actions and interactions of its individual units – the universities, and particularly their leaders. These individual efforts are not undertaken to create a 'sector' with particular features but to advance the interests of a university (more prestige, rising income, or better staff and students), and by the most effective means possible. The mechanism is self-help in a highly uncertain world, not the creation of a preferred type of university system. The nature of the outcomes – the market order, the 'sector' – is largely unintended. But it forms a compelling structure that no vice chancellor can ignore, whatever their public protestations to the contrary.

## ▶ Where has diversity as a 'good thing' come from?

The notion that universities should specialize and focus on what they are good at has a long history, particularly in the US. Initially formulated to justify a plurality of religious environments to match the respective churchly practices of students and staff, institutional diversity came to be seen as reflecting the wider social needs of an increasingly varied and multicultural society. Different university types with particular clusters of functions were a means of providing both responsiveness – to a changing economy and society – and stability as the system evolved (Trow, 1979). Students had more freedom to choose a university culture and mission that suited them best.

The spread of types of provision, it was felt, encouraged social mobility, promoted efficiency, and enhanced institutional freedom. In some cases, such as California, with its 'master plan' of colleges and universities fulfilling allocated and specified roles, from initial education to post-doctoral studies, market choice was underpinned by strong state intervention at the local level. As in many other sectors of US enterprize, the open market was seen as best achieved and maintained by a strong and often detailed planning and regulatory framework. Diversity as a policy was regarded as allowing experimentation to be low risk for the system as a whole. Failure could be confined to single institutions, while success was easily transposed elsewhere by highly mobile staff. The result is that, despite recent evidence of declining diversity, the US system of higher education generally has catered for high levels of access, as well as becoming pre-eminent (or elitist) in scientific and other research.

The arguments in favour of institutional diversity can be summarized as follows (Stadtman, 1980) as it:

- increases the range of choices available to learners;
- makes higher education available to virtually everyone, despite differences among individuals;
- matches education to the needs, goals, learning styles, speed and ability of individual students;

- enables institutions to select their own missions and to confine their activities to those consistent with their location, resources, levels of instruction and clienteles;
- responds to the pressures of a society that is itself characterized by great complexity and diversity; and
- becomes a precondition of college and university freedom and autonomy because the greater the differences among institutions, the more difficult it is for a central authority to convert them into instruments of indoctrination rather than of education.

The propositions for institutional differentiation – particularly the idea of responsiveness to the changing social and economic environment, and which appear to be even more germane in the rapidly changing modern world – have a democratic feel. They are not dissimilar to pluralist interpretations of liberal democratic systems, and their support for them, as typified by their multiple points of access, and formal separation and interdependency of powers and institutions. In part this linkage of institutional diversity with democratic openness and societal development derives from two strong intellectual models in the US. One is associated with the writings of the nineteenth-century French sociologist Emile Durkheim, and the reception of his work into the US through structural functionalists, such as Talcott Parsons. It was a perspective that adopted from the biological sciences the model of society as a functioning body or system, in which different parts undertook respective key functions, but interdependently relying on the efficient functioning of every part, for the healthy maintenance of the unified whole (organism).

The second tradition is more economistic and posits a powerful connection between competitive markets and institutional diversity. Institutional diversity is regarded as analogous with product diversity in commercial markets, and the more that it is increased then the greater will public preferences be fulfilled and society benefited (Dill and Teixeira, 2000). This form of thinking may underlie the increased public policy toward higher education in many societies in recent years of introducing market competition. Markets, or 'quasi' markets, are regarded as an effective mechanism for the allocation of funds to universities, whether these are public funds that are allocated competitively in the form of differential grants to institutions on the basis of success in, say, attracting more students, or on the basis of possessing better researchers following evaluation of track records (where the state acts as proxy purchaser for the individual buyer or the wider public), or private monies that are allocated directly by the consumer through user-pays policies.

Therefore, governments tend to see simulated competition as increasing programmatic diversity in the system as each university is forced to focus on its strengths. We shall see, however, that the causal linkage between the building-up by governments of market-like processes, and institutional and systemic diversity, is by no means well-evidenced. On the contrary, it is at least arguable that, rather than market-like processes, strong regulatory intervention at the public policy level, for example, in maintaining binary sector policies (between different types of higher education institution, such as the polytechnics or the *fachhochschulen* and the universities, in the UK and Germany respectively), may be more effective. Yet the dominance of the neoliberal critique of central planning and strong state steerage of national higher education systems as bureaucratic, distorting and inefficient, makes it unlikely that recently unified and marketized university systems (as in Australia and the UK) will be reformed back into more explicit and separate branches of the welfare state. At the very least, as we noted in Chapter 4, there is likely to be persisting tension between governments seeking to recognize and possibly support 'their' multinational world-class 'champions' in a more 'hands-off' manner, despite the latter's increased emphasis on more private or corporate organizational interests than wider national or public ones, and the temptation by ministers to more overly reintegrate universities within the state as part of promoting national economic competitiveness in an increasingly competitive and knowledge-based global economy. Either way, the pressures for convergence rather than diversity between universities are strong, and may be intensifying, as we shall examine shortly.

Moreover, rather than creating horizontal diversity of functions and niches, the marketization of higher education tends to reinforce vertical stratification of standing and prestige among institutions. The elite institutions are even better able than before to gain the best students and the most research funds, and to maintain their positions over the claims of other, often newer, institutions. The latter, although seeking to emulate the top universities, are required to generate standing from the less-regarded and less-rewarded activities of teaching and learning. And, although this produces systemic diversity of a sort, it is based on, and reproduces, static rankings and perpetuates the second-class status of university teaching in contrast with that of research. The key policy task is to find mechanisms that conduce innovation, particularly in teaching and learning, as a means of securing both wider functional diversity and change, and as a means of making more dynamic the current static hierarchies of prestige that currently prevail.

There are two further points to mention at this stage on the issues of the marketization of higher education, and on the matter of institutional stratification or hierarchy and its relationship to systemic diversity. First, although university systems have become more competitive in many countries in recent times, they hardly constitute full-blown markets. Universities are restricted by government in the prices that they can charge for much of their undergraduate portfolios, and often on the amount of product (places) that they can 'sell'. Public subsidies and governmental aversion to the political risks of allowing institutional failure or closure also distort market processes, as do impediments to student (consumer) information and mobility (shopping around). Undergraduate student mobility is perhaps most marked in the UK, but in countries such as Australia and even the US, local state and city boundaries exert powerful constraints on student choices of university.

Universities are also less unified or corporate than most business organizations, despite recent reforms in many advanced societies (and irrespective of their employee views on these matters!). They are not as able to respond to changing environments with the same sense of collective purpose as found in many other parts of the private sector. They remain publicly subsidized, non-profit organizations for the most part, made up of disparate, relatively autonomous, independent-minded, and often highly unionized, cynical and complaining professionals. The governance of universities is a complicated mixture of various types and cultures of managerialism (often derived from outdated business orthodoxies), versions of collegiality and rule by commune, and political manipulation and power plays. At the very least this mixture debilitates and disperses organizational direction and the ability to change.

Second, university systems are generally characterized by reputational hierarchy, with considerable levels of variation in status and resources between institutions. In theory, it is possible that such stratification could reside with, or even advance, systemic diversity. Yet, as we shall see, when hierarchical stratification is deeply-embedded, the prospects for diversity are effectively reduced. Students and others seek to avoid lower-ranking institutions if they can (in some cases they may wonder, given the official encouragement of accessing the 'top' universities, often in the name of advancing 'diversity', whether it is worth going to some of those with apparently low esteem at all). The active promotion by governments of hierarchy (by allowing top-up fees, or condemning 'micky mouse' degrees in the low status universities) seems at variance in such circumstances to professed governmental strategies of furthering institutional diversity.

Moreover, in some countries there has been recent encouragement of mergers and other forms of amalgamation. In Australia, for example, mergers were a key part of reforms to overcome binary policies and to have a unified national university system in the late 1980s and early 1990s. In the UK there have also been statements (and finance) periodically from funding councils and governments welcoming the prospect of institutional amalgamations. It may be regarded as somewhat contradictory then also to level the charge that universities are insufficiently distinct in the range of programmes or functions that they undertake.

Birnbaum (1983) suggests that institutional diversity enables students from across the achievement range to choose the university or college whose expectations about likely performance matches their own. They are more likely to feel comfortable in a peer environment where goals and behaviour are reasonably familiar. Yet it could be argued that such an approach solidifies existing patterns of stratification and may do little to encourage social mobility over a large distance. Too formal a pattern of diversity, particularly if linked to distinctive and stratified patterns of student recruitment, may merely help to consolidate existing configurations of inequality. Similarly, as a public policy, it may please elite institutions by freezing the hierarchy of prestige and power between universities into at least a semi-permanent arrangement. If every institution knows its place there is less chance of dynamic challengers emerging to threaten their dominance. These are points that we will return to later.

For the most part, however, the underlying assumption in much of the literature on diversity is that specialization enhances institutional effectiveness. This was particularly the case in the US in the 1970s and early 1980s when the influence of structural functionalist theory was at its height in the social sciences. Writers such as Parsons and Platt (1973), and Birnbaum (1983), emphasized the integrative and adaptive benefits to society of differentiated and specialist educational institutions reflecting and meeting the needs of an increasingly complex division of labour in advanced industrial economies. It was, as we noted above, a view that matched the pluralistic interpretations of democracy in the political sphere. If all colleges and universities had the same goals, organization and social bases of student recruitment, it was felt that the US system of higher education could not have excelled in both social access and scientific advance. Birnbaum, for example, argues that there is evidence that most higher education institutions cannot perform all functions well. Focusing on some goals inevitably means that less attention will be given to others. The effectiveness of the system is enhanced with institutional differentiation and the undertaking of specific missions and goals.

Consequently, diversity provides organizations with a fertile source of data not available to those operating in homogeneous and centrally planned systems. The outcome is less fear of innovation, which not only is potentially beneficial in a competitive sense to the individual institution, but also provides a form of 'public good' in that the risk of change for the whole system is lowered and the chances of dynamic and productive change are that much better. These advantages are seen as particularly important as educational systems seek to cope with increased levels of participation and yet at the same time aim to advance their intellectual and research esteem. A set of uniform institutions all undertaking the same roles, as opposed to greater specialization and organizational diversity, is seen as making such functional reconciliation that much harder (Trow, 1979).

The problems faced by institutions in fulfilling both elite (scientific) and mass (access) functions are outlined by Clark (1983). These needs, in his view, are sufficiently contradictory and generative of distinctive cultures that different types of college are required to cover their span. Some observers have gone further by arguing that both the elite and mass sectors are essentially complementary and dependent on each other. The elite sector requires the political, financial and social ballast of the mass sector; the mass sector depends on the values, standards and research of the elite to be educationally sound (Trow, 1979). They differ, nonetheless, in that elite institutions depend more on intimate and often residential forms of socialization of students than the often larger mass institutions, where there is more emphasis on training, work-related studies, and the transmission of skills (Scott, 1995). Yet, increasingly, both forms are taking on some of the aspects of the other.

Kerr (1963), for example, famously describes the 'multiversity' to indicate that universities were becoming more alike in the extending range of functions that they were undertaking and in the increasing instrumentalism – which he broadly welcomed – of their servicing of economic and other external interests. Older and more philosophical notions of the 'idea of a university', the sense of its guiding purposes as found in the European traditions and the works of writers such as Newman and Humboldt (see Chapters 1 and 2 of this volume), were discarded as less useful or necessary in the pragmatic and multifunctional US environment. Rather, universities were what they did. And this meant largely serving the variety of needs generated in the increasing complexity of social and economic life.

In this view diversity was developing internally to growing institutions, not in the specialization of roles between them. As well as teaching and research, universities were engaged in a variety of business and community 'outreach' activities. Moreover, universities could not really pick and choose what they wanted to do. Apart from the financial risk, contractors, not least in local and regional settings, were looking to universities on what we might term these days as a 'one-stop shop' basis. Universities were thus becoming engaged in a full range of activities. Institutions were starting to look similar, and it was this multifunctionalism rather than specialization that maintained system diversity. System diversity was being supported by what has been termed internal 'programmatic diversity' *within* ever-expanding universities, rather than by institutional diversity. However, it is not clear that this type of programmatic diversity delivers the benefits associated with the institutional specialization that we have outlined above (Goedegebuure and Meek, 1994). Kerr's view of the university as having continually to reflect the requirements of society at large found some echo, if not a strict parallel, in the work of Parsons and Platt (1973). As Delanty (2001) has recently noted, this is an important effort to apply Parsonian structural functionalism to higher education. The university in this schema provides the overall social system with a level of impartiality and trust necessary for both social cohesion and scientific and related advances. Its autonomy helps continually to establish and re-establish the cognitive structures of society that are necessary to the rationality of modern culture. And yet its neutrality helps establish social (moral) integrity. In this sense, both functions – the cognitive (scientific) and the social (trust) – indicate how universities service the overall needs of the social system, albeit at a very high level of structural abstraction and generality. Universities as an institutional configuration reflect the complexity and diversity of progressively knowledge-based or 'postindustrial' economies. In turn, these sub-system functions help maintain the overall unity of the social system. Unlike Kerr, however, Parsons and Platt tend to see the effectiveness and efficiency of these functional undertakings as best achieved by institutional differentiation rather than institutional multifunctionalism, committed as they are to a biological or organic model in which systemic differentiation, and role distinctiveness and complementarity, generate overall social (or 'bodily') integration.

## ▶ Binary, segmented and unified systems

Until the late 1980s and early 1990s university systems in a number of countries other than the US were characterized by formal or legal distinctions between 'sectors' or components. In some cases these had been established for some time. In late nineteenth-century Germany, diversification and specialization in higher education had resulted in a layered system, known as 'segmentation'. Certain elements of the system were opened up or new institutions were created, but in a manner that left the existing universities largely untouched, not least as finishing schools for the offspring of the already welloff. Rather than increased access to universities, technical, teaching and commercial institutes were formed to cater for the specific skills necessary for an industrializing society. These institutes drew their students predominantly from the lower social classes. This was a level of formal diversity that happened to a much lesser extent in the US (Mitchell Ash, 1996; Muller, 1987).

In the cases of Australia and Britain in the 1960s this type of formal diversity was known as a 'binary system'. Generally its development reflected the growing demand for higher education with the development of knowledge-based economies, and a view that this required, alongside the traditional universities, the creation of more vocationally and professionally relevant, less expensive, and more teaching-orientated colleges and 'polytechnics'. They were designed to be more publicly accountable and managerial in their practices and closely linked to the other elements of the postsecondary and adult sector. Their creation, however, signified an unwillingness by political leaders to take on the universities – many, after all, had graduated from them – and a preference to build up what was seen as a more modern and economically relevant 'public sector' alternative, and one able to appeal to social groups that had little tradition of accessing higher education. The minister who introduced the binary system in the UK in the mid-1960s presented the polytechnics as the major instrument for the government's drive to link higher education with industrial and economic needs. In terms of privilege, funding and standing, however, the two sectors were both different and unequal, despite governmental protestations that they were different but equal.

The creation of binary systems was also a key indicator that national educational policies were too important to be left to the universities and that greater state steerage and accountability were required if a country was to be globally competitive. This was particularly noticeable in the UK, following the decline and devastation of the war years and the recognition that education and skills could provide a way back to worldwide clout and economic effectiveness. In the case of research, seen steadily as the key to knowledge-based economic advantage, in the UK it took some time for the financial controls of the scientific community to be prised loose. By the early 1970s, and reinforced by the trenchant Rothschild Report into the public funding and purposes of university research, curiosity-driven research was seen as too uncertain in its instrumental payoffs to stay for long outside national strategic policy frameworks. With the cuts imposed on the universities in the 1980s, the Universities Grants Committee (UGC) was asked by government to be more selective in the distribution of research funds. It was at this time that the teaching and research funding streams to the universities became separated, and research funds became dependent on track records as indicated by success in regular research assessment exercises (Salter and Tapper, 1994).

This form of differentiation fuelled speculation that it was possible to conceive of universities as distinguished by the relative amounts of teaching and research that they undertook. There was a proposal, which subsequently foundered, from the Research Councils that aimed at formally identifying three types of institution: R (research-based), T (teaching-only) and X (mixture of the two), which would have severely questioned the long-held view that research activity by staff was essential to the vitality and health of the teaching function. Rather, a further distinction became part of the currency (stimulated by the work of the Carnegie Commission in the US) in which scholarly activity in support of teaching programmes was delineated from basic and applied research. The latter, especially in its big science forms, it was felt required large amounts of public finance and would benefit from selective policies that concentrated the disbursement of funds. Scholarly activity, however, was less expensive, needed to be widely undertaken, and could often be supported from teaching rather than research budgets.

This formal arrangement was never adopted, although some have argued that increasingly in the 1990s and into the new millennium, it has surreptitiously influenced university funding policies as research funding has become ever more concentrated. As overt policy, of course, institutional segmentation of this kind not only falls foul of the oft-stated belief in the necessity of the research–teaching nexus in universities, but is seen also as failing to recognize that, outside the big sciences especially, a wider dispersal of research funding among universities may provide greater 'bangs per buck' than more selective approaches. While the claimed beneficial and indeed vital links between teaching and research are not easy to substantiate, as Jarvis (2001, p. 14) has remarked, 'few universities wish to be regarded as only teaching institutions since research has been seen as a major indicator of the quality, even the essence, of the university since the Enlightenment [and] professional practitioners are increasingly undertaking research into their own practice and are generating new knowledge'.

Moreover, formal university differentiation has the propensity to 'freeze' research and university hierarchies in ways that could militate against innovation and dynamic change, particularly if this is strongly expressed through national funding policies. Outside the UK, too, similar attempts at more formal differentiation of institutions have foundered. In Canada, provincial intermediary bodies have either been created or reinforced in recent years to execute policies of rationalization and differentiation, and to re-examine institutional missions. Yet universities have successfully resisted attempts that some of them abandon their research and concentrate on teaching (Fisher and Rubenson, 1998).

In any case, formally stratified systems in the late 1980s and early 1990s were falling out of phase with the general ideological currents of the time. The state, particularly after the fall of communism in eastern Europe, and with the increasing influence of worldwide economic integration and other signs of globalization that appeared to undermine the historic powers and sovereignty of the nation state, was becoming more of an enabler or contractor than a micro-involved actor. It became less an owner and direct provider of services than a procurer of incentives and market-oriented structural reforms, and a regulator. Binary and other formally stratified systems were regarded increasingly as incompatible with wider forms of liberalization and deregulation, and with the aim of encouraging university responsiveness to the competitive demands of consumers and markets. Binary systems were seen as at cross-purposes with the fostering of institutional initiative and entrepreneurial orientations, as cloaking heterogeneity and the rise of considerable differences within sectors, and as stimulating 'academic drift' towards the traditional university model. By the early 1990s the binary system was covering up more institutional differentiation than it revealed – differences within the respective sectors were being artificially restrained as well as the borders becoming ever fuzzier – and a more competitive, diversified sector seemed more appropriate to the fluidities of a globalizing, knowledge-based society (Scott, 1995). It was better to let the market conduce diversity, flexibility and innovation, which would surely follow as institutions found their niche and responded to the bracing breezes of enhanced competition.

We shall see, however, that the notion that diversity is better promoted by the market than by formal systems of differentiation introduced by governments is flawed. There is little doubt that, as university systems take on more 'mass' characteristics as part of national strategies to respond successfully to the challenges of the global world economy, they become of greater interest to governments. As Scott (1995, p. 15) has observed, 'the historical record suggests that elite systems, whether or not state-funded, enjoy a high degree of autonomy, while mass systems, even if they become less dependent on the state, inevitably (and beneficially) attract political attention'. Yet the rub is that the growth of market reforms to university systems, in a context of political arrangements where direct policy levers available to the state generally appear less potent and more complex, has made diversity less likely. Not only do markets tend to encourage uniformity – for reasons that we shall explore later – their reliance in the absence of strong (and therefore highly contestable) regulatory frameworks diminish the necessary state powers for formal stratification that may be the only means to guarantee a clear level of mission distinctiveness. Although governments produce policy responses, not least on research funding, that are aimed at enhancing segregation, these do not prevent a movement toward institutional uniformity.

In the above context it was perhaps not surprising that the binary system collapsed after around 25 years of existence in both Australia and the UK, and that polytechnics and colleges became universities (in the case of Australia, after a number of mergers). In academic terms it had become increasingly difficult to distinguish the two types. Students in the so-called vocational college or polytechnic sector were more interested in the subjects of business, humanities and the social sciences, than in the more technological and applied sciences as originally envisaged. Moreover, managers and staff had aspirations for 'parity' with the universities and the shaking off of rather irksome forms of local political control and intervention. Among politicians, the notion of initially setting the colleges and polytechnics 'free' through legislatively provided incorporation, and then establishing formally 'a level playing field' with the traditional universities by allowing wider use of the university title, reflected the growing market-oriented ideas of the age among governments.

Not that market deregulation was seen as incompatible with greater accountability for the use of public funds or a greater responsiveness to 'customers'. In the UK at least, there was the added temptation for governments to slake their desire to bring the universities in to closer alignment with the accountability and managerial practices of the polytechnics and colleges. A problem, however, is that predicting organizational change under market conditions is quite hazardous particularly when, as we have outlined above, the organizations in focus are as loosely coupled as the universities, and the 'markets' that they operate in are considerably constrained and flawed. Predicting that such bodies will start to become more specialized and the system more diverse under these conditions is extremely brave and possibly foolhardy. As we shall see, there are at least equally compelling arguments that, in the context of reinforced reputational hierarchy, the market – or at least more competitive environments for institutions – will conduce institutional convergence rather than divergence.

Nonetheless, governmental views were that the creation of unified university systems, along with increasing market reforms, such as user pays and increased competition for declining public funds, would stimulate institutional diversity. The theory was that in this new climate universities would come to recognize the hopelessness of trying to do everything and would specialize and focus on their own particular niche. To do any thing else would be to dilute strengths, encourage mediocrity and hazard survival. Moreover, a more meritocratic sense of what a good university was – not least including the more visible virtues of entrepreneurialism and employer relevance – would help overcome rigid hierarchies of university prestige. Yet this has not happened. Binary may have gone, but stratification remains (Scott, 1995). Fuelled by an increasing selectivity in research funding, in the UK at least, 'league tables' of university rankings show still a relatively neat dividing line between the old and the new universities, which reflects both unequal status and levels of funding.

Scott (1998) has suggested that elite universities have shown a marked reluctance to focus entirely on their scientific functions – and have responded to political, financial and social imperatives to widen access. At the same time, encouraged by the regular research evaluation assessments of institutions by HEFCE, a research culture has become more widely disseminated among the ex-polytechnics. This is explained not only by institutional ambitions, but, as more research is undertaken outside university settings – as it becomes contracted and applied (it becomes more so-called mode 2 science, see Gibbons *et al.*, 1994, and Chapter 5 of this volume) – the distinction between research and teaching starts to dissolve, and research starts to lose its elite connotations. Researchers are a less privileged group and in the 'knowledge society' a great many activities have a research component. Scientific communities have become more open, characterized by networks of collaborators both inside and outside the university and by the rise of social concerns about the risks of scientific application. Professional workers have become more interested in undertaking research in the context of their work-settings, undertaking 'professional' doctorates, for example, and with an 'applied knowledge' that can lessen the intellectual authority of academic subject specialists. As a result, the democratization of the university – the increased interpenetration of the social and the scientific – has reinforced the development of Kerr's 'multiuniversities' and the likely decline of overt institutional specialization.

However, as well as the enhanced democratization, postmodernity and contestability of knowledge, and the rise of the social functions of the university, it is necessary to examine further the role of the market in enhancing processes of university homogeneity rather than differentiation. To do so will require that we are clear about the motivations that drive institutions and their leaders, and how these differ from the 'public good' statements and intentions of such individuals for what they perceive as the most desirable features of university systems. Before we do that, however, we examine the dimensions of elitism and mass higher education and their relationships to wider social processes.

## ▶ Human capital and social reproduction

A feature of a number of accounts, particularly official ones, of the purposes of the modern university is an emphasis on what has been described as 'human capital theory' (Dearing, 1997; Marginson, 1993). Simply stated, it posits the view that in an increasingly knowledge-based economy most value derives from the education and skills of a nation's people. Productivity switches from the tangible factors of production – land, capital, machinery and so on – to individuals. Moreover, the competitive advantage of nations tends to rest upon the ability to generate commodities that are high up the global 'value chain' and dependent on communication and information technological advance, rather than low-cost production and 'races to the bottom' (Porter, 1990). This requires highly educated and trained people, flexible, adaptable and willing to continue to learn. It follows that the best investment for a country is in its people – and that means investment in universities, colleges and other forms of educational provision. As such there should be a reasonable correlation between expenditure on higher education and national competitiveness and economic growth. (This appears to be the case, but it has never been easy to prove conclusively that educational investment is a cause of economic development. It is at least empirically plausible that increased spending on higher education actually follows economic growth rather than is its cause – see Wolf, 2002.)

During the 1960s human capital assumptions began to be included in the publications of the United Nations and its agencies and eventually became integral to developmental strategies, although it was increasingly recognized that economic development depended on the right or relevant type of education being applied. Doubts have continued about the ability of the universities to reform their curricula and research orientations to more explicitly facilitate economic growth and to deliver what employers want and, in part at least, this helps to explain the growth of private and corporate universities in the 1990s. In terms of institutional diversity, however, human capital theory gave greater credence to the 'capabilities curricula' of the newer universities and the importance of the teaching function. A reasonable expectation might have been a greater shift in the prestige and hierarchical standing of universities, based increasingly on criteria of contemporary relevance rather than antiquity. Yet this appears not to have happened. Why?

In part it follows the heightened attention that governments of all political persuasions have given to commercial and applied research, particularly the development of technoscience and what has been termed mode 2 science, where innovation and application (commodity/product) have become almost instantaneous, or converged. Funding for research, especially for forms of 'biggish science', inevitably has gone to those institutions with strong research infrastructures, which are the older universities, despite the claims for increased research funding for the 'near-market' traditions of the newer universities. Another reason may lie less in human capital theory than in those accounts that regard universities as essentially engaged in the reproduction of inequality and cultural capital. In this view, the purpose of leading institutions is to socialize people into the right dispositions for the top positions in capitalist and advanced society, having initially recruited predominantly from the higher social classes, and then to allocate them to the employment sector accordingly. Elite universities, and their dominant positions in stratified university hierarchies, in this view are essential for the social screening of individuals for their suitability for the occupational division of labour required for capitalist reproduction. This process has the advantage, too, of broadly maintaining social and other class privileges while being undertaken under the guise of neutrality, merit and democratic openness.

Perhaps the best-known proponent of this view is Bordieu (1977). Bordieu offers a different perspective to the one that sees education as closely linked to meritocratic opportunity and social mobility. Rather, education, and especially higher education, is regarded as a key process for reproducing inequality. This follows from the assumption than the main role for schools, colleges and universities is to continually recreate the mechanisms that help to allocate individuals to positions of economic power, social status and to possess the instruments of political influence. The social relations of inequality are not reproduced directly by educational institutions, but predominantly through the exercise of what Bordieu terms 'cultural capital'. Education is itself stratified in such a manner as to provide unequal access to the intellectual and social characteristics that are the primary criteria in the determination of individuals to places in the occupational division of labour. Thus, elite universities tend to recruit students from the higher social classes as ones displaying the behavioural and attitudinal – as well as intellectual – potential to go on to become members of the leading positions in society. Close intimate and intellectual engagement with such students helps inculcate the cultural and credential features that betoken elite recruitment and success.

Of course, the utilization of observable and meritocratic criteria for employment selection, and the operation by autonomous institutions of similar criteria for educational success, mean that there can be no direct one-to-one correspondence between existing members (and families) of the privileged classes in one generation and those in subsequent ones. Even the wealthiest and the brightest sometimes produce offspring that can be stubbornly incorrigible to achieving educational success, despite the variety of silver spoons that may be placed at the disposal of such individuals. But generally, the privileged classes are able to provide the cultural milieu and other support that enables their children to take their places through the intervening processes of, particularly, higher education. Institutional stratification is the means by which individuals also become stratified and selected for employment.

We should be clear that Bordieu is seeking to explain the structures of inequality and the reproduction of processes by which people become selected for their (unequal) positions in the class structure. He is less concerned with the proposition that the already privileged are able to secure similar advantages for their children. Even if perfect and open competition reigned, in a theoretical if impracticable cultural void, the stratification of educational institutions would still enable the organization of inequality to be reproduced, although presumably in a more hazardous manner.

Oxford and Harvard, for example, would still provide the essential mechanisms for recruitment into the leading positions and the assurance to employers that they were recruiting the right people. In the meantime, students graduating from lesser universities (in these terms) or with more 'vocational' qualifications would display the background and characteristics – and motivation – to be employable in a range of so-called lesser occupational positions.

Symbolic signs and systems – including qualifications from a particular type of educational institution – are part of the cultural processes of distinction and differentiation, of inclusion and exclusion, which help to stratify society. In higher education this operates through the use of ostensible neutral instruments, such as examination performance, credentialism and formally open selection. In Bordieu's terms, elite institutions, in which the higher ranks of the professions are formed, are connected with a particular form of class 'habitus'.

Bordieu's 'reproduction of social capital' approach may go some way in helping to explain why political leaders in many advanced societies have been reluctant to resist the elitism of stratified university systems. Funding policies, particularly the increasingly selective approach to research, appear to indicate recognition of the imperative to ensure that institutions are sufficiently differentiated to meet the requirements of an equally differentiated and unequal social system.

Yet there must be more to the story than this. Bordieu's model suggests an extraordinary rigidity in university stratification systems. It is not beyond the bounds of reason, for example, that employers may come to value the skills and competencies of graduates with economically relevant qualifications and experience from more vocational universities as the economy becomes more competitive and, if, traditional elite universities fail to adapt. Moreover, left-inclined governments have shown increased willingness to be at least critical of elite universities that fail to respond to social access policies and which under-recruit from a broader social base. Concentration of research and other funds, too, may reflect less a direct willingness to support traditionally privileged universities by governments than recognition that a general expansion of universities is expensive to the public purse. Big science especially is evermore expensive to fund, and the nature of mode 2 knowledge production and application indicates that international networks of collaboration by reasonably well-funded 'national champions' may be the only sensible way forward. Fast-emerging countries, such as China and Singapore, are among those that have seen, in mergers and the selective funding of excellence in a few chosen universities, the means for expanding their science and technology base in pursuit of innovation and economic growth at higher levels of the global 'value chain'. 'World class' universities

– that is, a select few – are seen as necessary in securing comparative advantage in a more competitive and integrated worldwide economy.

## ▶ Self-help and institutional diversity

We noted above that the relatively high levels of institutional diversity in the US have generally enabled a successful coverage of both elite and mass forms of higher education. As well as impressive levels of access and social inclusion in university participation, the US has not been short of Nobel Prize winners and excels in a range of research activities. As governments in other countries seek the means for a more highly skilled workforce to stay ahead in the comparative advantage of nations in the increasingly knowledge-based world economy, it is not surprising that they look to encourage diversity on the US model. In the UK, for example, a Labour government presides over an increasingly 'mass' university system and has set a target for the end of the first decade of the twenty-first century of 50 per cent of people to benefit from higher education by the time that they reach 30 years of age. As part of this aim it has regularly argued for increased diversity among higher education institutions. It seems to offer a way of absorbing a more heterogeneous clientele, of meeting the growing demands of employers, and yet enhancing the nation's research base within the public funds available, particularly in concentrating resources for science and technology, areas that are seen as essential for economic competitiveness and innovation.

Yet in both the US and the UK there is now a tendency for increased institutional uniformity rather than diversity. If diversity is occurring, it is to be found within institutions as they struggle to meet the challenges of teaching and research, access and science, elitism and mass. The picture is one of spinning plates on sticks, with the sticks being frantically twitched before a plate crashes to the ground. The UK sector's various and increased functions may be covered but not in the ways that generate the benefits of institutional diversity outlined earlier. Why should this be?

One reason, as we have noted already, is the extension of market processes to university systems. Policymakers have generally assumed that this is the best means for extending institutional diversity. They have increased competition for additional funding, and have frequently used evaluative tools, such as teaching quality assessments or tables of institutional research performance, to strengthen this. The result, however, has been reinforced hierarchical stratification, and emulation by the less-regarded institutions of their 'betters', not least in growing their research activities. Despite efforts by policymakers to continue to concentrate the distribution of public funds for research by being more selective on the basis of performance evaluations, at least some marginal success has served to encourage aspirant universities to keep on investing in research, although they continue to be exhorted by ministers to abjure and focus on their particular strengths, mainly in teaching. The pursuit of private income, such as through commercial research or overseas full fee-paying students, which carries considerable imperative as public funds relatively decline and student recruitment markets for a number of newer universities appear to be softening, may also reinforce these convergent tendencies, as the client groups are themselves fairly similar in their views of what constitutes a preferred university. 'League tables' of universities, if anything, reinforce these tendencies.

One reason often advanced for this move to institutional homogeneity is the existence of common academic norms and values in the system, not least as held by faculty, who, even in the newer universities, have generally received their education and intellectual induction in the older universities. The stronger the influence of such norms, the lower the diversity. Similarly, others have suggested that formal professional training and subsequent membership of professional and disciplinary networks produce a convergence of outlook among the practitioners in such occupations (Di Maggio and Powell, 1983).

A rather different approach has been to look at the workings of the higher education market for 'positional goods' (Marginson and Considine, 2000). In an account that is similar to the one outlined above by Bordieu, elite institutions are viewed as providing access for their students to the best jobs and positions in society, and to the commensurate rewards that these provide. Inevitably these are scarce and help constrain the top universities from producing too many graduates. But the 'positional goods' produced by such universities are founded particularly on reputation – for having the best academics, the most promising students, the leading research, and the best access to the most desirable jobs. Other universities thus recognize that the speediest path for their own standing is not to buck the system but broadly to follow it. The rules of the game are just too powerful. They thus seek to at least approximate to the profile of the 'best' universities.

An interesting argument is to suggest that the establishment of national quality assurance and other regulatory regimes that involve peer review furthers these processes. Disciplinary leaders, who are mostly from the top-ranked universities, tend to dominate both the composition and the approach of such bodies, even when teaching and learning is under the microscope, particularly when the focus is on subjects rather than the wider institutional context. Other academics and managers cannot ignore their interpretations of what counts as quality even if they were so disposed (Meek *et al.*, 1996). Moreover, at the supranational level, such as the EU, intergovernmental efforts to provide greater consistency and convergence in programme lengths and quality standards may also further homogeneity. Nor is it easy for organizations to suddenly specialize by changing mission and structure, given the costs of capital investment, the risks of environmental scanning (not least as government priorities seem to change so rapidly), and well-settled external and internal views as to what a university should be doing.

Universities are reputation-maximizers, and 'academic drift' from the technical and the vocational may reflect what the American sociologist David Reisman once called the 'snakelike academic procession', in which institutions at the head are models for those that follow. Yet we still need to know why this is the case and what the processes are for explaining emulation. The main explanation for institutional convergence may lie in the systems of competitive realism that are found in the 'managed markets' that now characterize higher education sectors. These orders of competitive realism are formed from the self-interested actions and interactions of their individual units – the universities – and especially their leaders. The dispersed and largely autonomous efforts of such leaders, in an age of increased executive and corporate responsibility for the wellbeing of universities, are not undertaken to create a university system with particular features but to advance the interests of their university (for survival, higher status) by the most effective means possible. The nature of the outcomes – the market order – is largely unintended, but it forms a compelling structure for all institutional leaders. A way to understand these processes is to adopt models from microeconomic theory that, in turn, have been applied in certain 'neorealist' accounts of international relations (Waltz, 1979).

## ▶ The system of competitive realism

The model that we use is an example of what is sometimes referred to as parsimonious. That is, it is simple and deliberately abstract, not because it is believed that empirical descriptions are necessarily exactly like that, but because it is heuristic – it enables us to explain phenomena better. As such, the theory does not purport to outline the characteristics of universities in every detail, or to describe all the individual motivations of institutional leaders, but to offer a structural account of why institutions act in the way that they do. The intentions of actors are assumed, not realistically described. The assumption is that universities seek to survive – in the best way possible – in a highly competitive, market-based environment where survival is not assured. This radical simplification, nonetheless, helps to provide a theoretically useful account of why institutional behaviour leads to uniformity and is at variance to the needs of the university system overall – defined as institutional diversity – as perceived by governments, and even by collective associations of universities themselves.

In referring to nation states in international political systems, Waltz (1979) observes that, out of their respective interactions, nation states develop a structure of an international order that rewards or sanctions actions that conform or not to what is required to succeed in the system. The game that a state has to win is defined by the structure that determines the kind of player who is likely to prosper. And those nations that succeed in the world order, with particular sets of characteristics, sometimes innovative, tend to be followed. The same is true for universities. In market-based, decentralized 'economies', individual university actions and interactions – acting for themselves, not 'the system' – create the market structures – often not intended – that then act back upon them as forces in their own right. These forces can be ignored, but only if an institution loses the will to live.

This is not to suggest that the act of survival explains every action by universities or that they are all the same. They differ in power and wealth but not necessarily in the tasks that they face. In market systems there is a tendency for like units to ally (the Russell Group of elite universities in the UK, for example), whereas in more government-directed systems the tendency is for unlike units to collaborate on the basis of functional differentiation, and this in turn is likely to increase the extent of their specialization. This collaboration is particularly noticeable if governments are able also in such state-categorized systems to sustain the legitimacy and standing of the respective sectors. In market systems, the question that universities ask themselves about collaboration is less whether all parties gain, but whether that particular university gains most. Too close or regular an interdependence between institutions in unitary, market-based systems generates vulnerability. In such circumstances individual universities cannot act for the system good, but can only compete and be independent, advancing only their own interests as rationally conceived. Coalitions thus constantly change.

In formally segmented systems, such as the binary one, universities and polytechnics are less likely to worry about comparative advantage – are they gaining more than their competitors – than absolute gain (are they getting anything from the arrangement). As such, they perceive few risks in collaborating on the basis of different strengths. In public resourcing terms, the coordination and other costs of market systems for governments are generally low but the risks of institutional failure are high, while in government-typified hierarchical systems the costs of funding and steering the system are high for the state, but the risks of institutional collapse are less.

The mechanism is self-help by largely autonomous institutions and their leaders in a highly uncertain world, not the creation by them of a preferred type of university system. Although universities vary in status, capabilities and attraction, functionally they are very similar. The resultant structure generated by the actions of individual universities rewards those that adapt most closely to what is required to succeed. And that is research-based status and strong market appeal to the best-performing students (generally from the higher social classes). In market systems universities do not become more specialized and expert at their particular niche (the underlying assumption behind market reforms of higher education over the last decade or so). Rather, they converge and try to become alike – mainly through the process of the newer, less prestigious universities seeking to emulate their so-called betters. Despite attempts to introduce even more selective policies (such as the concentrated funding following the last UK Research Assessment Exercise, and despite the extensive rise in nearly all universities of higher quality research), universities cover their bets. They become more alike. They try and do it all.

The reason derives from what Waltz (1979, p. 95) calls the 'socializing' logic of anarchy (market freedom). Failure to emulate the successful practices of the leading universities (that is, to conform to the logic of anarchic competition) leads to the opening up of a 'relative power gap' and consequently raised vulnerability. For example, in international relations, when Prussia defeated Austria (1866) and France (1870) through a superior form of military organization, other states were forced to emulate or to become vulnerable. Survival requires convergence or functional homogeneity. Strong universities are in effect 'power-makers' and can change the behaviour of weaker institutions, while the latter are 'power-takers' who have no choice but to follow the stronger universities. The picture that emerges is a positional one, based on power and prestige, not the individual characteristics of individual institutions. Emulation promotes the maintenance of the system by continuously seeking to reduce the power gap between universities, making it more difficult for one or more of the most powerful to effectively seize control of the whole system.

This strategy of emulation by the less well-ranked institutions, however, may be necessary but not sufficient for survival. Weaker universities (like states) generally need to ally to help balance or offset the strength of the leading universities – but not as a collective or system requirement, but in the interests of their own survival. In government-ordered and hierarchical systems, on the other hand, units become more specialized and more differentiated. And this differentiation leads to closer collaboration as specialization proceeds. In market conditions, however, networks form out of collective insecurity and the need for competitive edge. Consequently they are often temporary and opportunistic. As a result patterns of hierarchy tend to be stable and constant, and require revolutionary or dynamic innovative change to be fundamentally altered. And this persistence and continuity is explained by the structural influences of the market.

The problems experienced by UK governments in seeking to facilitate institutional diversity are in part largely of their own making. Their extension of the market to higher education militates against institutional differentiation. Rather than sustaining diversity, market forces encourage institutional uniformity. Conversely, diversity seems to require forms of government planning and direction that are now less fashionable. Trying rigidly to earmark institutions for particular functions is no longer possible. Relying on the market to create diversity is not effective. Nationally planned institutional diversity is best put to one side, and better the effort stepped up to secure innovation and collaboration in a competitive, insecure environment on the basis of institutional survival and self-interest. Competitiveness and (perhaps paradoxically) the collaborative ventures that competition stimulates are the keys to sustained innovation. And sustained innovation is a potential government policy that is achievable and consistent with their other market-based reforms. Away with diversity, and in with innovation!

## ▶ Conclusion: innovation and dynamic competition

In the current resource climate in the UK and elsewhere, although increased competition is generating defensive collaboration, it seems geared to achieving continuous cost reductions rather than to seeking genuine innovation (such as more effective applications of technology to university teaching). It is an example of what Gibbons (Chapter 5 of this volume) describes as 'static' as opposed to 'dynamic' competition. Static competition predominantly is concerned with achieving a recurrent process of efficiency gains through collaboration by organizations using similar technologies, methods and organizational design. That is, there is no technological or innovative breakthrough that gives one or more organizations a decisive advantage. There is no equivalent of the DVD player being introduced by one firm or collaborative venture to threaten others that specialize in cassette recorders; they compete either by reducing production and other costs for their particular cassette recorder, or through small variations in design and functionality. Static competition forms hierarchies between competing organizations, and organizations, because they are different, tend to gravitate around average practice. Sector leaders tend to be the largest units with the best means for achieving efficiency gains, from economies of scale, for example, which means that the 'market-takers' are in a continuous race to catch up. Hierarchies tend to be fixed and any institutional mobility generally is short-range between those in close proximity in market positioning.

In dynamic competition, however, units are in what Gibbons describes as 'search mode', seeking new technologies and methods to improve their competitive situation. It is a process of innovation and can be radical. Yet radical change is risky and collaboration is a means of reducing risk and uncertainty. This is not entirely eliminated as organizations have to join the networks that are most likely to deliver and they, in turn, have to have the capabilities to transform innovation into effective business forms. This may mean units switching alliances quite readily on the basis of creative and other evaluations. But because superior creative and business innovation does not necessarily lie with sector leaders, successful innovation is one means by which the structural underpinnings to an established hierarchy can be successfully challenged and overcome. And this potentially allows for radical repositioning in sector hierarchies. In time those companies outside the ranks of the successful innovators will need to adapt and to conform in order to survive.

Whether universities can collaborate in ways that develop the equivalent of the internal combustion engine or the DVD player, and generally move to a level of continuous value destruction and creation that characterizes capitalist economies generally, remains to be seen. But problem-based searches for innovation in the context of dynamic competition – which can then be resourcefully applied in pursuit of self-interested competitive edge – may be the only way in which established stratification may be challenged. The competitive, 'catch-up' nature of the new market environments, however, suggests that institutional diversity arising from such innovative processes is likely to prove a short-lived arrangement. But institutional hierarchical ordering does become more dynamically changing and is less fixed.

Of course, institutional diversity by itself may, or may not, be beneficial. We need to be clearer about what it is intended to produce and then examine whether the claims are validated. Moreover, the benefits may not flow from diversity so much as from the factors that produce some forms of diversity. For example, as Dill and Teixeira (2000) point out, innovations that generate diversity that is quite socially beneficial might include the extension of academic programmes to new student constituents, such as part-timers or those suffering from low forms of geographical or social accessibility to such programmes. Similarly public benefit and social value could follow from the inclusion of better forms of organization or implementing new factors of production, such as the application of information technology to learning and teaching where this reduces costs and enhances quality.

Where innovation as a generator of socially beneficial diversity becomes the focus, then policy emphasis should switch to examining the market and other conditions that are most likely to produce it. Some form of competitive structure would appear necessary for innovative behaviour, although its degree is open to question. Some argue, for example, that monopoly market conditions enable organizations to engage in secure investment in, say, new products, while others have pointed to the benefits of more competitive market conditions, but with elements of regulatory protection (such as fixed periods of patenting protection) to enable institutions to obtain reasonable advantage from their risk-taking. After all, if innovations are capable of being adopted by others too easily, with virtually all the costs and risks taken by the innovator, then universities will feel disinclined to take such routes. Consequently the regulatory as well as other market factors that are most likely to result in both publicly and corporately advantageous innovations, which in turn may lead to more dynamic, more diverse, and less concretely stratified university systems, would appear well worthy of sustained analysis.

University systems would become more competitive and creative, and the relative rankings of universities more fluid, if innovation, rather than mergers or functional diversity, was given greater public funding and incentives. Support for groups of universities seeking step-change leaps in technology, organization, delivery and so on would improve the system, result in more satisfied clients and keep everyone on their toes. The increased competitiveness of the system that would follow would, in turn, create a greater momentum for innovation and competitive advantage. The pursuit of planned diversity – despite its iconic standing in university systems worldwide – is a chimera that may be best put away in favour of regulatory and market incentives for innovative risk-taking.

# 7 Borderless Higher Education

*Svava Bjarnason*

## ▶ Introduction

The past decades have seen an increasing challenge to the conventional model of the university as found in Humboldt and Newman and as based firmly in the traditions of research and liberal education. New providers of higher education are emerging, increasingly privately owned and operating 'for profit', sometimes using the title 'university', and often delivering across distances and territories with the help of the latest developments in communication and information technologies. All this helps to test the national predominance of the longer-established universities. There is an increasing permeability of borders in higher education, both geographical and conceptual, which results in borders that are less strongly delineated than before. These new developments are inevitably changing the scope and scale of higher education. Growth in 'borderless' higher education means that new configurations and partnerships are emerging. In many cases these increase the capacity to meet the growing demand for higher education for an increasing proportion of the population, often in the absence of public funds.

Drivers of these developments include (but are certainly not limited to) the growth of knowledge-based economies and the recognition by governments that increased human capital investment is required for national competitiveness, the individual desire for good employment and social mobility, and an increasing emphasis by employees on the need for lifelong learning. These factors, coupled with recent developments in the use of new technologies, have provided major impetus to provide additional capacity to reach the growing pool of potential learners. As we shall see, increasingly such provision seeks to shake off the inconveniences and limitations of space and place.

The perception that governments are motivated to seek increased investment in tertiary education to build the knowledge base of their economies in order to sustain economic development rests on an economic perspective that is supported by the World Bank in a recent report on higher education (2002). This posits that knowledge is one of the most important motors of economic growth in emerging economies and that universities have pivotal roles in creating the fundamentals for the widespread and continuous learning that all societies now need in order to be relatively prosperous. The report goes so far as to enjoin governments in developing countries to keep the regulatory regimes inhibiting virtual and private providers to a minimum and encourages the establishment of networks with foreign-accredited public and private institutions.

Demographic trends in many western countries reveal considerable growth in the numbers comprising the 'third age' – men and women over the age of 50 who are living another 20 to 30 years and who are both mentally and physically active. This, coupled with the trend for employees to change career paths more frequently in the span of a working life, bringing the requirement for constant skills upgrading and retraining, encourages governments to promote programmes that facilitate greater participation in lifelong learning.

The growth in information and communications technologies (ICT), and enhanced abilities to deliver higher education to more people over wider distances, have provided particularly useful means for both universities and new providers to satisfy increasing demand. But there is also considerable experimentation underway, apart from that requiring major technological investment, that reflects a more dynamic and innovative sector and which is helping to change some of the conventions and confines of higher education at the turn of the twenty-first century.

This chapter illustrates some of the developments in this increasingly 'borderless' terrain. It begins by exploring the current 'market' for higher education and goes on to suggest some possible scenarios. It explores current activities from a number of different perspectives, including types of providers, geography, and the nature of new models of collaboration. The conclusion provides an analysis of the relative impact of borderless ventures and an exploration of their implications for universities.

## ▶ Borderless(ness)

The term 'borderless education' was coined by a team of Australian researchers that undertook one of the first studies of the new media and its implications for higher education (Cunningham *et al.*, 1998). These themes were explored further in 1999 when the Australian Department for Education, Training and Youth Affairs (DETYA), and the (then) Committee of Vice Chancellors and Principals (CVCP) in the UK, now Universities UK, commissioned two separate studies to look more closely at the growth and role of new higher education providers in the context of the increasing use of new technologies to deliver across large distances (Cunningham *et al.*, 2000; CVCP, 2000).

The immediate image that the term 'borderless' evokes is a lack of geographical borders, or at least easy and regular mobility across them. Yet it embodies a much broader conceptualization. The nature of 'borderless' higher education, as developed in the aforementioned studies, encompasses a range of borders that are becoming increasingly permeable or artificial. These include those of:

* *time*, as learning opportunities are increasingly available 24 hours-a-day, seven days a week. Technologies enable learners to participate in both synchronous and asynchronous learning activities, with colleagues located almost anywhere in the world;
* *place*, as traditional modes of distance learning, often enhanced by technology, provide learners with the opportunity to study regardless of their physical location. This includes transients such as serving members of the armed forces, or business people travelling the globe, and what the Australian team termed 'learners earner', individuals who study at home after their workday ends; and
* *level*, with the boundaries between education and training, and between universities and colleges, becoming increasingly blurred. Courses leading to degrees are being taught in institutions other than universities (such as further education colleges in the UK, and vocational education and training colleges in Australia), while continuing professional development (CPD) courses are equally gaining market share (in the new trade lexicon) as professional bodies increasingly require their member practitioners to keep abreast of new methods and approaches.

These borders, and others, are under pressure from a myriad of forces, many driven by the advance of new technologies and the potential that they bring for changing methods and modes of delivery. Influences for change also arise from the quickening processes of internationalization and globalization, as outlined in previous chapters. These include an ever-increasing notion of an international higher education 'marketplace', and easier student and academic mobility. As well, the growth of supranational forms of governance, such as found in the European Union (EU) or through the operations of bodies such as the WTO, are leading to greater interest by governmental policy-makers in coordinating regulatory and accreditation regimes across nations, and in promoting international collaboration between universities.

These developments are challenging the prominence of the conventional universities in this increasingly diverse global marketplace. Publishing houses, and private, 'for-profit', corporate and virtual universities, are but some of the new types of providers actively trying to enter the higher education market.

## ▶ The global higher education 'market'

The idea that education does not lend itself to being traded or considered a commodity is clearly increasingly confounded by evidence that it is fuelling a growth market in education services. These activities are not confined to new commercial providers, as many more traditional universities are very active in international 'trade'. Professor Frank Newman, Director of the Futures Project at Brown University in the US, has argued with Courturier that:

> Higher education has become far more competitive, shaped more by the market, less by regulation . . . Frustrated by the slow pace of change, policymakers no longer feel the need to protect institutions from competition, turning instead to the power of market forces as the lever needed to reform higher education . . . The key is finding policy solutions that help steer the market in ways that benefit society and serve the greater public good. (Newman and Courturier, 2002)

It is in this context of competition and change that borderless developments are located. Governments and university leaders increasingly are turning their attention to a more global higher education market, both to build capacity within their countries when public domestic higher education is financially constrained, and as a tradable export opportunity.

This section presents an overview of the various approaches and activities that traditional institutions are engaged in internationally. The four modes of delivery used in the General Agreement on Trade in Services (GATS) framework (see Chapter 4 for a more detailed discussion) are helpful here. Exploring the nature of borderlessness through these four modes provides particular insight into the crossing of geographical borders. It also outlines the different types of collaborative ventures that are emerging (particularly in establishing a commercial presence abroad) and which are helping to blur the line between education and training.

### Mode 1: Cross-border supply

This mode encompasses distance learning and the use of new technologies where the learners remain static and the provision crosses the borders. A report by the US firm Eduventures indicates that fully online distance learning provision is growing substantially in the US, generating over US $1.75

billion in tuition fee revenue in 2002 (Gallagher and Newman, 2002). The percentage of total postsecondary enrolments of students learning wholly online (in the US) are projected to be over 5 per cent by 2005, representing over US $4 billion in revenue. Although we are referring to US developments here, other countries are also beginning to witness rising proportions.

Of course, distance education has a very long and established track record, although technological developments have given it enhanced capability and prestige. As well as conventional universities and their new challengers another type can be found. These are the 'global mega-universities' and include the large 'traditional' distance learning universities, such as the Open University in the UK, the China TV University, and the Indira Gandhi National University in India (Daniel, 1996). These institutions attract over a million students, mostly studying in the country in which the institution is located, but increasingly attracting students from a wider global diaspora.

**Mode 2: Consumption abroad**

Historically the notion of 'borderless education' conjures up a picture of the wandering scholar or the internationally mobile student. Student mobility still comprises the largest and most financially lucrative mode of borderless provision. Travelling to study abroad is generally accepted as an integral aspect of the higher education experience. A recent Australian study suggests that global demand for international students is set to rise from 1.8 million in 2000 to 7 million students in 2025 – a nearly fourfold increase (Bohm *et al.*, 2002). Asia is the key contributor to this growth (led by China and India), representing 70 per cent of demand in 2025 as compared to 27 per cent in 2000. European student numbers are estimated to be relatively constant, which suggests a global market share decline from 32 per cent to 13 per cent.

National and supranational governments provide considerable sums of financial support to facilitate student mobility (see Chapter 2 on the European schemes). One of the largest European programmes is ERASMUS, which contributed to the mobility of over 100,000 students in 2002, supported by a budget of 200 million euros. A scheme announced in 2002 aims to bring non-European international students into Europe; ERASMUS WORLDWIDE (with 200 million euros for 2004/8) is projected to have 2000 students travelling to Europe by 2004 on its mobility scheme. Consumption abroad, through the economic multiplier effect, makes a significant contribution to the local economies of host countries, while some students also remain after study and contribute as employees.

**Mode 3: Commercial presence**

In this mode of supply, providers establish a physical presence in another country through a variety of different means, such as branch campuses or through partnerships with local providers. In a recent study, IDP Australia presents a typology of the different types of programmes that reflect the various organizational structures adopted in these situations (Adams, 1998). These include:

- *twinning*, where an institution offers a qualification in conjunction with a local provider situated in the receiving country. The 'twin' organization might be a private provider, professional body or another institution offering tertiary education (university or college level);
- *franchising*, with an offshore institution effectively licensing the in-country provider to provide a programme of study, which is quality assured by the offshore institution;
- *offshore or branch campuses*, where the offshore institution sets up a physical presence in the host country and seeks formal accreditation status, either in their own right, or in partnership with a local provider;
- *moderated programmes*, where a local institution offers a programme developed by academics in a local institution which is then quality assured by an offshore university;
- *joint awards*, which are courses or degrees recognized by at least two institutions generally located in two different countries; and
- *distance learning*, particularly in a more traditional model of distance learning which uses print-based material or satellite or video, where a local partner provides both a level of learner support and the basis of the commercial presence.

Establishing actual numbers of student enrolments represented by these different models of commercial presence on a global basis is difficult. IDP Australia statistics for 2002 suggest that offshore enrolments have increased 13.9 per cent against the previous year, which is the international mode with the highest growth among Australian universities. Of the approximately 150,000 international students enrolled in Australian universities, 28.6 per cent are studying at offshore campuses and 6.9 per cent are enrolled in distance learning programmes.

## Mode 4: Presence of natural persons

This (rather unfortunately titled) mode of supply refers to those instances where the academic travels to the location in question to provide an educational service. The peripatetic academic model is certainly not new. However, this mode is one that may well be set to gain momentum. In the next decade a generation of professors and senior academics will retire and will need to be replaced. In the absence of sufficient domestic supply of academically qualified staff, in subjects such as mathematics and economics particularly, where the numbers undertaking doctorates is declining quite rapidly, some countries will seek to recruit from abroad (or more so than currently is the case).

An increased international mobility of academics inevitably will contribute to the plight of many developing countries, by drawing their best academics to richer countries. A number of developed countries also will be at risk of losing their brightest and best as employment terms and conditions in other countries, particularly the US, look increasingly attractive. Governments will need to develop robust policies to respond to these pressures and to ensure that there are sufficient numbers of qualified academics to meet national needs. In Canada, for example, the government has introduced a programme called the 'Canada Research Chairs' with CA $900 million invested. This programme has a target of 2000 new research chairs and total investment of $9 billion by 2010, with matching private sector funding. It is likely to have considerable impact in enticing overseas academics.

The current negotiations under the GATS process will force the hand of many governments and university leaders to clearly articulate a position on policies and strategies to either facilitate or deter international mobility and educational trade. A 'one size fits all' approach will not suffice internationally as each nation state will need to determine the capacity of its current providers to meet perceived future education needs. Policies determined in this framework will have considerable impact on how the sector continues to develop – and how borderless it will become.

▶ **Future scenarios**

If one looked into the future to suggest how increasing globalization and trade in education services might change the higher education terrain – what might we see?

We can identify four possible scenarios (Middlehurst and Bjarnason, 2001). These combine a number of different elements, such as variations in the type of provider; the type of course provided; quality assurance mechanisms; and business models (such as, is it for-, or not, for-profit).

These scenarios are purposely provocative and value-laden. They reflect in part many of the concerns raised against the marketization and globalization of higher education, and portray four fairly distinct outcomes extrapolated from current developments. They are presented here as a 'point of departure' from which the various themes in the rest of the chapter are developed.

## Scenario One – Invaders' triumph

In this scenario, large and dominant foreign players seek entry to, and increased share of, higher education markets globally. These 'higher learning businesses' originate primarily in the United States, the UK and Australia and take a variety of forms. Some of these businesses are purely commercial operations, others are hybrid consortia with public and commercial elements, and others are existing universities expanding their online and distance education. On the horizon are other for-profit players offering innovative forms of education.

These foreign players are targeting the profitable sections of global markets: undergraduate and postgraduate courses in business, healthcare, engineering and information technology, and also the lucrative CPD markets where employers will absorb the costs. These organizations offer face-to-face teaching at private campuses/centres in many regions, close to cities, or via online learning.

## Scenario Two – Trojan horse

Scenario Two sees universities and colleges from outside the country/region seeking partnerships with local providers. The content of programmes is designed abroad, but delivery of teaching and support of students is provided by local institutions. Examinations are online or externally organized. Online options are also available for the delivery of teaching and support of students through the international 'e-university', set up as a joint venture between three large western countries, involving universities from these countries, and with funding support from governments and venture capital from the private sector.

Programmes cover the full range of university curricula, some of which are supplied by professional institutions and large companies. Many students are paying high fees for programmes that are perceived to have international employment value.

## Scenario Three – Community champions

An international publishing company, with government and international donor support, has invested in its country's local and regional distance-learning universities to enable them to extend the range of their technologies and pedagogy to meet the needs of their areas. This enables a new model to be developed of a network of community centres, located in villages and towns, close to hospitals, schools and other local amenities.

Distinctions between different levels of education have become less relevant; the motivation is to encourage as many people as possible into learning. Friendly learning guides assist individuals to access what they require and to plan individual programmes. Specialist guides are employed and can be reached in different ways; face-to-face, through call centres or online. Students and professional people from other countries are also welcomed as learning guides alongside the national ones and this has created innovative opportunities for international collaboration (as well as a research agenda on intercultural and intergenerational learning). Community projects often form a vehicle for learning. The Centre is open 24 hours a day, all year.

**Scenario Four – Explorers international**
Professional associations (in nursing, IT, teacher education and business in particular) have joined together across national boundaries to establish a new educational consortium. The consortium provides modules on relevant subjects (taught either in longer programmes or short modules) drawn from several sources. Students (now called associates) can study in several different countries if they are seeking face-to-face tuition and work-related learning in different cultural contexts.

Some of these professional associations provide their own accreditation, while others partner with universities for accreditation purposes. The primary target for these programmes are managers, from both the private and public sectors, who need to broaden their experience and who are seeking portable international qualifications.

While these scenarios are clearly fictional in nature, current developments provide ample illustration as to the potential viability of each. The following sections of this chapter provide examples of some of the different types of provider currently active in the borderless higher education terrain and emerging configurations as new collaborative ventures unfold.

## ▶ New providers

The nature of a changing terrain is that the players effecting change are not necessarily those one might expect. Some are quite familiar and are accepted as legitimate and even benevolent, while others are new, rather different, still evolving in their role, and tend to be viewed by governments and other institutions with scepticism. The UK Business of Borderless Education report (CVCP, 2000) identified a four-fold classification of higher education providers:

1. public;
2. private, not-for-profit;
3. private, for-profit; and
4. corporate

*Public education providers* are those institutions that have predominantly been funded from the public purse. As we have noted in previous chapters, the extent and current trajectory of such funding varies between countries with different state traditions, as does the extent of broader university–state relationships. Such providers will include a broad range of tertiary institutions, including colleges, polytechnics and universities.

*Private not-for-profit providers* have existed for many years, often founded by social elites or religions for cultural reasons. They generally do not receive much, if anything, of public subsidies and depend primarily on tuition fees, as well as church, corporate or philanthropic support. Often they are relatively small institutions, focusing on a very limited spread of disciplines. Private not-for-profits are particularly prevalent in the United States, where much larger and more prestigious institutions of this type, such as Harvard, can be found.

*Private for-profit institutions* constitute a relatively recent model, but one that is proliferating globally – particularly in central and eastern Europe, some African countries, and in South America. The private for-profit institutions come in a number of different guises, from small single discipline-based institutions, to those with very large multidisciplinary multi-campuses (such as the University of Phoenix in the US). In a recent paper, Levy describes the latter as forming education 'chains', where a provider duplicates a profitable venture in one place to a variety of geographical locations, using a common curricula and structure (Levy, 2003).

In some instances both public and private not-for-profit providers can also operate as for-profit providers, particularly when they establish programmes abroad. This particular approach has provided some rather unusual partnerships, such as large public providers partnering with smaller colleges overseas. Levy (2003, p. 8) argues that such examples provide evidence of a win/win situation for the institutions, students and governments:

> The foreign institution expands its reach geographically and often socio-economically and garners tuition [while] the local private college gains a legitimizing link, curriculum, and the ability to offer a diploma or degree that may lack state recognition but can have job-market or international value.

*Corporate universities* do not fit easily into any of the previous three categories as they often offer courses solely to their employees and not the general public. However, they have gained considerable momentum since the late 1980s (primarily in the US), and have spread globally over the past decade.

Taylor and Paton (2002) identify four models of the corporate university. They are structured on essentially two axes: at one end the emphasis is on training company staff in basic skills and the necessary knowledge to undertake their work roles, while at the other end the focus is on a higher level of education (such as the Masters of Business Administration, or MBA), and may even involve research activities. The first axis lends itself more to modes of delivery utilizing distance and e-learning, and the other more to campus-based delivery.

The corporate 'university' adds to overall capacity to meet the increasing demands of the knowledge economy and lifelong learning, but does so primarily through organizational structures that differ considerably from the forms found in conventional universities (even though the latter are beginning to change towards more corporate arrangements). Increasingly the larger corporate universities are partnering with a wide range of other educational providers – both public and private, and including traditional universities.

## ► Competitors and collaborators

A number of the so-called 'new' providers that have emerged as key players in borderless higher education provision on closer inspection appear not so new after all. In fact, some have been involved over a number of years, but are beginning to forge new relationships with more traditional providers. These include publishing houses, specialist content providers, education brokers and portals, as well as corporate universities. Many are beginning to forge new relationships with more traditional deliverers.

Some of these new providers have made considerable progress in collaborating with existing higher education institutions while others might well be considered as more direct competitors. It will be useful at this juncture to outline the range of activities and roles undertaken by various providers, and to follow with specific examples of particular players and partnerships.

### Publishing houses

Publishing houses are longstanding collaborators with higher education, but are increasingly becoming competitors. At the very least, their relationship with the traditional university is changing. Large media firms have begun to develop a wide range of learning opportunities, both in-house and in collaboration with universities and other educational organizations. In the last five years, a small number of major publishing houses have developed considerable capacity in-house for delivering (independently and in collaboration) higher education provision. Indeed, one publishing company (Harcourt) set out to establish itself as a virtual university only to eventually fail in the endeavour and to be taken over by another publisher.

The nature of collaboration and competition between universities and the publishing houses varies. Some have involved leveraging the international distribution chains of the houses to market existing university provision more globally; others have been established through partnerships that enable the houses to essentially gain accreditation in partnership with a university for the development of curricula-based resources (and copyrights) that the publishers hold. In other cases the partnerships with universities are more deep-seated and include jointly developing curricula and programmes that can be easily marketed online, thus reaching beyond the traditional span of either organization. Some publishers choose to remain primarily as repositories of text and artefact that provide equitable access to learners as a public good. These business models are not mutually exclusive, and indeed some publishing houses operate on a number of different levels. The important point is that a small number of publishing houses are becoming increasingly ubiquitous in their partnerships with higher education institutions and are beginning to exert considerable influence on the sector globally.

## Brokers

Brokers of educational services are also appearing in the mix of new providers, and also as partners with traditional higher education institutions. There are essentially three different types of educational broker. The first is well-established and facilitates more traditional distance learning activities. This includes brokers that provide a central marketing and distribution location for a wide range of providers to offer distance-learning courses. These brokers are often regional or national in scope and support the educational experiences of learners in large countries with small and dispersed populations (such as in Australia and Canada). Learners are able to identify the level of courses available as well as to determine more about the kind of institutions offering them.

The second type builds on the framework of the first, but extends its activities in a more proactive and entrepreneurial manner. Brokers here act on behalf of the institutions, often by actively marketing courses internationally. In some instances, brokers of this type will identify an international market for a particular programme that is not currently on offer from participating institutions and will then commission its development, sometimes to meet the needs of a specific international 'client'. The 'client' in this instance is often a corporate body with a requirement for a bespoke course for small niche or individual use that would not be economic for them to develop alone.

The third type of broker provides a hybrid of services that includes not only access to courses but also a wide range of services to both institution and learner. These service often include:

- access to (often customized) learning platforms;
- assessment services;
- market data;
- technology support in developing appropriate materials;
- training for personnel involved in marketing, admissions and technical support; and
- customer service for learners often situated in dispersed locations.

### Specialist content providers

Specialist content providers represent a relatively new area of growth as providers of higher education. Often based on subject or disciplinary themes, primarily in information technology, these companies provide discrete packages of content that are often considered as at the leading edge. The quantity of the content provided varies considerably, from short-term training courses (taking a matter of hours), to long-term programmes of study extending over years. The smaller, discrete, elements are generally added to existing curricula on programmes of study offered by their traditional university partners. Longer-term programmes developed by the specialist content provider usually stand on their own, with a recognized certificate by the company in question.

This is certainly not an exhaustive representation of the new providers currently active in borderless higher education. Rather it provides an illustration of the range of activities of some of the major players that have emerged to challenge the primacy of traditional institutions. To understand the implications of these developments more clearly, it is necessary to have an understanding of how new and traditional providers are coming together to change the educational landscape globally.

### ▶ Global collaborators

Numerous examples could be selected to exemplify the scope and nature of global collaboration in higher education. The following provides working examples that illustrate different modes of services (based on the GATS framework) as well as different models of delivery (online, branch campuses and so on).

Some caution in our approach is necessary. There is often a certain amount of 'hype' involved in an announcement of a new and potentially exciting partnership or offering in the area of borderless education. Many of the activities of the new providers are as yet unproven, as a service, product or venture. Indeed there are numerous examples of high profile ventures that have proved unworkable (for a variety of reasons) and that have not stood the test of time (even for a rather short period). One such company – Fathom – ceased trading in early 2003, although it started out with large ambitions and a exemplary set of partners.

The motivations of partners behind collaborative ventures vary widely. Examination of the stated mission, aims and objectives of some of the leading international networks or consortia reveals the following key objectives:

- to build internationalization into the educational experience through student and academic exchange programmes and curriculum change;
- to create a critical mass of expertise in particular areas of research or in teaching a particular discipline;
- to widen access to higher learning locally, regionally, nationally and internationally;
- to learn from partners, either through benchmarking good practice or from experience;
- to pool resources and knowledge; and
- to assist in developing capacity for higher education in poorer countries.

However, further aims and objectives, which are not made explicit in the documentation in the public domain, might equally include:

- leveraging existing 'brands' globally and marketing a strong national reputation internationally;
- making an economic return;
- gaining the necessary accreditation powers or recognition if the provider is not an accredited entity; and
- bypassing regulatory issues in other countries by partnering with a recognized or accredited institution.

### Universitas 21 and U21 Global

*Universitas 21* is one of the most prestigious of the international consortia in borderless higher education. It originated in 1997 as an international network of research-intensive universities and has worked methodically toward the development of a range of activities based on collaboration, collegiality and entrepreneurialism. The partner institutions are from Europe, east Asia, North America, Australia and New Zealand (see below). Student exchanges, fellowships for teachers, researchers and administrators, and the establishment of a 'libraries group', are examples of the fairly traditional approach taken in its early years. However, since 2000 there have been more innovative developments, such as the creation of a shared curriculum in accountancy and with plans to extend the approach into architecture and teacher training.

*Universitas 21* recently has entered into online learning with the formation of *U21 Global*. This new venture is a partnership with a large Canadian-based company, Thomson Corporation, and has a distinctive business model, with Thomson taking responsibility for marketing programmes, as well as for a large proportion of curriculum development and learner support. Partners in this venture include:

*Europe*
- University of Birmingham
- University of Edinburgh
- University of Glasgow
- University of Nottingham

*North America*
- McGill University
- University of British Columbia
- University of Virginia

*Asia*
- National University of Singapore
- University of Hong Kong
- Peking University
- Fudan University

*Australia/New Zealand*
- University of Melbourne
- University of New South Wales
- University of Queensland
- University of Auckland

*Universitas 21* represents what might be considered a fairly traditional alliance between well-established, traditional research-led universities. However, the *U21 Global* arm looks much more borderless and extends the traditional university model in quite novel ways through the partnership with Thomson Corporation. The approach goes further than most other university–media/publishing partnerships in which, as we noted above, the added-value of the latter companies is their global marketing reach and strong content resources. The very hands-on approach from Thomson, developing a high proportion of curriculum content, has caused some disquiet among the original partners of *Universitas 21*, with academic staff and students expressing concerns over quality assurance and the risk of reputational degradation for participating institutions. *U21 Global's* response has been to create *U21 Pedagogica*, an in-house quality assurance mechanism with representatives drawn from the major partners, a relatively unique feature of the current terrain of borderless developments. As outlined in Chapter 4 on regulatory issues, recognition and accreditation are critical in global higher education, and without it, ventures will have difficulty in surviving. An interesting speculation generated by the development of *U21 Pedagogica* is whether it will float away to become a lead player in the international domain of quality assurance agencies, or whether it will remain harnessed to its parent.

## NextEd

Founded in 1998 and based in Hong Kong (now also in Sydney), *NextEd* represents yet another model of collaboration within the world of borderless higher education. Its business model is different again from that of *Universitas 21*, as *NextEd's* primary function is that of broker, although it has some novel features. *NextEd's* partners are categorized into three types: education partners; technology partners; and associate partners. These include private and public education institutions, corporate and professional associations, and training organizations. Its location is also its strength – located near the Asian market and focusing on that market ensures that it brings a very strong competitive knowledge to any partnership concerned with that region.

In its primary role as broker, *NextEd* provides a number of services, including training, customer services, and technological design and support. Intimate knowledge of the fast-developing Asian market, and their Hong Kong and Sydney locations, makes them ideally suited to broker for Australian and New Zealand universities in particular. It has enjoyed a particularly strong relationship with one of the world leaders in technology-supported distance education on a global scale, the University of Southern Queensland. *NextEd* also serves as the key resource for the Global University Alliance, which has participating universities in Canada, New Zealand, the US, the Netherlands, the UK and Australia.

*NextEd's* 'associate partners' reflect a somewhat different mix, including two large English language training organizations (both based in the US), as well as with Internet education portals in China (one of which is a commercial arm of Peking University), the China–Australia Chamber of Commerce, and the publisher of the largest English language newspaper in China. *NextEd's* technology partners include Blackboard, which is widely acknowledged as one of the leading providers of educational learning platforms globally, and Impart Corporation, a supporter of the Instructional Management System (IMS) that is endeavouring to work toward standard guidelines and tools to aid in the management and access of online learning materials and environments.

## NIIT and ITT

This collaborative effort also features relatively unique elements. First, one of the partners is located in India and the other in the US – in many of the current global partnerships the collaborators are primarily western institutions with a view to creating reach into the Indian or Asian markets. A second unusual element is that this partnership involves a specialist content provider from Asia. Third, it has secured an articulation and credit transfer agreement with an accredited for-profit US institution, and has university partners in Australia, the US, the UK and New Zealand.

*NIIT* is one of India's leading software and information technology companies, and it has developed a two-year certificate and diploma programme that is offered through some 3000 education centres in 28 countries. The certification is, however, not recognized by the Indian government and therefore has little academic standing in that country. Partnerships with accredited institutions are critical therefore for *NIIT* graduates to gain international academic recognition for their primarily vocational, sector-relevant, studies. As a result, *NIIT* has established relationships with the University of Canberra in Australia, Auckland Institute of Studies in New Zealand, the University of Sunderland in the UK and Southern New Hampshire University in the US, which enables graduates from *NIIT* to gain credit for their studies from the institutions in question. The agreement with the four universities requires that students travel to the member institutions in order to complete their degrees.

*NIIT* recently announced a new partnership with *ITT* Educational Services, a for-profit provider in the US, which will enable students to complete their studies wholly online. This offers significantly increased flexibility for students who are able to gain international accreditation without the added cost of overseas study. *ITT* Education Services operates over 70 centres in 28 states, and accounted for 15.2 per cent of all electronic and electronic-related bachelor degrees awarded in the United States in 1999–2000.

**Fathom**
Based in the United States at Columbia University in New York, Fathom represented one of the most eclectic consortia in the borderless territory. Its mission was (at least) two-fold: to provide public access to a wealth of resources and to create opportunities for learners to access accredited courses. Fathom positioned itself as a knowledge network linking a global community of learners with educational and cultural resources.

As a founding partner of Fathom, Columbia University saw its development as one element of a three-strand University strategy aimed at bringing technology into higher education more widely through knowledge development and management, pedagogy, and delivery. However, Columbia announced that Fathom would cease trading in April 2003.

The business model was complex. As a corporate entity Fathom played a variety of roles as:

- *broker* for a wide range of courses, both free (non-accredited) and available on a fee-paying basis (accredited by the respective institutions);
- *producer* of e-learning materials, drawing on an extensive resource of graphic design professional and course production;
- *portal* for a variety of electronic-based learning opportunities; and
- as a *quality assurance body*, through the Fathom Academic Council.

Members of the consortium included:

*US*
- Columbia University
- The University of Chicago
- The University of Michigan
- Woods Hole Oceanographic Institution
- The RAND Corporation
- The New York Public Library

*UK*
- Cambridge University Press
- The London School of Economics
- The British Museum
- The Victoria and Albert Museum
- The Natural History Museum
- The British Library

This large group was distinct from Fathom's original partners who represented an equally diverse group, including an international television and media provider (BBC Worldwide), corporate eLearning providers (Smart-Force), online publishers (XanEdu), as well as a number of more traditional universities in the US and Canada, such as the University of British Columbia, and the University of California at Los Angeles. Other partners included the Elderhostel organization and the American Association of Retired Persons.

Perhaps tellingly, the glossy publication showcasing Columbia's digital media initiatives (of which Fathom was one), suggested that the initiative 'brings teaching tools, business opportunities and more exposure for Columbia faculty', which begs the question of what its real objective was – to provide a unique resource of materials for lifelong learning opportunities, or to promote Columbia's research profile and to raise income? These cross-purposes may have proved too difficult to sustain.

In concluding this section we note a significant preponderance of partners located in three countries: the US, the UK and Australia. There are exceptions to this trend with an increase in Asian partners in China, Singapore and Hong Kong. The continental European university system is underrepresented in this analysis – probably because the market mostly demands English language instruction, and Continental institutions are only slowly moving in this direction.

However, analysing the physical location of the institutions does not provide the whole picture, as an important issue is whether the alliances are there principally to facilitate exchanges of people and information between the partners (who, for the most part, are drawn from western developed countries), or whether their purpose is to access a global market with partners located in widely dispersed territories.

Our discussion of borderless developments and organizations is not exhaustive, not least because we are dealing with a fast-moving area. There are a growing number of national e-university ventures, for example, that are being developed, some with national delivery aims (as in Finland), and others with international objectives (such as UKeUniversities Worldwide). There are also large private providers, such as the Apollo Group International and University of Phoenix Online, which are purposefully targeting growth in developing countries such as India and Brazil.

## ▶ Conclusions: future directions for borderless higher education

This chapter has set out to illustrate that the boundaries of higher education are becoming more porous as traditional constraints, such as those of territory (the physical and national location of the learner and teacher) and levels of study (whether technical, vocational and higher, for example), are becoming less easy to demarcate rigidly. New forms and organization for providing higher education are appearing to challenge the monopoly positions of the longer-standing universities. An increasingly heterogeneous landscape is beginning to appear. These developments help to raise questions such as 'what constitutes *higher* education' and ultimately 'does it matter'?

The borderless developments described here indicate that conventional university domains and privileges are coming under challenge, if not – yet – under siege. The US management pundit, Peter Drucker, argues that the death knell may well be ringing for universities, and that 'thirty years from now the big university campuses will be relics. Universities won't survive' (Drucker, 1997, p. 127). However, as pointed out in earlier chapters, universities have been around for at least 900 years, even if most are more modern creations, and to suggest that as institutions they will cease to exist within decades is, perhaps, precipitous. They may well change – some even dramatically – but not beyond recognition.

Developments in borderless education provide both opportunities and threats for existing conventional providers. The four scenarios outlined above provide glimpses of how new configurations of higher education might come together to meet the needs of both governments and learners, and they indicate both competition and collaboration between new and old providers as possible options.

It is clear, however, that countries and higher education institutions will need to be innovative and proactive to seize opportunities. A senior education consultant from the World Bank suggests:

> While there is no rigid blueprint for all countries and institutions, a common prerequisite may be the need to formulate a clear vision of how the higher education system can effectively contribute to the development of each country and how each institution elects to evolve within that system. (Salmi, 2000)

Governments across the world recognize the need to have an educated population to help to create a just society and to drive their economic engines. However, the financial resources to build the required infrastructure and to support the educational processes do not always exist, particularly in the developing countries and in other countries in transition.

Indeed, there is a risk that in many of the developed countries the unit of resource for many universities is shrinking to the point that they must increasingly look to other sources of income to cross-subsidize and underwrite their activities. This pressure on governments to expand higher education is providing increased opportunities for new (often private and for-profit) higher education providers as a means of enhancing domestic capacity, without excessive requirements for public expenditure. A number of developing countries, for example, offer wide-ranging proposals for liberalization under the current GATS round as a means of easing the way for foreign education providers to operate within their territories.

The purposes underlying an institution's involvement in borderless activities can vary. Commercial considerations may be accompanied by more egalitarian and academic ones that are regarded as more acceptable to traditional academic values, such as to enhance research exchanges, to expose academics and students to a wider body of international knowledge and experience, or to help build institutional capacity in developing countries, and so on. These positions are undoubtedly held sincerely, although it is not always easy to see how thoroughgoing they are in practice, or to overlook the financial advantages that often accrue to institutions from engagement in the borderless business.

An example of egalitarianism, and an institutional desire to provide open and free access to a body of knowledge on a global basis, is the MIT Open-CourseWare project. It was established in 1999 with the express aim of making the MIT course materials used at both undergraduate and postgraduate levels available without charge. Although not offering MIT awards, the project, with US$11 million start-up funds from two US philanthropic bodies, provides access to technology-enhanced course materials that can be utilized by a wide number of academics and students, and as such it may justify its purpose of 'democratizing and transforming [the] power of education'. Two points may need to be made. First, the project indicates that what universities possess that is most valued, by both students and by many of the new borderless providers, is the ability (often a protected monopoly capacity) to make degree awards (rather than the possession of course material as such). Second, in recognition of this first point, MIT may be smart to use the free distribution of material as a good promotional mechanism that eventually may enable it to maintain or enhance the competitive advantage of the real 'product' that is sells, namely its degree awards.

A further (not inconsiderable) inequity in the MIT approach is that the distributable resource is wholly technology based and there exists tremendous disparities between countries and social groups in obtaining access to communication and information technologies. The recent World Bank (2002) report alluded to earlier indicates that developing countries have just 5.9 per cent of the world's Internet hosts and over 80 per cent of its population. North America, however, has 65.3 per cent of the world's Internet hosts but just 5.1 per cent of the population.

Among other concerns raised by the development of borderless education we can also include the following:

- Will national governments, in looking to the new borderless providers to expand capacity without a call on the public purse, adequately regulate them?
- Are institutions able to transform their structures and processes in order to use technology and online learning most effectively in enhancing student (and staff) learning experiences, whether on a commercial, borderless or conventional basis?
- Will the new borderless providers simply 'cherry pick' the most popular and lucrative subject areas, and operate on the lowest cost basis possible, without adequate libraries or research activity, and thus threaten quality?
- Will international collaborative ventures really bring new resources for institutions, and opportunities for learners, that might not otherwise be available, or will they be loss-makers and divert funds from necessary domestic purposes?

How, too, will nation states respond to the dilemmas posed by the expansion of borderless higher education? In an age of increasing globalization and supranationality will nation-state authority to legislate the shape and form of higher education within their borders become eroded and ineffective? The liberalization of trade in education services within the GATS negotiations places particular and unfamiliar responsibility on governmental trade policymakers to take considered and knowledgeable decisions for their national higher education sector.

The nature of the learner in this borderless context is also shifting the focus from the more traditional first degree and the school-leaver, to older learners undertaking postgraduate study or continuing professional development, or re-training to pursue another career. These learners often do not require, or wish to have, the full social trappings of an on-campus educational community – they have more immediate and instrumental needs and, in any case, they have less need for the early maturation experiences of younger students, at least as these are generally found on university campuses.

The last decades of the twentieth century witnessed considerable experimentation in higher education partnerships, structures and provision. This is likely to continue in the new millennium and is likely to be more competitive, market-driven and global than before.

# 8 Teaching and Learning in the Global Era

*Yoni Ryan*

## ▶ Introduction

Previous chapters have examined the effects of globalization on university systems, regulatory regimes and emerging models of higher education provision. They provide valuable background for a more specific evaluation of the pedagogical implications of globalization processes. In essence, this chapter attempts a microanalysis – what particular aspects of globalization have affected university learning and teaching practices and theories? This involves asking 'how has teaching actually changed at the turn into the new millennium, a decade after the pioneering applications of information and communication technologies (ICTs) to higher education?' A further pertinent issue is whether the role of the 'academic' is also being transformed.

Some manifestations of the effects of globalization are more obvious than others. For example, although the international mobility of teaching and research staff is a longstanding characteristic of universities, recent decades have witnessed much larger volumes of student mobility across international boundaries for higher education qualifications, most notably from south and east Asia to English-speaking western countries such as Australia, the US, Canada, the UK and New Zealand. Examining the effects of these movements on teaching and curricula is a major task of this chapter.

A key characteristic of globalization, which has directly influenced teaching and learning, is found in the huge and rapid application of ICTs in educational systems – to enhance effectiveness in administrative and support structures, to enrich learning, and, perhaps more significantly, to increase the efficiency of teaching. The new technologies, of course, both drive globalization processes, and are in turn propelled by them. In the business world, for example, corporations and financial systems have used the technological revolution to expand globally, and to reinforce corporate culture and knowledge; the search for worldwide markets in turn drives further development of higher performing information and communications platforms.

For universities, learning networks that have been made possible by the worldwide web and digital technologies, have significantly enhanced off-campus learning opportunities for 'anywhere, anytime' education. The convenience of studying without a routine time/place engagement at a campus location, and the time savings associated with not travelling, have helped to reduce major obstacles for time-poor students, particularly in metropolitan areas, where the greatest expansion in off-campus enrolments has occurred. However, we need to examine further the impact of ICTs on the higher education sector as the research to date in this area is still patchy.

Also, we need to look more specifically at ideas of the curriculum and conceptions of knowledge as held by academics, and at the consequences of these for their approaches to teaching practice, and how these are being influenced by increased technology and international student mobility. This also involves looking closely at how academics conceive of their role, since this too informs their pedagogical methods and ultimately the quality of the student learning experience.

## ▶ Student mobility and its effects on teaching

As indicated above, the most obvious feature of globalization in higher education is accelerated international student mobility and its consequences for the national profiles of student populations, particularly in western English-speaking countries. Nowhere is this more evident than in Australia, where the student body is now more international than in any other country except Switzerland. Further, the racial composition of Australia's international students differs markedly from that of the dominant domestic population. In 1991, at Monash University, one of Australia's largest, the student population was 91 per cent domestic, and, of the 2900 international students, all were studying onshore (in Australia). By 2000, 21 per cent of students were international: the majority of the 9300 international students were based in Melbourne, but nearly 3500 were studying offshore (outside Australia), at Monash's overseas campuses in Malaysia, and at partner institutions in Vietnam, Singapore and Hong Kong, or externally (Brace, 2002).

In some Australian universities the proportion of international students is even higher – over 30 per cent at Curtin, and around 50 per cent at RMIT, in 2001. Universities have thus become financially vulnerable to any shifts in enrolment, either to other universities in Australia, or to other countries. In the US, the overall proportion of international students is considerably lower, at just over 4 per cent, although actual numbers are huge, at around 582,000. In the UK, the total of foreign higher education students was 232,000 for 2001, and numbers have steadily increased for over a decade.

The national backgrounds of onshore international students differs between countries – Australia recruits largely from Singapore, Hong Kong, Malaysia, China and Indonesia, which are countries within 'short-haul' travel time, while in the US, historically attractive particularly to those from Korea, Japan and Hong Kong, Indian students became the predominant group in 2002. In the UK the volume of Chinese students is rising dramatically, as visa regulations progressively are relaxed. Onshore cohorts are further differentiated by level: the majority of US internationals are in graduate programs, while Australia attracts degree and sub-degree enrolments: the 'mass market'. The effects on student flows from abroad to the US of more stringent visa requirements for students and others imposed following the 11 September 2001 attacks on that country are not yet clear. Foreign students' choices of programmes may also be affected by US government prohibitions on biochemical and cyber security research.

International students are both a symptom of globalization, and a driver of globalizing tendencies, including through population shifts. Their economic contribution to national economies has prompted legal and immigration policy changes, although governments are sensitive to popular calls for immigration restrictions on wider social grounds. In Australia, to support what has become the country's sixth largest export earner, regulations limiting the number of hours of paid work that international students are permitted to undertake during their studies have been loosened, notwithstanding the concerns of some citizens about the presumed loss of jobs for Australians. Further, international students are now allowed to apply for residency if they work in Australia following their graduation, where previously they had to return to their home country to apply. Easing immigration policy in this way has proved a powerful marketing tool for Australian universities. The UK has followed suit in easing restrictions on employment for students from abroad, not least to retain the UK's share of the market.

The presence of international students in large numbers on campuses has forced changes in teaching methods in many universities, and stimulated major curriculum change. The 'internationalization of the curriculum' has become a key strategic objective, and while it has often been interpreted in purely commercial terms, increasing the numbers of fee-paying students is steadily impacting on curricula. Universities are recognizing that much subject content is too domestically oriented in an era when graduates – domestic as well as international – are facing the prospect of more globally mobile careers, or, even if working locally, doing so for organizations operating in cross-national contexts. International law, global telecommunications, and engineering are examples of sectors that now require knowledge of international standards and different national cultures and codes for successful employment.

Increasing international student flows have changed also the programme profile of many universities. Strong preferences for information technology and business programmes by international students have skewed enrolments towards those areas. Since these are the departments where the emphasis is less on basic or theoretical research, and where industry relevance, and sector experience for teachers and researchers, are considered more valuable than doctoral knowledge, universities have struggled to recruit in the face of the competitive salaries offered by industry and commerce. Perhaps making a virtue of necessity, universities generally have turned to employing more part-time staff from industry itself. These 'practising professionals' have also been attractive to many of the for-profit colleges and universities discussed in Chapter 7, which generally focus on vocational programmes.

Language difficulties among the large proportion of students who are not native English speakers, and the 'non-theoretical' nature of information technology and business subjects, have influenced a move towards more graphical presentations of material (the PowerPoint mania) and away from the traditional oral lecture. A further shift to the use of slides on the Internet, to enable students to access materials 'anytime, anyplace', has reinforced this approach.

As academics have sought to handle larger numbers of international students, especially from Asia, the presumption that learning styles and cognitive approaches in higher education were homogenous and universal has been severely challenged. Western university learning has been characterized as critical of established knowledge, as vocal, vigorous and argumentative in expression, as individual in achievement, and as exploratory – 'how do I know what I think until you hear what I say?' Yet cognitive scientists, educators and cultural studies scholars, such as Smith (1999), Cryer and Okorocha (1999), and Choi (1997) have identified culturally derived learning styles that contrast strongly with this western conception of university learning. Most interest has centred on Confucian learning because for various political, economic and cultural reasons, a large proportion of international students originate from Chinese communities in Asia. Confucian learning is said to favour deep respect for the authority of the teacher and for print text, and favours the replication of received knowledge rather than the generation of new ideas. Learning is conceived as a group collaborative or collective activity, avoiding the focus on the individual that characterizes the verbal teacher–student interrogation typical of the 'western' seminar.

These features of alternate learning styles underpin the 'problems' that western academics complain of in teaching Asian international students – reticence in demeanour and in oral discussion in class, non-integration in mixed domestic and international classes, and more recently, in accusations of 'plagiarism' (from a western perspective) or 'reproduction of received wisdom' (from a Confucian perspective).

Countering these teaching problems has forced many academics to re-examine their teaching methods. Combined with the challenge of ever-larger classes in popular programmes, and diminished funding for teaching, the growth in international student numbers has accelerated the trend to a reduction in face-to-face contact hours, and has shifted the teaching pattern away from small group tutorials to lectures and independent study activities that can be undertaken in student groups outside a classroom. Patterns of study are therefore changing, and edging 'off-campus'. Nor is student mobility confined to international students; recent US studies indicate that over one-third of domestic students transfer between institutions over the course of finishing a programme.

While the most obvious effect of international student mobility is discernable in the classrooms of countries such as Australia and the UK, the flow is not entirely one way. The semester abroad programme has long been a feature of US liberal arts colleges, but is now being promoted by UK and Australian universities as part of more concerted internationalization agendas that encourage student exchanges. Generous sponsorship by Scandinavian governments, for example, has brought Norwegian and Swedish students to Australia for a year's exchange. However, relatively few scholarships are available in Australia and the UK for exchange study, which generally has restricted exchange opportunities to those students from higher socio-economic groups. Indeed, international student mobility can be construed as essentially privileging those from professional occupational families.

Physical mobility is not the only way for students to gain an overseas education, however. The aggressive expansion of UK and Australian institutions into the lucrative markets of Asia has brought western models of university education into those countries. Most often, the model takes the form of a hybrid distance–local programme of intensive or block teaching over several days, delivered by 'fly in, fly out' teachers from the provider universities, and supported by local tutors and prepared teaching materials. In 2002 for example, Hong Kong, seen as a toehold to the People's Republic of China, had 550 offshore programmes delivered to over 60,000 students. UK institutions offered 57 per cent of these courses, 31 per cent were from Australian universities, and only 7 per cent were from US colleges (Jegede, 2001). These figures reflect historical ties to the UK, its strong reputation for quality education, and aggressive marketing from Australia, compared to the relative lack of market interest from the US.

From the student perspective such programmes offer an overseas degree at much less cost than travelling abroad, despite their high fees compared to local tuition rates, and living costs for staying at home are generally lower. Although there is concern about the quality of some of these programmes, and certainly few are supported by the range and quality of facilities that are available to the home students of the provider institution, the curriculum is western-oriented, which for many students is part of their attraction. Many local commentators deplore the potential for cultural imperialism posed by offshore courses (see Jegede and Shive, 2001), and for their general failure to acknowledge and incorporate local modes of knowledge and contextual issues.

Nevertheless, student demand remains strong, and Asian and Middle Eastern governments have proved eager to encourage western education models, to shift their own populations towards a greater private contribution to educational costs, and to reform what are considered to be highly regimented and stultified education practices which engender conformity rather than creativity. In Singapore the authorities have facilitated the establishment of branches of elite non-profit US institutions specifically to stimulate the critical thinking and problem-solving abilities perceived as typical of US graduates, and have repudiated the rote learning, examinations-driven approach previously favoured in local institutions, which Jegede and Shive (2001, p. 30) refer to as having 'factory-like routines', and 'compulsory pacing'. It is difficult not to see western teaching models becoming more widely diffused. How this will affect different learning styles is not yet clear, but perhaps the best outcome would be for a productive blend of collaborative and individualistic attainment, which combines the best of group and personal achievements.

## ▶ New technologies and globalization

Although predictions of the demise of the residential or physical campus with the advent of the Internet have proved groundless, new digital technologies and the worldwideweb have altered teaching and learning practices in most discipline areas, although this does not appear to be the case at first glance. Preliminary national surveys suggest that little has changed in university classrooms, even in developed countries where Internet penetration in the general community is high. In Australia, for example, Bell *et al.* (2002) conclude that wholly online courses constitute a tiny fraction of all courses offered by Australian universities, and only 5.8 per cent of courses depend on the Internet for delivery of content. A UK survey of Commonwealth universities revealed that just over 10 per cent of universities had integrated online technologies into their programmes in any significant way (Observatory on Borderless Higher Education, 2002).

Yet such surveys underestimate the extent to which digital technologies are routinely incorporated in teaching and learning, certainly in the ancillary services provided by libraries and enrolment departments, but also in the form of learning resources. The failure to define exactly what is meant by 'online teaching and learning' and 'e-learning' clouds the validity of survey

data, and a failure to agree metrics to evaluate the efficacy of online learning slows uptake. For instance, institutions in the Australian survey were
asked to nominate all their subjects into one of three categories, with the
lowest category being that with no unit information on a website for that
unit. Data collection was thus compromised by a lack of knowledge at the
central level of what was occurring within classrooms – 'no unit website' was
simply equated with 'no use of the Internet'. Yet there are few university staff
who do not refer students to the rich resources available on the Internet in
all discipline areas, whether these are databases or more specific learning
materials. Many protest only that web resources are so dominated by US-
based search engines which favour US sites, and that the US hosts the richest
treasure store of web materials (Wilson *et al.*, 1998).

ICTs have of course changed the *activities* of academics in dramatic ways.
Exhorted to 'put their courses online', they taught themselves the often
clunky early versions of learning platforms, or were drafted into 'sheep dip
training' on a template, or took the line of least resistance, learnt Power-
Point, and simply uploaded 'slides' of their 'lecture' into dot points for
bemused students to download. Those who attempted to develop rich
interactive materials, which capitalize on the potential of multimedia to
engage a generation of media-sophisticates, quickly found that thoughtful
pedagogical use of multimedia requires time, energy, and the skills of
graphics/audio/video/programming experts, and that those skills are rare in
universities, because pay rates for such skills are much higher outside. By
the late 1990s, credible evaluations and a flood of 'first-hand experience' articles lamented the high costs of e-learning development, and the time that
the team development approach requires.

At the same time, quality assurance in education has become a western
government and management mantra, sometimes in tandem with hymns of
praise for 'quality audit' processes. This has helped to generate the emergence of teaching and learning development professionals, who work with
discipline specialists to design courses and to produce specific learning
materials. 'Winging it' in a lecture without adequate preparation has become
less possible, since the typical 'Unit Outline', presented at the beginning of
a semester, and detailing each week's topics, has gained the status of a
legally enforceable contract between the university and the student.

The high costs of producing quality multimedia have hastened the
entrance of commercial print publishers into web and CDROM production.
Since early generic materials proved unpopular with staff, publishers such
as McGraw-Hill Higher Education are now partnering with course management systems' companies like eCollege to produce online exercises and
simulations, and supplements to publishers' textbooks. These materials,

described as 'content cartridges' by some companies, can be customized by academics for integration into courses. If the 'learning objects' are well-conceived and are accepted, the waste that has characterized many virtual learning projects generally remaining unknown outside a particular department, or a single university, should decrease (Alexander *et al.*, 1998; Morrison and Newman, 2003).

It is not only global commercial publishers that are worldwide in reach. The *Universitas 21 Global* consortium (discussed in more detail in Chapter 7) has mooted an ambitious learning object and content management system to underpin its online teaching. The consortium would collaborate to develop and share e-learning materials, thus amortizing the costs across all participating universities. However, with the publisher Thomson Learning as a partner, more commercial development of teaching materials may follow.

The idealistic MERLOT project promised an alternative. It was conceived, with support from philanthropic grants, as a non-profit, peer-reviewed repository of open source online teaching materials to be freely used by academics. However, it appears to be struggling in a university sector that has become marketized, and its recent alliance with EDUCAUSE suggests it may convert to a for-fee business model to survive.

Whether e-learning 'objects' are developed by commercial publishers, or as commercial ventures of not-for-profit universities, or by non-profit agencies, generally matters little at the level of teaching and learning practice as compared to the impact of changes in formats. Electronic learning objects change the nature of teaching *acts*, requiring teachers to think deeply about the structure of their programmes, about the continuing efficacy of the lecture/tutorial/laboratory model, and inevitably about their own contribution as teachers. Is their distinctive professional expertise the possession of research knowledge? Is it the ability to identify relevant and well-conceived learning materials, and to combine them in specific ways for particular cohorts of students – in other words to judge and then 'mediate' knowledge? Or is it to provide the human dimension to the cognitive and social processes that are education?

These are questions that are taxing all academic staff as they grapple with the shift from the university as a 'cottage industry' (Elton, 1995) to one as an increasingly non-privileged education site among many others in a postindustrial knowledge economy. They are particularly pertinent for the application of digitized course management or learning management systems that have become a standard feature of most universities. These have promised efficiencies in digitized data storage, in relational databases, and in the calculator power to automate administrative systems, and to link these to teaching activities – to assist grading, to generate databanks of learning resources, and to help communication with students. No single platform has yet been developed that integrates the many complex processes encompassed in a university, but the promise remains.

Although many of these systems – or elements of them – originated within the technology departments of universities, their development has relied on commercial approaches, generally beyond the capacity of most universities, which have found difficulty in building volume, particularly during the heady years of the dot-com boom which sucked staff and other resources to the commercial sector. The result is that development of learning management systems has progressively transferred to commercial North American companies like Blackboard, Campus Pipeline, eCollege and WebCT, which now distribute worldwide a platform designed for the US higher education model, which assumes cheap Internet access, and which requires academics in other countries to adopt US terms ('courses' for 'subjects' or 'units') or to adapt the platform at additional cost. These systems are criticized by academics for lacking an educational basis, for being more suitable for 'training' programmes, and for lacking the flexibility needed in a comprehensive university with diverse discipline approaches. MIT's Open Course Ware initiative (discussed in Chapter 7) promises to provide a more flexible platform, but until that is fully developed, commercial Learning Management Systems (LMS) platforms will continue to prevail. The wider adoption of their templates and their underlying 'delivery' pedagogy are likely to further standardize teaching and learning practices worldwide.

That globalization has yet to result in, for example, Physics 101 – a course authored and delivered by 'the world's best physics professor' – being beamed to millions of students and many universities worldwide from, say, a corporatized university headquarters in Arizona, is attributable not simply to the recalcitrance and resistance of academics who refuse to surrender their hegemonic control of university curricula, and who cannot master new technologies, as some have claimed. Nor can we blame the blinkered inability of university managers to foresee a future in which online technologies will shape all institutional systems. Indeed, managers have adopted, at great financial cost, computer systems which enable comprehensive data collection, and which automate the more tedious service elements of university study – enrolment, payment of various fees, library searching, and so on. Teaching staff – though not without complaint – have quickly adopted the communication potential of the web, and its capacity as an enormous repository of learning resources, both to supplement their on-campus teaching, and to alleviate the disadvantages of distance education. Discussion forums, email list notices, even synchronous chat rooms and videostreaming, are increasingly accepted as teaching methods.

Most academics have recognized, however, that a only a small minority of students are comfortable with an education that is 'wholly online', in which all content and interaction occur in cyberspace and cybertime, that is, at 'any time'. Rather, students prefer a 'bricks and clicks' experience, a hybrid model that provides time and place convenience through access to resources off-campus, but which does not eliminate the physical and community experience of the campus enclave, a 'space' for the specialized activity and group learning that most young adults need, and most older adults want. Hence, staff and students are reluctant to 'go wholly online' as they perceive their degree as an education, not just a qualification (Smith, 1999; Warner *et al.*, 1998).

What is less explicable however, is the persistence of the 'not-invented-here-syndrome' in relation to online teaching resources, particularly as it is now widely accepted that 'getting a course online' increases academic workloads, both in the initial preparation of materials, and in the ongoing maintenance and updating of websites and links. There is strong resistance to the notion of an American-sourced Physics 101, which in part is understandable, but which nonetheless reduces rational sharing of online teaching resources. Partly this attitude derives from the competitive business environment in which western universities operate, as universities feel pressured to brand their distinctive mission, and their teaching and learning styles, rather than rely on 'imports' produced elsewhere. It follows too from the curricula autonomy university teachers expect as a corollary of academic freedom, to present their particular 'take' on a discipline.

It is also a consequence of complex intellectual property regimes in which teaching materials are variously the property of the employing university, or the academic and the team that produced them. Teaching content has become a saleable product, thus introducing an ethical dilemma for many academics between, on the one hand, the intellectual value of wide and free distribution of material, and, on the other, notions of intellectual property and the right to its commercial exploitation. (Paradoxically the authorship and sales of commercial textbooks seems to elicit no such qualms.) Costs are also an issue. Current copyright laws and business models require universities to purchase licences to use many online resources, and they cannot, in many jurisdictions, recoup these costs from students. It is therefore easier to direct students to print texts, to 'home-grown' resources, or to public access sites.

When regulatory environments come to terms with globalized business approaches and allow both cheap access to online learning resources and also protection for the intellectual property of the contributors, or when the idealism of MIT's OpenCourseWare Initiative (to place all its learning materials online for unrestricted use) re-enters academia, the usefulness of the web for university teaching and learning will increase exponentially.

In the meantime, the Internet will propel globalization of teaching and learning in more constrained ways – by facilitating communication across the boundary of the physical campus, and across the borders between nation states, as well as between university and industry. It will, albeit more slowly, drive the development of richer multimedia explanations of physical phenomena for science, engineering, medicine and technology, and interactive manipulations of data and systems in simulations that generate new knowledge. Learning is already becoming more active – more kinaesthetic than verbal, as teaching embraces the capacity of new technologies to 'virtually' replicate systems and experiments, allowing students to manipulate graphic representations of text formulae and processes that previously were explained in static text forms.

There are, however, some unintended consequences of student use of the Internet, not the least of which is the supposed 'explosion' in 'cut and paste plagiarism'. Sites such as *SchoolSucks.com* charge to supply a ready-made essay or term paper for desperate students, but free online articles and information sites also provide a quick solution for those unwilling to pay for an assignment. Because so many western students today undertake paid work during their university study, and because in many disciplines frequent assignments have replaced or supplemented examinations, the pressure to produce assignments in short-time frames has produced this new form of cheating, to avoid failure in an era of high and escalating tuition fees.

So alarmed have university managers become by this trend, that to protect the integrity of their degrees, many have joined forces to employ the technical capacities of the web and powerful search engines to defeat student use of those search engines, via such web crawlers as *turnitin*, a plagiarism detection device which compares student papers with internet resources and other assignments. *Turnitin* has won endorsement from Universities UK, and a consortium of Victorian state universities in Australia.

A further and unintended consequence of Internet-based resources is that, worldwide, students are increasingly restricted in accessing resources, as library budgets decline and librarians desperately cull subscriptions. Commercial publishers have gradually bought up publishing rights to the journals of professional associations, and 'bundle' titles in their full text digital forms. Using digital catalogues, students are eschewing non-digital resources from more obscure publishers, for print-on-demand articles that may be less appropriate to their topic (Bell, 2003). Moreover, search engines such as *Yahoo!* are more likely to direct students to non-scholarly sources, with sorry consequences for in-depth and accurate learning. Most online resources also originate in western countries – an African student seeking online articles is unlikely to find much in the way of local authorship, even if she can afford the connectivity costs of online searching. So

ICTs, in furthering globalization, also enhance the dominance of western scholarship.

As well as generating convenience and time savings for students, learning networks of another sort challenge traditional patterns of teaching and learning: in the developed world at least, extensive information is available outside the university, at little or no cost, which forces institutions (along with the great public library systems of the world) to reconsider their role as major repositories of knowledge. These alternative sources are a product of globalization, as they comprise mainly for-profit organizations that gather and exchange information for a fee. They style themselves as 'knowledge economy' bodies and see their role as paralleling and indeed challenging that of the university. Universities are often exhorted by governments to forge alliances with these organizations as part of encouraging greater public–private partnerships. Such links, however, have significant pedagogical impact, not only in extending the use of digital resources, but also hastening the process of curriculum reform towards more contemporary knowledge forms, and away from methods that emphasise historical and accretive learning processes. A consequence is a paradigm shift in the nature of the knowledge taught in higher education, which raises important questions such as 'what is *worth* teaching? *what* is to be taught?' and also 'how is it to be taught?' (Barnett, 2000; Gibbons *et al.*, 1994).

## ▶ Globalization and the pursuit of the vocational

The nature of work in the West, and increasingly in less developed countries, has changed with globalization, and this too has affected higher education teaching and learning.

First, as sectors become dominated by handfuls of large multinational companies, their workforces become more subject to directives from headquarters, and are required to update industry skills and company product knowledge continuously. Education institutions have been coopted to assist corporate universities and the training divisions of global corporations in these processes, and this in turn has led to quite dramatic increases in the proportion of older students attending western universities, and to an aging of the student profile. In almost all western English-speaking university systems, 'mature' (generally those over 21 years of age at commencement) students now outnumber recent school-leavers. In 1991, for example, 53 per cent of Monash University students were school-leavers; by 2000, this proportion had dropped to 47 per cent. The 'aging' of the student population has also increased off-campus enrolments as mature students are more likely to seek the convenience of not having to attend regular classes – 12 per cent of Monash students were enrolled externally in 1991, but by 2000, this figure was 17 per cent and growing (Brace, 2002). Part-time numbers have increased similarly.

Second, the consumer culture fostered by globalization, along with the proposition that higher education is a personal as well as a public good (that is, graduates benefit from increased lifetime occupational earnings), and therefore justifies individual financial investment, have turned many younger students into 'learner-earners' – enrolled notionally full-time, yet undertaking paid work during their semester-time study periods, rather than solely during vacations. In the US, the UK and Australia, the majority of students now work part-time, often for over 14 hours per week (AVCC, 2001). Study and the university experience has become only one facet of the lives of young students, a situation beginning to resemble the many competing commitments usually associated with the lives of mature-age students. Traditional 1960s campus activities, such as political clubs, sport associations and debating societies geared to adolescents with time on their hands and hungry for emotional and intellectual exploration, have lost their appeal to contemporary student cohorts. According to research in both Australia and the US, students have become 'disengaged' (McInnes et al., 2000).

'Learning' thus occupies less of a student's time. Accommodating work commitments has reinforced demands for learning resources to be available outside classrooms, off-campus, and especially online. Two decades or more ago, with free or low-cost education, it was possible to persuade students that they had a full-time commitment to the 'work' of study, and that each subject required at least 10 hours of study outside class time. Now such propositions appear risible to most students. Their learning time is compressed into 'study binges' around assessment. In turn, academics are 'chunking' content into short modules, catering to the time pressures and shorter attention spans of their learners, a situation far removed from the image of languorous days reading under dreaming spires.

There is no evidence yet of the long-term effects of these changing patterns of learning on intellectual achievement. We simply do not know whether short-burst learning leads to a diminution of cognitive capacity for the sustained intellectual effort that leads to major discoveries. Only a few cognitive scientists have begun to question whether the actual length of time over which neurological processes engage in the 'study' of a subject affects cognition itself and the long-term 'patterning' of deep knowledge structures associated with higher education. We do not know if 'disintermediation', the removal of the teacher from many of the learning activities performed by students, will lead to the notion of knowledge as simply one form of consumption, to be 'enjoyed' privately and at convenience.

These current trends in educational practices in higher education are linked to the ideological and systemic changes that underpin globalization, which seek to standardize national systems in more privatized economies. It is not difficult to draw direct connections between the standardization of education systems, the commodification of knowledge, and the rising notion of university education as a 'business in a borderless world'. The clear value of a degree in maximizing employment to an individual – and with individuals helping to pay for it – has spurred a more utilitarian view of the benefits of higher education.

Mass participation at the tertiary level, starting in the 1960s but reaching heady heights in the 1990s, has helped to stimulate entrepreneurial interest in education as a product good with mass potential at the convenience end of the market. This argument is explored more fully and extremely in Ritzer's *McDonaldization Thesis* (1998). In the early 1990s, many observers linked this potential mass market with ICT delivery – knowledge could simply be 'packaged' and downloaded to computers worldwide to allow millions to gain qualifications and to boost their own and their countries' economic performance. A decade later, there remain voices which persist in this simplistic vision of education as solely the transmission of codified knowledge or information, although it is gratifying that the World Bank has now conceded that its aspirations for western degrees delivered to the masses through the African Virtual University, to take one example, was an overenthusiastic reaction to the heady atmosphere of the dot.com boom (Wolff, 2002). It is now conceded that local adaptation and implementation of online education is required for success.

The entry of large for-profit education companies, traded on (mainly US) stock exchanges, has further embedded the notion of knowledge as a personal economic good, and of a degree as an individual financial investment. Though such companies have themselves been relatively cautious so far in expanding overseas, some such as Sylvan are now moving into Latin America and Europe. In the main, however, for-profit US universities have contained their ambitions within the North American market, which they understand. The more likely candidates for international ambitions are publishing companies, which, as indicated above, increasingly supply standard instructor packs including slides, exercises, and websites which can be simply adopted by academics.

## ▶ The changing academic role

Most industry sectors have responded to competitive demands for efficiency by changing work patterns, including more part-time and some would say more casualized employment, in which previously holistic roles are 'unbundled' into narrower specializations. Some of these tendencies are apparent in universities too. This has been possible through atomization of the academic role. In Elton's 'cottage industry', an academic had sole responsibility for designing, developing, administering, teaching, testing and marking a subject area. In what has ironically become more like a large manufacturing process (see Campion and Renner, 1992), course design is now more often undertaken by a core of permanent full-time academics, in conjunction with specialist education developers and media experts. Casual or part-time staff are then used to deliver and support learning more directly.

At more research-intensive universities, part-time and casual employment remains more on the lines of a traditional apprenticeship model, and postgraduate students support the teaching of undergraduate programmes as a means of both supplementing their income and adding teaching experience to their working biographies, while undertaking their primary task of understanding how to research. In universities geared more to the provision of education and training for professional occupations, and in the US for-profit college chains, outside sector practitioners are engaged more to bring relevance and insights about current work practices to students. Pragmatically, of course, such employment practices also allow greater 'flexibility' in teaching budgets, as hourly rates for term-time only teaching and short contracts cut costs and fixed commitments.

The increasing stratification of higher education systems has also generated greater differentiation in academic roles. In research-intensive universities, which are relatively well-endowed, and largely exclusive in student entry requirements (despite the social engineering efforts of governments such as the UK) a full-time senior academic is still able with reasonable autonomy to apportion time between teaching, research, and consultancy or community service. But such universities increasingly comprise the minority within mass education systems.

For many universities, teaching absorbs a more significant proportion of academic time, if not time in front of a class, then time spent 'managing' the heavy administrative burden of large classes, hiring and guiding a string of tutors and guest lecturers, and developing course programmes others will actually teach. A course coordinator also assumes the role of marketeer, obliged by the competitive environment to maximize student numbers and the 'first preferences' of high scoring students whose recruitment elevates the prestige of the programme. The coordinator is also a financial manager, balancing budgets through casual appointments, judging how large lectures can be, and searching for ways to transfer costs. Cynically perhaps, but moves to workplace-based learning can be seen as a cost-shifting mechanism by universities, as much as a genuine pedagogical attempt to increase the relevance of student learning and to provide employers with 'job ready graduates'.

In consequence, time for research is snatched in the interstices of these various tasks, and the time available to academics for contributing to public debate has diminished. In some universities (often 'new' and recently ex-colleges or polytechnics), and in the for-profit universities, which focus on professional programmes for which there is strong mass market demand, teaching is the only role expected of most staff. Where such universities have entered the fee-paying international market (which may be one of the few means of staying financially viable), full-time academics are expected to prepare for, market, and often administer the programmes offered through franchises, twinning programmes, and branch campuses – and yet still maintain the standards they would observe on the domestic front. This is a new, unanticipated academic role – and one for which many academic staff have shown they are not well prepared.

For many academics, particularly in the less prestigious institutions, this disaggregation of their historical role and the assumption of more commercial and business-like responsibilities have entailed a difficult adjustment in their self-conceptions as autonomous professionals (Coaldrake and Stedman, 1999). Further, their individual 'worth' to the university is increasingly defined not by their discipline knowledge, but by their direct earnings in terms of numbers of students taught under operational grants or in fee-paying popular courses.

### ► Conclusion

Much good has already emerged, albeit haphazardly, from greater attention to international contexts in university curricula, and from student immersion in other cultures, fostering more tolerance for difference, and finding a common cause across nations in the objective and dispassionate pursuit of knowledge. Considerable benefits already have been achieved in using ICTs to enhance student learning, and to extend educational opportunities to those unable to attend conventional university campus-based programmes. Care must be taken, however, to preserve what was of value in teaching and learning practices, particularly the intensive dialogue that was possible in less 'mass market' circumstances. Paradoxically, this may be possible through the more sophisticated and effective use of the technologies that threaten the one-to-many lecture mode.

Inevitably, however, western models of teaching and learning, diffused through the new technologies that have made globalization possible, will ultimately prevail over alternative forms found outside the West. Chief vehicles will be the commercial publishers operating internationally, and technology companies building and exporting large systems software. More ironically, globalization will have been aided and abetted by the commercial arms of some of the great public and not-for-profit universities desperately seeking new income in response to governments' demands that they become less 'public', and more 'profitable'

# Bibliography

Adams (1998) 'The Operation of Transnational Degree and Diploma Programs: The Australian Case', *Journal of Studies in International Education*, 2, 1, 3–22.

Albrow, M. (1996) *The Global Age* (Cambridge: Polity Press).

Alexander, S., McKenzie, J. and Geissenger, H. (1998) *An Evaluation of Information Technology Projects for University Learning* (Canberra: DETYA).

Appadurai, A. (1990) 'Disjuncture and Difference in the Global Cultural Economy', *Theory, Culture and Society*, 7, 295–310.

Archibugi, D. and Iammarino, S. (2001) 'The Globalization of Technology and National Policies', in Archibugi, D. and Lundvall, B. (eds), *The Globalizing Learning Economy* (Oxford: Oxford University Press).

Asmal, K. (2002) 'Higher Education and Globalization – A View from the South', Address to the Nuffic Conference on *The Global Higher Education Market*, The Hague, Netherlands, March.

Australian Vice Chancellors Committee (AVCC) (2001) *Paying Their Way* (Report accessed at www.avcc.edu.au/policies-activities/teaching-learning/students, September 2002).

Balmer, B. (1996) 'Managing Mapping in the Human Genome Project', *Social Studies of Science*, 26, 531–73.

Barnett, R. (2000) 'Reconfiguring the University', in Scott, P. (ed.), *Higher Education Re-Formed* (London: Falmer Press).

Becher, T. (1989) *Academic Tribes and Territories* (Buckingham: Open University Press).

Becher, T. and Kogan, M. (1992) *Process and Structure in Higher Education* (London: Heinemann).

Bell, M., Bush, D., Nicholson, P., O'Brien, D. and Tran, T. (2002) *Universities Online: A Survey of Online Education and Services in Australia* (Canberra: DEST).

Bell, S. (2003) 'Has Google Won?', *Chronicle of Higher Education*, January (online edition).

Birnbaum, R. (1983) *Maintaining Diversity in Higher Education* (San Francisco: Jossey-Bass).

Bohm, A., Meares, D. and Pearce, D. (2002) *Forecasts of the Global Demand for International Higher Education* (Sydney: IDP Australia Publications).

Bordieu, P. (1977) *Outline of a Theory of Practice* (Cambridge: Cambridge University Press).

Brace, D. (2002) 'Student Transformation?', *Monash Magazine*, Spring/Summer, 18 (Melbourne: Monash University).

Braithwaite, J. and Drahos, P. (2000) *Global Business Regulation* (Cambridge: Cambridge University Press).

Brennan, J. (1999) 'The Evaluation of Higher Education in Europe', in Henkel, M. and Little, B. (eds), *Changing Relationships between Higher Education and the State* (London: Jessica Kingsley).

Campion, M. and Renner, W. (1992) 'The Supposed Demise of Fordism: Implications for Distance Education and Higher Education', *Distance Education*, 13, 1, 7–28.

Choi, M. (1997) 'Korean Students in Australian Universities', *Higher Education Research and Development*, 16, 3, 263–82.

Clark, B. (1983) *The Higher Education System* (Berkeley: University of California Press).

Clark, B. (1998) *Creating Entrepreneurial Universities* (New York: Elsevier).

Clarke, M. (2000) *Regulation* (Basingstoke: Palgrave Macmillan).

Coaldrake, P. and Stedman, L. (1999) *Academic Work in the Twenty First Century* (Canberra: DETYA).

Commonwealth Department of Education, Science and Training (2002) *Higher Education at the Crossroads* (Canberra: DEST).

Commonwealth Of Learning Report (2001) *Issues and Choices* (Vancouver: COL).

Cryer, P. and Okorocha, E. (1999) 'Avoiding Potential Pitfalls in the Supervision of NESB students', in Ryan, Y. and Zuber-Skerritt, O. (eds), *Supervising Postgraduate Students from Non-English Backgrounds* (Buckingham: SRHE and Open University Press).

Cunningham, S., Tapsal, S., Ryan, Y., Stedman, L., Bagdon, K. and Flew, T. (1998) *New Media and Borderless Education* (Canberra: Department of Employment, Education, Training and Youth Affairs).

Cunningham, S., Ryan, Y., Stedman, L., Tapsall, S., Bagdon, K., Flew, T. and Coaldrake, P. (2000) *The Business of Borderless Education* (Canberra: Department of Employment, Education, Training and Youth Affairs).

CVCP (2000) *The Business of Borderless Education: UK Perspectives* (London: Committee of Vice Chancellors and Principals).

Daniel, J. (1996) *Mega-Universities* (London: Kogan Page).

Dearing, R. (1997) *Higher Education in the Learning Society. Report of the National Committee of Inquiry into Higher Education* (London: HMSO).

Deem, R. (2001) 'Globalization, New Managerialism, Academic Capitalism and Entrepreneurialism in Universities: Is the Local Dimension Still Important?', *Comparative Education*, 37, 1, February, 7–20.

Delanty, G. (2001) *Challenging Knowledge* (London: The Society for Research into Higher Education and Open University Press).

Department for Education and Skills (2003) *The Future of Higher Education* (London: HMSO, Cm 5735).

Di Maggio, P. and Powell, W. (1983) 'The Iron Cage Revisited: Institutional Isomorphism and Collective Rationality in Organizational Fields', *American Sociological Review*, 48, 147–60.

Dill, D. and Teixeira, P. (2000) 'Program Diversity in Higher Education: An Economic Perspective', *Higher Education Policy*, 13, 99–117.

Drucker, P. (1997) in Lenzer, R. and Johnson, S. 'Seeing Things as They Really Are', *Forbes*, 10 March, 127.

Elton, L. (1995) *Is University Teaching Researchable?* Inaugural Lecture (London: UCL).

Fisher, D. and Rubenson, K. (1998) 'The Changing Political Economy: The Private and Public Lives of Canadian Universities', in Currie, J. and Newson, J. (eds), *Universities and Globalization* (London: Sage), 77–98.

Galison, P. (1997) *Image and Logic* (Chicago: University of Chicago Press).

Gallagher, S. and Newman, A. (2002) *Distance Learning at the Tipping Point* (US: Eduventures Publication).

Garrett, G. (1998) *Partisan Politics in the Global Economy* (Cambridge: Cambridge University Press).

Gibbons, M. (2001) 'Governance and the New Production of Knowledge', in de la Mothe, J. (ed.), *Science, Technology and Governance* (London: Continuum).

Gibbons, M., Limoges, C., Nowotny, H., Schwartzhiau, S., Scott, P. and Trow, M. (1994) *The New Production of Knowledge* (London: Sage).

Goedegebuure, L. and Meek, V. (1994) 'Pyramids, Prisons and Picturesque Housing: A Discussion on Diversity in Higher Education', *Higher Education in Europe*, 19, 4, 37–50.

Gray, J. (1998) *False Dawn: the Delusions of Global Capitalism* (London: Granta Publications).

Habermas, J. (1996) *Between Facts and Norms: Contribution to a Discourse Theory of Democracy and Law* (Cambridge: Polity Press).

Hall, P. and Soskice, D. (2001) 'An Introduction to Varieties of Capitalism', in Hall, P. and Soskice, D. (eds), *Varieties of Capitalism* (Oxford: Oxford University Press).

Harrison, S., Moran, M. and Wood, B. (2002) 'Policy Emergence and Policy Convergence: the Case of "Scientific–Bureaucratic Medicine" in the United

States and the United Kingdom', *British Journal of Politics and International Relations*, 4, 1, April, 1–24.

Harvey, D. (1989) *The Condition of Postmodernity* (Oxford: Blackwell).

Hay, C. and Marsh, D. (eds) (2000) *Demystifying Globalization* (Basingstoke: Palgrave Macmillan).

Hayek, F. (1978) 'Competition as a Discovery Procedure', in *New Studies* (London: Routledge).

Held, D., Megrew, A., Goldblatt, D. and Perraton, J. (eds) (1999) *Global Transformations* (Cambridge: Polity Press).

Hirst, P. and Thompson, G. (1996) *Globalization in Question* (Cambridge, UK: Polity Press).

IDP Australia Website http.//www.idp.com/marketingandresearch/research/internationaled (accessed 21.11.02).

Jarvis, P. (2001) *Universities and Corporate Universities* (London: Kogan Page).

Jegede, O. (2001) 'Hong Kong', in Jegede, O. and Shive, G. (eds).

Jegede, O. and Shive, G. (eds) (2001) *Open and Distance Education in the Asia Pacific Region* (Hong Kong: Hong Kong Open University Press).

Keohane, N. (2000) 'The American Campus', in Smith, D. and Langslow, A. (eds), *The Idea of a University* (London: Jessica Kingsley).

Kerr, C. (1963) *The Uses of the University* (Cambridge, MA: Harvard University Press).

Kidder, T. (1981) *The Soul of a New Machine* (Boston, MA: Little, Brown and Company).

Kogan, M. and Hanney, S. (2000) *Reforming Higher Education* (London: Jessica Kingsley Publishers).

Lacey, R. (1996) *Complexity and Creativity in Organizations* (San Francisco: Berrett-Koehler).

Latour, B. (1997) 'Socrates and Callicles's Settlement – Or, the Invention of the Impossible Body Politic', *Configurations*, 5, 189–240.

Levy, D. (2003) *Expanding Higher Education Capacity Through Private Growth* (London: Observatory on Borderless Higher Education).

Marginson, S. (1993) *Education and Public Policy in Australia* (Melbourne: Cambridge University Press).

Marginson, S. and Considine, M. (2000) *The Enterprise University* (Melbourne: Cambridge University Press).

Mason, R. (1998) *Globalising Education: Trends and Applications* (London: Routledge).

Maxwell, J., Provan, D. and Fielden, J. (2000) *State Controlled or Market Driven? The Regulation of Private Universities in the Commonwealth* (London: ACU/CHEMS Paper 31).

McInnes, C., James, R. and Hartley, R. (2000) *Trends in the First Year Experience in Australian Universities* (Canberra: DETYA).

Meek, V., Goedegebuvre, L., Kivinen, O. and Rinne, R. (eds) (1996) *The Mockers and the Mocked: Comparative Perspectives on Differentiation, Convergence and Diversity in Higher Education* (Oxford: IAU Press, Pergamon).

Middlehurst, R. and Bjarnason, S. (2001) 'Invaders Triumph or Community Champions?', paper presented to a *Society for Research into Higher Education* conference, Cape Town.

MIT (2002) *MIT OpenCourseWare Quick Fact Sheet* (Cambridge, MA: MIT).

Mitchell Ash (1996) 'Common and Disparate Dilemmas', in Muller, S. and Whitesell, H. (eds), *Universities in the Twenty-First Century* (Providence: Berghahn Books).

Moran, M. (2002) 'Review Article: Understanding the Regulatory State', *British Journal of Political Science*, 32, 391–413.

Moran, M. (2003, forthcoming) *The British Regulatory State* (Oxford: Oxford University Press).

Morrison, J. and Newman, F. (2003) 'The Technology Revolution', *The Technology Source*, January/February, accessed at http://ts.mivu.org/default.asp on 5/1/03.

Muller, D. (ed.) (1987) *The Rise of the Modern Educational System: Structural Change and Social Reproduction, 1870–1920* (Cambridge: Cambridge University Press).

Nelson, R. and Winter, S. (1982) *An Evolutionary Theory of Economic Change* (London: Belknap Press of Harvard University Press).

Newman, J. (1996) *The Idea of the University* (New Haven: Yale University Press).

Newman, F. and Courturier, L. (2002) *Trading Public Good in the Higher Education Market* (London: Observatory on Borderless Higher Education).

Nowotny, H., Sibbons, M. and Scott, P. (2001) *Re-Thinking Science* (Cambridge: Polity Press).

O'Brien, R., Goetz, A., Scholte, J. and Williams, M. (2000) *Contesting Global Governance* (Cambridge: Cambridge University Press).

Observatory on Borderless Higher Education (2002) *Online Learning in Commonwealth Universities Report* (London: Association of Commonwealth Universities).

OECD (2001) *Trade in Educational Services: Trends and Emerging Issues. Working Paper* (Paris: Organisation for Economic Co-operation and Development).

Parsons, T. and Platt, G. (1973) *The American University* (Cambridge, MA: Harvard University Press).

Popper, K. (1945) *The Open Society and its Enemies* (New York: Harper and Row).

Porter, M. (1990) *The Competitive Advantage of Nations* (Basingstoke: Macmillan – now Palgrave Macmillan).

Readings, B. (1996) *The University in Ruins* (Cambridge, MA: Harvard University Press).

Ritzler, G. (1998) *The McDonaldization Thesis* (London: Sage).

Robbins Report (1963) *Higher Education: Report of the Robbins Committee* (London: HMSO, Cmnd. 2154).

Roberts, J. and Associates (2002) 'Faculty and Staff Development in Higher Education: The Key to Using ICT Appropriately?', *Report of the Observatory on Higher Education* (London: ACU/UUK).

Robertson, D. and Hillman, J. (1997) *Widening Participation in Higher Education for Students from Lower Socio-Economic Groups and Students with Disabilities* (Report 6 to the Dearing Inquiry) (London: HMSO).

Salmi, J. (2000) *Pacing the Challenges of the Twenty-First Century* (TechnKnowLogia).

Salter, B. and Tapper, T. (1994) *The State and Higher Education* (London: Woburn Press).

Scholte, J. (2000) *Globalization* (Basingstoke: Palgrave Macmillan).

Scott, P. (1995) *The Meanings of Higher Education* (Buckingham: Open University Press).

Scott, P. (1998) 'Massification, Internationalization, and Globalization', in Scott, P. (ed.), *The Globalization of Higher Education* (Buckingham: Open University Press).

Scott, P., Sibbons, M. and Nowotny, H. (2003, forthcoming) 'Mode 2 Revisited: The New Production of Knowledge', *Minerva*.

Slaughter, S. and Leslie, L. (1997) *Academic Capitalism; Politics, Policies, and the Entrepreneurial University* (Baltimore: Johns Hopkins University).

Smith, D. (1999) 'Supervising NESB Students from Confucian Educational Cultures', in Ryan, Y. and Zuber-Skerritt, O. (eds) *Supervising Postgraduate Students from Non-English Backgrounds* (Buckingham: SRUE and Open University Press).

Smith, P. (1999) 'Client Focused Flexible Delivery', in *Open, Flexible and Distance Learning* (Geelong: Deakin University).

Stadtman, U. (1980) *Academic Adaptations* (San Francisco: Jossey-Bass).

Star, S. and Griesmer, J. (1989) 'Institutional Ecology, Transitions and Boundary Objects: Amateurs and Professionals in Berkeley's Museum of Vertebrate Zoology, 1907–39', *Social Studies of Science*, 19, 3, 387–420.

Swank, D. (2002) *Global Capital, Political Institutions, and Policy Change in Developed Welfare States* (Cambridge: Cambridge University Press).

Taylor, S. and Paton, R. (2002) *Corporate Universities: Historical Development, Conceptual Analysis, and Relations with Public Sector Higher Education* (London: Observatory on Borderless Higher Education).

Thompson, J. B. (2001) 'The Media And Politics', in Nash, K. and Scott, A. (eds), *The Blackwell Companion to Political Sociology* (Oxford: Blackwell).

Torstendahl, R. (1993) 'The Transformation of Professional Education in the Nineteenth Century', in Rothblatt, S. and Wittrock, B. (eds), *The European and American University since 1800* (Cambridge: Cambridge University Press), ch. 3.

Trow, M. (1973) *Problems in the Transition from Elite to Mass Higher Education* (Berkeley: Carnegie Commission on Higher Education).

Trow, M. (1979) 'Aspects of Diversity in American Higher Education', in Gans, H. and Associates (eds), *On the Making of Americans: Essays in Honor of David Reisman* (Philadelphia: University of Pennsylvania Press).

UKCOSA and CEC (2000) *Student Mobility on the Map* (London: UKCOSA/CEC).

Utterback, J. (1998) *Mastering the Dynamics of Innovation* (Boston, MA: Harvard Business School Press).

Veblen, T. (1962) *The Higher Learning in America* (New Haven: Yale University Press).

Waltz, K. (1979) *Theory of International Politics* (Reading, MA: Addison-Wesley).

Warner, D., Christie, G. and Choy, S. (1998) *The Readiness of the VET Client for Flexible Delivery* (Brisbane: ANTA).

Weber, M. (1968) *Economy and Society* (New York: Bedminster Press).

Webster, A. (1998) 'Strategic Research Alliances: Testing the Collaborative Limits', in Etzkowitz, H., Heatey, P. and Webster, A. (eds), *Capitalizing Knowledge* (New York: State University of New York Press), 95–110.

Weinberg, A. (1963) 'Criterial for Scientific Choice', *Minerva*, 1.

Whitley, R. (1999) *Divergent Capitalisms* (Oxford: Oxford University Press).

Williams, G. (1999) 'The State Financing of Higher Education', in Henkel, M. and Little, B. (eds), *Changing Relationships between Higher Education and the State* (London: Jessica Kingsley).

Wilson, M., Qayyam, A. and Boshier, R. (1998) 'Worldwide America? Think Globally, Click Locally', *Distance Education*, 19, 1, 109–23.

Wittrock, B. (1993) 'The Modern University: the Three Transformations', in Rothblatt, S. and Wittrock, B. (eds), *The European and American University since 1800* (Cambridge: Cambridge University Press).

Wolf, A. (2002) *Does Education Matter?* (Harmondsworth: Penguin).

Wolff, L. (2002) 'The African Virtual University', *TechKnowlogia*, April–June, 23–5.

World Bank (2002) *Constructing Knowledge Societies: New Challenges for Tertiary Education* (Washington, DC: World Bank).

# Index